"Don't Ask What I Shot"

HOW EISENHOWER'S LOVE OF GOLF HELPED SHAPE 1950s AMERICA

CATHERINE M. LEWIS

New York   Chicago   San Francisco   Lisbon   London   Madrid   Mexico City
Milan   New Delhi   San Juan   Seoul   Singapore   Sydney   Toronto

Library of Congress Cataloging-in-Publication Data

Lewis, Catherine M.
    Don't ask what I shot : how Eisenhower's love of golf helped shape 1950s America /
by Catherine M. Lewis.
        p.   cm.
    Includes bibliographical references.
    ISBN 0-07-148570-8
    1. Eisenhower, Dwight D. (Dwight David), 1890–1969.   2. Eisenhower, Dwight D.
(Dwight David), 1890–1969—Influence.   3. Presidents—Sports—United States—Case
studies.   4. Presidents—Recreation—United States—Case studies.   5. Golf—
United States—History—20th century.   6. Golf—Social aspects—United States—
History—20th century.   7. Golf—Political aspects—United States—History—20th
century.   8. Presidents—United States—Biography.   I. Title.

E836.L48   2007
973.921092—dc22   2007005453

1 2 3 4 5 6 7 8 9 10 11 12 13 14 15 16 17 18   FGR/FGR   0 9 8 7

ISBN-13: 978-0-07-148570-8
ISBN-10:   0-07-148570-8

Photo insert design by Pamela Juárez

McGraw-Hill books are available at special quantity discounts to use as premiums and sales
promotions, or for use in corporate training programs. For more information, please write
to the Director of Special Sales, Professional Publishing, McGraw-Hill, Two Penn Plaza, New
York, NY 10121-2298. Or contact your local bookstore.

This book is printed on acid-free paper.

For my daughter

CONTENTS

PREFACE

On January 24, 1953, four days after his inauguration, the *New York Times* reported that President Dwight D. Eisenhower, known fondly as Ike by both friends and strangers, had been spotted on the White House lawn practicing his short irons in the direction of the Washington Monument. Soon, reporters and tourists began gathering outside the gates of the White House to get a glimpse of their new president. They quickly learned that the late afternoon was the prime time for spying Ike practicing near his office. Aides confirmed that Ike would take a bucket of balls and work on his game for a half hour with his valet, John Moaney, shagging for him. These informal sessions became important substitutes for a full round at Burning Tree Club or Augusta National Golf Club, two of the many private golf courses where Ike preferred to play.

Golf was on Ike's mind constantly—he often took practice swings in his room before his morning appointments began. Rarely was he seen in the afternoons without a golf club in his hands and his golf spikes on; sometimes he even moved meetings onto the lawn to keep from missing his practice sessions. After Ike suffered his first heart attack, in 1955, a reporter asked about how his recovery was progressing, to which Ike replied,

"Pretty well, pretty well, but I'm having trouble getting around the ball." For most of his public life, Ike's golf game was intimately connected to his well-being.

For years, visitors to the White House's inner sanctum could see one of Ike's most enduring legacies: spike marks on the floor of the Oval Office. They are invisible now, because both Richard Nixon and Ronald Reagan had the floors redone, leaving what *Golf Digest* writer Tom Callahan described as only "a glimpse of a sweet past." Not everybody, though, was nostalgic about the damage Ike left behind. John F. Kennedy, his successor and a far better golfer than Ike, once complained to "60 Minutes" producer Don Hewitt, "Look what that son of a bitch did with his golf cleats."

Kennedy was not Eisenhower's only critic. Ike tolerated a fair amount of flak from Democratic members of Congress and foreign leaders for his proclivity for golf. Yet he never stopped playing nor did he lose his sense of humor about the game. Labor leader Jacob Potofsky of the Amalgamated Clothing Workers of America once remarked, "You know, Mr. President, we're keeping track of the number of times you play golf," to which Ike replied, "You go right ahead. I only wish I could play more." Fidel Castro predictably disdained Ike's sport of choice, calling golf "a game of the idle rich and exploiter of the people."

In the spring of 1955, Ike found himself with a more formidable adversary. On March 3, a front-page *New York Times* headline read, "President vs. Squirrels and Senator." Apparently, the White House squirrels that had been hand-fed during Harry Truman's presidency were destroying the surface of the putting green that Ike had allowed the United States Golf Association (USGA) to install on the lawn in 1954. Ike ordered the marauding rodents to be trapped and removed to wooded areas in Maryland and Virginia. Outraged by the spectacle of members of the U.S. Army chasing squirrels around the White House lawn, several Democrats, led by Senator Richard L. Neuberger of Oregon, started a "Save the White House Squirrels Fund."

To announce his plans, Neuberger delivered what may have been the most unusual speech of his career, and this was not a man known for his whimsy. To a nearly empty Senate chamber, Neuberger pleaded with the president, "Tolerate a few scratches and bumps on your private putting green in order to continue a fine and colorful heritage of the White House squirrels." He asked that a fence be erected to prevent the squirrels from coming onto the green and also asked Ike to support a rescue program so that "squirrel families can be brought together again in happy reunions." Under public pressure, the administration finally announced that it would allow the squirrels to remain on the White House grounds. Eventually, Neuberger donated $202.48 that he had raised for the squirrel fund to the Wildlife Management Institute. For the first time in his life, General Dwight D. Eisenhower—who had served as the supreme commander of the Allied Expeditionary Forces in Europe during World War II, head of the American Occupation Zone in Germany, chief of staff, president of Columbia University, the first supreme Allied commander of the North Atlantic Treaty Organization (NATO), and president of the United States—admitted public defeat, albeit with a grin on his face.

Stories about Ike and his golfing exploits are largely lost to the American public today. Historians and journalists who write about the 1950s rarely focus on the culture of sports. Instead, the decade is remembered as an era populated by either June and Ward Cleaver or a maniacal Joseph McCarthy. Ike is often portrayed as a bystander watching the nation change before his eyes. One enduring image of this era—drawn by famed *Washington Post* political cartoonist Herblock—depicts Ike as a doddering old man who is unsure of what is happening around him. But a closer look tells another story and reveals a contradiction of epic proportions. Ike was the last president born in the nineteenth century, and his presidency set the country's agenda for the next fifty years. The issues his administration grappled with—race relations, suburban growth, and the arms race—continue to shape national politics to this day. The values Ike embraced would be tried, tested, and found inadequate to meet the complex challenges of a changing world. Yet he was beloved by the American public, enjoying high approval ratings and earning respect across the political spectrum throughout much of his presidency.

As a historian and author, I was surprised when I came across a series of front-page newspaper articles that pictured Ike golfing with various politicians or celebrities. As I would soon find out, my surprise was misplaced; it became difficult to find an image of him *without* a golf club in his hand. Curiously, the accompanying articles rarely had anything to do with the image. For instance, photos of Ike in full golf dress illustrated articles on subjects as varied and important as the Korean War, H-bomb testing, U.S. policy in the Middle East, or planning for the new interstate highway system. No matter the tone or topic of the article, Ike was frequently depicted as a smiling, casually dressed, relaxed president tooling around a golf course. After finding literally dozens of these images juxtaposed with the headlines of the moment, I began to wonder how the media's portrayal of the president in this way must have affected the American people and foreign governments. Did they wonder if Ike was taking the issues of his presidency seriously? Or conversely, did his golf game give them confidence in his leadership? As I began to look into these and other questions, a complex picture of the 1950s emerged, one that can be clearly seen through the lens of Eisenhower and his favorite pastime. Recently, historians such as David Halberstam, Peter Guralnick, Pete Daniel, and others have turned their attention to this enigmatic decade, hoping to understand its contradictions. Ike on a golf course may be a crucial key to unlocking many of them.

ACKNOWLEDGMENTS

I want to begin by thanking Jill K. Sauser, my colleague and friend, who mined through magazines, newspapers, and other sources to find articles published on President Dwight D. Eisenhower and golf. The many stories and anecdotes found in this book are mainly the result of her careful research and stellar organizational skills.

B. G. Dilworth, my agent, deserves enormous credit for making *Don't Ask What I Shot* the book that it is. Nothing I say can thank him enough for his insight, good humor, and perseverance. He is one of the best in the business, and I am honored that he took so much pride in this project.

I would like to single out the staff at the Eisenhower Center in Abilene, Kansas. Throughout the writing process, Herb Pankratz helped me identify pertinent collections on Ike's favorite hobby. My research began and ended with his guidance. Dennis H. J. Medina, the museum's longtime curator, and Nathan Myers, who had only been on the job for three weeks, gave me a personal tour of the museum's golf holdings and shared their broad knowledge of the former president. B. J. Splichal in the reception office greeted me each morning and helped me navigate through the center. In the library, Chalsea Millner and Catherine Cain pulled dozens and dozens of manuscript collections for me to review. Kathy Struss helped locate and scan photography. Finally, Mark and Elizabeth Glennerster and Jolly Bean, proprietors of Abilene's Bed and Breakfast, went out of their way to make me feel welcome during my research trip in July 2006. Their Midwestern hospitality was in full bloom during a fierce heat wave.

Patty Moran at the United States Golf Association helped me locate materials on Eisenhower and his influence on golf. She is a consummate librarian and a good friend. It's always worth a trip to Golf House just to spend time perusing the library and chatting with her and the rest of the staff. The staff at the Robert W. Woodruff Library at Emory University provided reference support, and I am particularly grateful to Chris Palazzolo and Gayle Williams for resolving last-minute problems with citations.

Glenn Greenspan and Jill Maxwell at Augusta National Golf Club assisted me in locating obscure facts about Eisenhower's time at the club and in the city. They have, for much of my career, always been quick to respond to my inquires and provide just what I need. Nobody could ask for more.

At Reid Memorial Church in Augusta, I would like to thank Jan Blisset, Boyd Lien, Kay Pruitt, and Phillip and Helen Christman. They were so kind to help me locate the memorials to Eisenhower throughout the church and city. Tom Beck, Director of Recreation and Parks for the city of Augusta, deserves special thanks for answering last-minute questions about Eisenhower Park. My friend and colleague Lynn Watson-Powers also deserves recognition for taking a half-day field trip around Augusta to locate sites related to Eisenhower. She also kindly read and commented on Chapter Six and made important edits.

Doc Giffin at Arnold Palmer Enterprises kindly arranged my correspondence with Arnold Palmer, who was a close friend and frequent golfing companion of Eisenhower. Zoila Torres of SoliDesign scanned and touched-up all of the images.

Many thanks to John Turner, a professor of history at Colby College in Maine, for helping to find a particularly useful article from the *Economist* that opens Chapter Three. I'm also grateful to my colleagues at Kennesaw State University and the KSU Foundation, including Paul Dover, John D. Fowler, Thierry Leger, Karen Paonessa, Kay Reeve, Howard Shealy, Richard Vengroff, Dave Waples, and Wesley K. Wicker, for their support for my research and their enthusiasm for this project. I would be remiss if I did not recognize and thank the staff in Interlibrary Loan at the Sturgis Library at Kennesaw State University. Amy Thompson, Michelle Smith, and Jonathan Lu worked hard to help me locate books and articles in a timely manner, often exceeding my expectations. I am forever grateful for their efficiency.

Thomas Mann, author of *The Oxford Guide to Library Research*, and David Kelly, the sports and recreation reference specialist, helped me navigate the massive collection at the Library of Congress on several occasions, identifying numerous books and articles that helped me round out my research. Jeff Bridgers of the Prints and Photographs Division at the Library of Congress helped me find numerous images of Eisenhower and his life and times, and for this I am forever grateful.

Charlie and Dorothy Yates and their family shared their private collection of Eisenhower memorabilia and told me behind-the-scenes stories about Eisenhower that gave me a more complex and human portrait of the man. I am also grateful to the Atlanta Athletic Club for sharing its Eisenhower collection with me. The letters, telegrams, and photographs have helped me find stories about Ike that I had not known. Gordy Keen, a longtime member of Merion Golf Club, also sent me the 1960 Eisenhower Cup program, for which I am grateful.

I had several readers who did much to shape and improve the manuscript. My father, James Richard Lewis, and brother, Richard Anthony "Tony" Lewis, both edited early drafts and offered valuable suggestions. As I discovered long ago, it is useful to have two professors, one trained in English and one in art history, sitting at your dinner table. My discussions with them helped shape my thinking about Ike and this enigmatic decade. Finally, Stacy Braukman served, once again, as a fine copyeditor. Her careful attention to detail and good humor helped improve the manuscript in ways that I can never repay.

At McGraw-Hill, Mark Weinstein was the first person to see the merit of this project. I am also grateful to Doug Corcoran, my editor, who offered much enthusiasm for the book. Julia Anderson Bauer, Ann Pryor, and so many others helped bring the book to life. Last, but never least, I want to thank my husband, John Companiotte, a noted golf historian and author in his own right. His keen critical eye and spirited conversation about Ike and the fifties kept me thinking and revising until the last moment.

ONE

GOLF BEFORE IKE

One may not agree that golf builds more character than any other game, but who will deny that it takes real fortitude to stay with the game and conquer it? Oddly enough, the game we all allegedly play for fun cannot be taken lightly.

— HENRY FORD II

Dwight David "Ike" Eisenhower emerged as a national hero after leading the Allied victory in Europe against fascism during World War II, and this fame helped him secure two terms as president, from 1953 to 1961. He was, even to his enemies, not Mr. President but Ike. This nickname symbolized his easy smile and no-nonsense manner. While in the White House, his obsession with golf provided easy fodder for critics; they accused him of spending more time rolling a little white ball down green fairways than attending to the affairs of state. Yet, in the face of this criticism, Eisenhower prevailed, enjoying widespread public support and high poll numbers throughout his presidency.

Golf, too, benefited from his popularity. If the elitist and unathletic game of golf was Ike's sport of choice, that was good enough for most Americans. Frequently photographed with a golf club in his hands, Ike was largely responsible for the midcentury growth in the sport.

Golf boomed twice in America during the twentieth century. The sport first gained a foothold in the early 1890s, just a few years after Eisenhower was born. The United States Golf Association (USGA) was founded in 1894, and the first U.S. Open was played the following year. During the 1920s, when Ike played at the U.S. Army's Command and General Staff School at Fort Leavenworth, Kansas, golf was enjoying its first period of dramatic growth. Noted golf course architect Donald Ross designed or renovated more than two hundred courses during the decade as the game gained new adherents. The Jazz Age also produced the first genuine golf hero, Robert Tyre "Bobby" Jones Jr., who, as an amateur in 1930, became the first and only golfer to win the four major championships in a single year, an achievement that became known as the Grand Slam.

Not surprisingly, however, participation in the sport declined dramatically during the Great Depression and World War II. In 1927, 2.7 million members belonged to 5,500 country clubs. By 1939, the numbers had been reduced to 593,000 members at 4,700 clubs. More golf courses closed than opened during the 1930s. In the early 1940s, the industry suffered from a lack of personnel, materials, and maintenance as wartime exigencies consumed financial and human resources. Even the fabled Augusta National, which later became a beloved vacation spot for Ike and Mamie, was converted into a cow pasture in support of the war effort. But as the country entered a period of unprecedented prosperity after 1945, golf enjoyed a renaissance.

After the war, men and women took up the sport for numerous reasons: it gave players an opportunity to enjoy the outdoors, it was something the whole family could do together, and it was quickly becoming a tangible status symbol of the much-heralded American prosperity. The sudden influx of returning soldiers, some of whom had been introduced to golf while stationed on military bases or during exhibition matches attended by celebrities, came home eager to try the sport. Thousands of women, who had enjoyed unprecedented independence during the war, embraced golf as a means of preserving at least a semblance of the autonomy they had experienced in the public sector between 1941 and 1945. In addition, new methods and equipment made golf course construction more efficient, and more golfers meant that additional courses were needed to accommodate demand.

Photographs of Eisenhower enthusiastically playing his favorite courses during his presidency also kindled the nation's interest in the sport. If golf was worthy of Ike's participation, then it must be good for anybody. Ike was widely popular among the American people, regardless of their political persuasion. "I Like Ike" was not only a political slogan but the consensus concerning the president. His obsession with the game—combined with the postwar rise in leisure time, the availability of new equipment, the advent of televised sports, and the popularity of players such as Ben Hogan and a young Arnold Palmer—proved influential in the sport's second renaissance.

The two golf booms were also part of a larger emphasis on physical fitness, sports, and recreation. Time on

3

the job was shortened progressively in the first half of the twentieth century, allowing for more leisure time. In 1850, before the Civil War, nonagricultural workers in the United States averaged a seventy-hour workweek. By Ike's twentieth birthday, in 1910, that number had declined to fifty-five. Nineteenth- and twentieth-century reformers William A. Alcott, Russell Trall, Catharine Beecher, and others published numerous articles on the importance of diet, exercise, and health care reform as Americans saw a growth in discretionary time and income. Beecher's *Physiology and Calisthenics for Schools and Families*, published in 1856, advocated fitness regimes for schools and hospitals. The Young Men's Christian Association (YMCA), founded in England in 1844 and in the United States in 1851, came to symbolize the confluence of Christianity and muscularity in America in the latter part of the nineteenth century. The organization recruited members at 348 gymnasiums that were spread throughout the nation by 1892.

The Association for the Advancement of Physical Education was established in 1885, five years before Eisenhower's birth, followed by the Society of Directors of Physical Education in 1897 and the Association of Directors of Physical Education for Women in 1910. The revitalization of the Olympic Games in 1896 and the rise of amateur athletic clubs also reflected these new trends. Research on cardiology, which became vitally important to Eisenhower in the middle of the twentieth century, had its roots in the nineteenth. In 1877, Dr. E. H. Bradford published a report demonstrating that Harvard students who had been rowers lived longer than nonathletes. Many Americans, including Ike, embraced the new focus on health and turned their attention to sports.

4

But the term itself meant different things to different people at the turn of the century. Baseball and prize-fighting, for example, appealed primarily to members of the working classes, especially new immigrants from Poland, Russia, Ireland, Austria-Hungary, and Italy who came to America between 1880 and World War I. Golf, tennis, yachting, cricket, and polo—all associated with country clubs—were closely allied with the affluent and native born. These sports embodied patrician, corporate, and Victorian values of modesty and sportsmanship. But such values were in flux. In the 1880s, social commentator Hobart Chatfield-Taylor argued that men were divided into "the workers and the loafers" and sport was for the "weak-minded." A mere ten years later, the "new creed of health and happiness" had transformed sport into a sign of masculinity. Certain sports became, in the words of historian Richard Moss, "redemptive leisure," which served as antidotes to the world of business. But golf posed a special problem.

In 1926, as Ike was perfecting his game, reformer Robert Hunter wrote, "Less than thirty years ago the game was looked upon as something effeminate—an unmanly sport suited to the pink-coated fops and dandies who played it. And what moral courage was required in those days to walk the town streets or board a train dressed in knickers and carrying a bag of clubs." Yet, men such as Andrew Carnegie embraced it, claiming that golfers were "worshipers of God of the open air." And like Ike, Carnegie saw that golf tended "to make men dearer friends than ever." The focus on the lessons of golf, which Ike would so eagerly embrace, are echoed by Charles Blair Macdonald, who wrote that "no game brings out more unerringly the true character of the man or teaches him a better lesson in self-control."

5

Golf, then, became one of many sports from which Americans could choose at the turn of the century, though its origins are much older. Golf in the British Isles, from the fifteenth century forward, was popular with men and women of all classes. Writing for *Scribner's Magazine*, Henry Howland explained that "the game is a leveler of rank and station. King and commoner, noble and peasant, played on equal terms in days gone by, and rich and poor, clever and dull, are 'like as they lie' when matched in skill." Not until golf came to the United States did it become exclusively associated with the wealthy. In 1786, the South Carolina Golf Club in Charleston (now the Country Club of Charleston) was established as the first golf club in the United States. The second club, the Savannah Golf Club, was founded in Georgia several years later. Early mention of this club was made on September 22, 1796, in the *Georgia Gazette*. Historians have dated the club's beginnings as 1794 and ending at the start of the War of 1812.

Despite the formation of these early clubs, golf would not take a firm hold for another hundred years. Other sports appealing to mass audiences, including horse racing, baseball, cycling, and prizefighting, were more popular. Still, sports associated with wealth and privilege gained more adherents during the late nineteenth century. The first national tennis championship was held in 1881 at the Casino Club (in Newport, Rhode Island), a club so exclusive that Chester A. Arthur, president of the United States from 1881 to 1885, was once turned away for "his inadequate social standing." Historian Benjamin Rader explained the importance of elite games in the United States in the late nineteenth and early twentieth centuries: "In a society characterized by an exceptionally fluid social structure, expensive sports provided a means by which the wealthy, especially the parvenu, could distinguish their numbers from the masses. The wealthy therefore tended to look upon sports requiring merely a field and a ball with contempt; these were the diversions of ordinary people. Instead, they lavished their attention on thoroughbred racing, yachting, polo, track and field, cricket, tennis, and golf, games that might require large amounts of free time, costly facilities, elaborate equipment, and sometimes travel to faraway places."

The reintroduction of golf to the United States is closely associated with Robert Lockhart, a New York linen merchant, and John Reid, manager of J. L. Mott Iron Works. Lockhart has been called "the introducer of the game of golf in this country," while Reid became the "missionary who so ably carried on its perpetuation." The two men were from Dunfermline, Scotland, and Lockhart's business permitted frequent travel between the United States and his home country. In 1887, he visited the Royal Burgh of St. Andrews and, at Reid's suggestion, bought six handmade clubs and two dozen gutta-percha balls from Old Tom Morris's shop. On February 22, 1888, Reid invited four friends to play three holes of about a hundred yards each in an old cow pasture in Yonkers, Westchester County, New York. The event was so successful that Reid ordered more clubs and in April decided to expand the course to six holes over the rough pasture. On November 14, 1888, four of the men who played that game in Schott's meadow (Harry Holbrook, Kingman H. Putnam, Henry O. Tallmadge, and John B. Upham) later joined Reid at his home for dinner and founded St. Andrews Golf Club. Lockhart was elected first active member, and

7

the club agreed to move the course to an apple orchard, hence the nickname the Apple Tree Gang. Although there were courses that predate Lockhart's and Reid's St. Andrews course, many historians mark 1888 as the true beginning of golf in the United States.

On December 22, 1894—six years after the founding of the American St. Andrews Golf Club and four years after Ike's birth—representatives from five golf clubs met to form the Amateur Golf Association of the United States, which eventually became the USGA. The five charter members were the Country Club in Brookline, Massachusetts (1882); Shinnecock Hills Golf Club in Southampton, New York (1891); Newport Golf Club in Newport, Rhode Island (1893); Chicago Golf Club in Wheaton, Illinois (1892); and St. Andrews Golf Club in Yonkers (1888). (Newport would become one of Eisenhower's favorite vacation spots.) The USGA had four goals: to enforce uniformity in rules of play, to establish a system of handicapping, to establish an executive committee to serve as the final authority in matters of controversy, and above all "to decide on what links the Amateur and Open Championships should be played."

Theodore A. Havemeyer of Newport was elected the first president, and the group organized the first U.S. Amateur and the first U.S. Open (at Newport Golf Club, a nine-hole course) in 1895. The first U.S. Women's Amateur was held that same year at Meadow Brook Club in Hempstead, New York. Many of the early courses comprised six, eight, or twelve holes. Charles Blair Macdonald built the first eighteen-hole course at the Chicago Golf Club in 1893, the year of the Columbian Exposition. During the 1890s, golf became firmly established in the American consciousness. An article in the *New York Times* in 1894 reported, "Society is as prone to fads as are the sparks to fly upward. And the latest in outdoor fads is golf. Tennis, archery and polo have each had their turn, and golf is now coming in to replace them in the fickle minds of the Four Hundred." Dozens of private clubs were founded in this period, and the first public golf course opened in 1895 in Van Courtland Park in Bronx, New York. Golf remained, however, associated with wealth, power, and privilege.

Before World War II, golf was a game played by two very different groups who were divided by class and social status. Amateur men and women mostly played golf at country clubs where they were members. Professionals were frequently male employees of these same clubs who had trained as caddies and were occasionally permitted to travel and participate in exhibitions or compete in tournaments. While amateurs tended to be established scions of society, golf professionals typically were from more eclectic, often humble backgrounds. Ike would have been in this second class.

But the game was changing for professionals. Hoping to sell more sporting equipment in his department stores, Rodman Wanamaker established the Professional Golfers of America (PGA) in 1916 in New York City to formalize a national membership organization for club professionals that still exists today. Similar early efforts in New York, Boston, Philadelphia, Baltimore, Washington, Chicago, and St. Louis paved the way for the formation of a national organization. It was not until 1968 that touring professionals created their own organization, the PGA Tour, separate from the PGA of America, to manage their operations.

Professional golfers welcomed Wanamaker's efforts. In the early part of the twentieth century, professional golf was not nearly as lucrative as it is today. Purses for regional tournaments barely covered travel expenses, as prize money rarely exceeded $200. Club professionals' salaries averaged $25 a week, and many golfers in these early years made more money through side bets than by carding the lowest score. Jim Barnes, winner of the first PGA Championship (in 1916), remembered playing in tournaments that gave cakes and pies as prizes.

The spread of golf was aided by Wanamaker's largesse and the growth of railroads, especially those traveling south to places like Augusta, Georgia; Aiken, South Carolina; and Asheville, North Carolina. The automobile was a mere novelty until the 1910s, while trains offered speed and comfort. Luxury hotels with challenging courses were built along East Coast rail lines, ushering in the era of resort golf. Golf periodicals also started appearing at the turn of the century: *Golf* began in 1897, *Golfer's Magazine* in 1902, the *American Golfer* in 1907, and *Golf Illustrated* in 1914. Popular magazines such as the *Ladies' Home Journal,* the *New Yorker, Saturday Evening Post,* and *Collier's* began featuring male and female golfers on their covers. Benjamin Rader argued that golf expanded much faster than tennis: "Abetted by the rapid growth of country clubs in the 1920s, golf spread (as one wag put it) from the upper 'Four Hundred' to the upper 'Four Million'." He further noted that businessmen, cramped in crowded, busy offices, found a "pastoral retreat" on the golf course. But he offered yet another explanation: "Sometimes golf seemed only a pretext for convivial gatherings at the 'nineteenth hole,' the clubhouse bar."

Three British players—Harry Vardon, J. H. Taylor, and James Braid—dominated golf before World War I. But American players were making important inroads. In 1913, Francis Ouimet, a former caddie, thrilled the nation by winning the U.S. Open at the Country Club in Brookline, Massachusetts, signaling a sea change. World War I slowed the production of golf equipment and the playing of championships, but by the 1920s, golf was again booming. In 1913, fewer than 350,000 Americans played golf. By 1923, with active golfer Warren G. Harding in the White House, two million people had taken up the sport.

That same year, Bobby Jones won his first national championship, the U.S. Open. Born in Atlanta, Georgia, Jones would become an international hero. He played in dozens of tournaments between 1916 and 1922 but failed to capture a national title. While a student at Harvard University, Jones beat Bobby Cruickshank in a play-off at the 1923 U.S. Open at Inwood Country Club in New York to capture his first national championship. Over the next seven years, Jones won five U.S. Amateurs (1924, 1925, 1927, 1928, 1930), four U.S. Opens (1923, 1926, 1929, 1930), three British Opens (1926, 1927, 1930), and one British Amateur (1930). In 1926, as Ike was finishing his program at the U.S. Army's Command and General Staff School, Jones won the U.S. Open and British Open. His crowning achievement came in 1930 when he won the Grand Slam (the British Amateur, British Open, U.S. Amateur, and U.S. Open). All told, Jones played in thirty-one majors and placed first or second better than 80 percent of the time. It is hard to overestimate Jones's fame in his era. The *Atlanta Journal* once compared the golfer to "the Cyclorama, Stone Mountain, and Margaret Mitchell as

11

a top Atlanta attraction." Upon his retirement in 1930, Jones played in exhibition matches and twelve Masters Tournaments. Because of the advancing symptoms of a spinal disease, he played his final round of golf (at the Atlanta Athletic Club's East Lake course) in 1948, the same year Ike was invited by Jones and Clifford Roberts to become a member of Augusta National Golf Club.

After Jones retired and as the Depression gained momentum, the American public's interest in golf waned. Professional golfers in the 1930s were journeymen, mainly club professionals who balanced tournament careers with their responsibilities at golf courses. Only a handful of players, such as Walter Hagen and Gene Sarazen, were prominent enough to negotiate time off to play in exhibitions and tournaments. Playing in PGA-sponsored events was at best a part-time occupation. As a result of the growing financial crisis in the nation, professional golf suffered a decadelong decline.

World War II further hampered golf, as it did many sports. Golf equipment companies began contributing to the war effort: Titleist manufactured gas masks and MacGregor made parachute packs. Though it was a legitimate form of recreation, many Americans saw golf—more than other sports—as frivolous in the face of war. Setting moral issues aside, even if a golfer wanted to play, the rationing of gas and the limited number of caddies imposed additional constraints. On December 17, 1941, ten days after the Japanese bombing of Pearl Harbor, Leon Henderson, administrator of the Office of Price Administration, announced that rubber products would be rationed for civilians. The only response left to golfers was to conserve their golf balls or give up the game altogether. Some were unwilling to do either, evidenced by the golfers who stampeded sporting goods stores to purchase all of the balls that were on the shelves. Abercrombie & Fitch reported on December 18, 1941, that the New York City store had sold twenty-four thousand balls. On April 9, 1942, the War Production Board ordered golf equipment manufacturing to be stopped completely; a month later, an amendment allowed companies to make new clubs with materials on hand. Despite the changes, many golfers in the armed forces and on the home front refused to abandon the game. One story holds that a paratrooper under Ike's command carried a golf club with him on D-day to ensure that he would have the honor of driving the first golf ball in a liberated Normandy.

To further complicate matters, the golf tour was almost completely suspended during the war. The USGA, under the presidency of Harold Pierce, made that decision at a meeting in New York on January 9, 1942. Pierce argued, "With the nation at war the association is faced with a major question of policy. I feel the association should cancel its championships and devote its effort to war relief." His colleagues supported his position and issued the following resolution: "Resolved, that it is the sense of the Executive Committee of the United States Golf Association that the main aim of golfers and golf organizations should be to contribute to the greatest possible service to the nation for the duration of the war. Therefore, be it further resolved, that the Executive Committee of the United States Golf Association hereby cancels the four championships which it has scheduled for 1942—namely the Open, the Amateur, the Women's Amateur, and the Amateur Public Links Championship." Golf writer Herbert Graffis

13

explained how the USGA silenced criticism of the decision: "What to hell, don't you guys know your country is in a war?" The Royal and Ancient Golf Club of St. Andrews had already canceled the British Open.

Ed Dudley, the president of the PGA of America who would later serve as Ike's professional at Augusta National, was reluctant to follow suit, so the PGA Championship was played in 1942. It would later be canceled for 1943 and resumed again in 1944. Baseball, however, took a different path. When Judge Kenesaw Mountain Landis wrote to President Franklin D. Roosevelt, asking him what should be done about baseball, the president responded decisively, "I honestly feel that it would be best for the country to keep baseball going. There will be fewer people unemployed and everybody will work longer hours and harder than ever before. And that means that they ought to have a chance for recreation and for taking their minds off their work even more than before." Golf, associated with leisure and, in some minds, idleness, seemed inappropriate to many during a time of national crisis, whereas baseball, widely regarded as a democratic and national sport, was heralded as a legitimate diversion.

Promoters of the professional golf tour tried to keep events going in the midst of the war. In 1943, the PGA of America announced that only three official events, with a total of $17,000 in prize money, would be played. Golf, some believed, could revive its image and become associated with patriotic endeavors. Individual clubs were encouraged by the USGA to put a Red Cross box by the first tee to get golfers to donate a dime a round. USGA committeeman Edward Cheney calculated that sixty-three million rounds were played in 1941, indicating that such a program would bring $6.3 million to the war effort. Clubs also agreed to host individual Hale America tournaments to coincide with Memorial Day. Bobby Jones, who reportedly demonstrated a "swing as smooth as Dixie molasses," led the qualifiers at the Atlanta Athletic Club's East Lake Golf Club for the 1942 Hale America National Golf Tournament. Ben Hogan would go on to win the event that netted $25,000 in 1942 for Navy Relief and the United Service Organizations (USO). By comparison, the U.S. Open the year before had raised $12,567.

Coverage of the Miami Open in the *Miami Herald* revealed how most of the organizers responded to the new conditions: "The Miami Open is competing with the greatest news of the generation—the war with Japan. But its value will not be lost, its interest for the public entirely blotted out by the clouds of war. Your golf addict will be watching the daily reports of the play from coast to coast. The American sports fan never quite loses interest in athletic battles, come war or high water." But the organizers of such events did not simply conduct business as usual. Many arranged for prize money to be conferred in war bonds. For the PGA of America, this gesture was a way to both contribute to the war effort and keep golf alive. Moreover, players and promoters wanted to make sure that golf would not be perceived as self-serving. Ed Dudley, president of the PGA of America, went as far as to send a letter to President Franklin D. Roosevelt to reassure him that professional golf would support the war relief agencies in whatever way they could. Golf did contribute, with more than three thousand tournaments organized to benefit the Red Cross.

While golf temporarily declined in the United States, it was hit especially hard throughout the British Commonwealth. The British Open was not played from 1940 to 1945, and the Ryder Cup was canceled from 1939 through 1945. Many British players—Henry Cotton, Charlie Ward, and Arthur Lacey—set their clubs aside to help fight fascism. And the British government urged players to do their part at "Keeping Adolf at Bay." Numerous courses were badly damaged by German bombs, but they remained open for play. The players at Richmond Park were asked to abide by temporary rules established in 1941 that required golfers to "collect the bomb and shrapnel splinters to save these causing damage to the mowing machines" and were advised that "a ball moved by enemy action may be replaced." Golfers who played in Kent were told to carry guns in case of the sudden appearance of German paratroopers.

As supreme Allied commander, Ike played infrequently while in Europe during the war, but Ike's golf caddie, Army Lieutenant James "Jimmy" Preston, recounted one telling anecdote in a letter to his sister from 1943 when the general was stationed in Italy: "When I rolled out the map of the golf course he got that slight frown on his face and walked around the table two or three times. He wanted to see it from all angles, pointed at certain features and asked a lot of tough questions. This was designed by the Special Corps and yours truly; he hadn't seen any of it. I could tell he was pleased, but he didn't want to show it too much. We were almost finished when he spotted something and leaned down on the table. Then he looked at me and said we had a problem, that he and General Marshall were going to play on Friday, tee-off at o-nine-hundred hours. I said we'd be ready. The General said that I didn't understand and, pointing at the map said, 'this is a shot General Marshall can easily make. There needs to be one helluva bunker right there.' He was pointing with his finger directly in front of the green at Hole Four. I'll tell you, Sis, my face got real hot all of the sudden. I told him that Special Corps had advanced on into Greece and that I didn't have any help and that the Italians couldn't care less about it. I had to tell him that I didn't know if we could get a hole that large dug in time. You can imagine I wanted to crawl out of there. The General paced for about five seconds and you can see why he's the Commander. He called in an Army Air Force general and asked him who was the best low-altitude pilot in Italy. The Air Force general named a man who knew the answer to the question. The General said that the pilot was to contact me immediately for a special mission. And that was that. The Warhawk came in low just at dusk. It followed the line of flags leading up to Hole Four and over the flagged-off circle in the grass. It banked hard over the brown hills and I ran for cover behind a tree near Hole Three. The next run he was maybe forty-five feet over the target and I saw the bomb hit the grass and disappear into the ground for about two seconds. In that instant I thought it was a dud until the grass and dirt and rocks blasted out and rained down over everything. He flew over just once more, rocked his wings and the Warhawk became just a speck in the sky and was gone. I don't even know who he was and if he ever wondered what he was doing but it was as near to a perfect bunker as I've ever seen in the States. To make a long story short, Gen. Marshall lost to the General and I'll have to tell you that I did

17

everything but bite my tongue as General Marshall just about wore out his sand iron clawing his way out of the bunker on Hole Four."

While Ike led the troops against Hitler and Mussolini, golfers in America heeded Winston Churchill's December 30, 1941, speech to the Canadian Parliament: "In this strange, terrible war there is a place for everyone, man and woman, old and young, hale and halt; service in a thousand forms is open. There is room for the dilettante, the weakling, for the shirker, or the sluggard. The mine, the factory, the dockyard, the salt sea waves, the fields to till, the home, the hospital, the chair of the scientist, the pulpit of the preacher— from the highest to the humblest task, all of our equal honor; all have their part to play." Golf's role would be multifaceted. In 1942, the PGA of America bought two ambulances for the Red Cross and distributed golf clubs and balls to military bases. The USGA donated a new ambulance to the Royal and Ancient Golf Club of St. Andrews with a note that read, "The United States Golf Association sends from its annual meeting its sincere expression of goodwill to the Royal and Ancient Golf Club and its renewed hopes for a just peace for the world." The Women's Golf Association of Philadelphia collected 1,352 golf clubs, 200 golf balls, and 138 golf bags in a single week to donate to soldiers. By November 1944, the PGA had contributed $550,000 to war charities, service organizations, and soldier rehabilitation projects.

President Roosevelt named Olympian John B. Kelly, the father of Grace Kelly, assistant U.S. director of civil defense in charge of physical fitness. Founded in 1941, the Office of Civil Defense was a federal agency that coordinated state and federal efforts to protect the civilian populace, promote volunteerism, and bolster morale. Golf was only one part of Kelly's program, and he himself played periodically with professional Porky Oliver. In a speech to the USGA, Kelly outlined his position: "Eight million people will be going into the armed forces. My job is to look after the one hundred twenty-four million who won't or can't go. They can keep fit by playing golf. France was the most physically inactive country in the world, and look what happened to it." Kelly appointed Fred Corcoran, who at the time was managing the PGA of America's tournaments, to be his golf deputy. Corcoran's job was to encourage the USGA, the PGA, and golf clubs around the nation to host tournaments that could raise funds for the war. Corcoran recruited Bobby Jones, Craig Wood (the U.S. Open champion), and Ed Dudley to help promote and coordinate the Hale America tournaments. Jones's earlier work during World War I, raising $150,000 in a series of Red Cross matches played with Perry Adair, Elaine Rosenthal, and Alexa Stirling, made him a logical choice to aid in World War II. In a letter to O. B. Keeler, who reported on Jones during the teens and twenties, Jones explained his position: "The production job we face now is far greater than that of the previous war. It is going to require the most efficient use of all the resources we possess. The men who work with their hands are of vast importance, but the real McCoys are the fellows who know how to set up a production schedule and make it click—in short, the managers. And they need breathing spells in their thinking as much as the workmen need rest for their hands. They can walk, or pull the weights, or ride a bicycle for physical exercise.

19

But the best way for them to get exercise, fresh air, and mental relaxation at the same time is to play golf. They can't do much worrying on a golf course."

Many of the regular Tour players served in the war; in fact, by November 1, 1943, nearly 350 PGA members were in the military. Vic Ghezzi was stationed at Fort Monmouth, New Jersey; Joe Turnesa and Horton Smith were in the Army; Jimmy Demaret and Sam Snead were in the Navy; and Ben Hogan joined the Army Air Corps in 1942. Lloyd Mangrum, who would win the U.S. Open in 1946, was wounded at the Battle of the Bulge. For the players who did not serve—Byron Nelson due to a blood condition, Harold McSpaden for asthma, and Craig Wood because of a back injury—the PGA of America, as it had done during World War I, coordinated exhibition matches and visits to rehabilitation centers. Throughout 1942 and 1943, Nelson and McSpaden, called the Gold Dust Twins, participated in more than a hundred such events across the United States. Sponsored by MacGregor and Wilson, they often traveled with Bob Hope and Bing Crosby and frequently visited camps where their fellow professionals were stationed.

Hope, who would become Ike's close friend and frequent golfing partner, did much to popularize golf during World War II. Before Pearl Harbor, Hope, along with Crosby, participated in exhibition matches at the request of President Roosevelt to raise money for the War Relief Fund. The matches more closely resembled vaudeville routines than legitimate competitions, but the public and the troops loved them. Hope played often with Babe Didrikson Zaharias, one of the best female golfers of the era and a founding member of the LPGA. They both engaged the crowds with their banter, as Hope revealed in one story: "On a par-3 hole, if I hit first, she'd ask me, 'What club did you use, Bob?' I'd say a 4-iron. In a loud voice that the gallery couldn't miss, she'd laugh and tell her caddie, 'Give me an 8-iron.' " During an exhibition in Chicago, a spectator called out while Hope was addressing the ball, "Hey, Hope, your slip is showing." With perfect timing, Hope replied, "Your father's slip is showing." During the war, Hope often joined other celebrities in USO performances and exhibition matches. He would entertain the troops with golf jokes and a driver as his only prop and, in this way, introduced young men and women around the world to a game that they may never have played before. In recognition of Hope's efforts, Ike (then army chief of staff) awarded him the Medal of Merit after the war.

This was not the first time golf went to war. It had been a part of military life for several decades before World War II. Herb Graffis, author of *The PGA*, estimated that more than 200,000 men were introduced to golf at courses on military bases. What eventually became the site for Memorial Park Golf Course in Houston began as a place for recuperating soldiers to play golf after World War I. A. W. Tillinghast, who would later become famous for designing the San Francisco Golf Club, Winged Foot, Baltusrol, and the Philadelphia Cricket Club, designed the Fort Sam Houston Golf Course in San Antonio in 1921. Had Tillinghast been there six years earlier, he might have enticed Ike to play when the young soldier was stationed there in 1915. It was one of the best military courses in the country. Dozens of other golf courses were established by the military on U.S. soil and on bases throughout the world. Because the federal government subsidized the courses,

21

military personnel could play golf more affordably than civilians. Some soldiers, like the men at a naval construction unit in the South Pacific, were forced to improvise. In 1944, First Class Metalsmith Tim Sullivan, using homemade clubs, won a tournament on a course that the men designed. The trophy was made from a 105-millimeter shell.

Veterans hospitals in the United States also built golf courses, including one at Oliver General Hospital in Augusta, Georgia, to aid in the rehabilitation of injured soldiers. By the end of 1945, the Veterans Administration had documented nineteen hospital golf courses, with six others under construction. Golf was viewed as a sport with great recuperative benefits, as Ike would discover after his 1955 heart attack. Dozens of PGA members helped with entertainment and rehabilitation programs at facilities around the country. Eleven PGA sections reported in 1944 that exhibitions and tournaments raised $130,000 for golf at military hospitals.

Although golf was growing at military bases and hospitals, the war nearly brought about the demise of Augusta National Golf Club (ANGC). As with the PGA Championship, the Masters was canceled from 1943 to 1945. In a letter dated October 1, 1942, Clifford Roberts announced to members that ANGC would close because of World War II. Dues were suspended, and Bobby Jones and Roberts asked members to make a gift to the club of $100 annually to help cover the cost of maintenance, estimated at $12,000 per year. During the war, Roberts supervised the club (which Ike would join in 1948) from his office in New York. In 1942, Jones, who would serve as an Air Corps intelligence officer overseas, suggested that cattle be raised on the grounds to contribute to the war effort. By the next year, the club had a herd of 200, and Roberts purchased 1,423 turkeys. A November 20, 1944, advertisement appeared in the *Augusta Chronicle* promoting turkeys "on foot," "feather picked," or "dressed and drawn." The club may have been heartened to learn that Baltusrol Golf Club had made a profit from raising livestock on its two courses. Unfortunately, Augusta's livestock efforts proved far less successful, but the members hoped they had in some small way helped out on the home front.

In 1942, ANGC financed and supervised the construction of a practice range and a large putting green for the soldiers at nearby Camp Gordon. ANGC committed to design and maintain the facility, install floodlighting, and provide equipment and additional supplies. ANGC declared in a press release, "A man in an army training camp can't come to a golf course—at least, not often. So golf is coming to him." The Bobby Jones Driving Range, as it would be named, accommodated fifty golfers and eventually cost $2,669. Additionally, the members and golf shop made gifts to soldiers of golfing equipment and balls.

Despite wartime efforts to keep golf in the public eye, the war threatened the economic viability of both public and private golf clubs. As the *New York Times* reported in 1942, "The unprecedented current situation hits clubs after a decade of violent readjustment. Only a minority have recovered from the shock of the depression which began in 1929. Many a proud course . . . is now a suburban housing development; once they had a waiting list of members seeking to join, but the hard times of 1930 to 1933 put them in the hands of mortgage holders. Still other once-exclusive clubs have become semi-private." During World War II, many golf clubs were transformed to serve the war effort. Congres-

23

sional Country Club in Washington became a training facility for the Office of Strategic Services in 1943. Philadelphia Country Club allowed the Army Corps of Engineers to use their Spring Mill Course, host to the 1939 U.S. Open, to test chemicals for the purpose of camouflage. The Navy took over Lido Golf Club on Long Island.

The Greenbrier in White Sulphur Springs, West Virginia, housed Hungarian and German diplomats and foreign news correspondents from enemy countries until July 15, 1942. In 1944, the spa and resort at White Sulphur Springs became Ashford General Hospital, a place for Army officers to spend their leave playing golf, riding horses, and swimming. Prior to D-day, Ike and Mamie spent time there, and Ike was seen golfing and reading A Tree Grows in Brooklyn. Baltusrol Golf Club in Springfield, New Jersey, converted its fairways into a farm, hoping to ameliorate the meat shortage. Many clubs set aside land to build victory gardens. Golfing Magazine made light of the sacrifice: "If you are lying close to a cabbage and have played five or more strokes, the new rules allow you to play the cabbage from that point on." Other clubs helped in other ways, such as increasing dues and contributing the excess to the Red Cross, offering free rounds of golf to soldiers stationed nearby, hosting dances for soldiers, and donating clubs to scrap drives.

As victory seemed imminent, Ed Dudley and Fred Corcoran reinvigorated the professional tour. In 1944, twenty-two tournaments were played for a total of $150,500 in war bonds. Late in 1944, Clifford Roberts began working to restore Augusta National to playable conditions. Forty-two German prisoners of war, who had served as an engineering crew in Rommel's Afrika

Korps and were detained at Camp Gordon, completed much of the restoration. They built the bridge over Rae's Creek near the thirteenth tee, which was replaced in 1958 by a stone one dedicated to Byron Nelson. The club reopened on December 23, 1945, and, after a three-year hiatus, the Masters Tournament resumed the next spring. Clubs around the nation that had been largely neglected because of labor shortages had to recondition their courses. Most players did not care; they were willing to carry their own bags and overlook maintenance problems. The war was soon to be over, rationing would end, soldiers would be home, and golf could rebuild.

Byron Nelson's streak of eleven consecutive victories in 1945 was just what the nation needed to prove that golf would survive the war. It all began with the Miami Four-Ball in March. Over the next five months he won at Charlotte, Greensboro, Durham, Atlanta, Montreal, Philadelphia, Chicago (twice), Moraine (Ohio), and Toronto. The streak ended in August at Memphis, when Nelson finished fourth, despite shooting rounds of 69–73–66–68. Along the way, the victory march was chronicled in national magazines such as *Esquire, Life, Time,* and *Collier's,* and he was featured in newsreels shown in movie theaters across the nation. Wheaties even featured him on their cereal boxes. The news coverage of Nelson's accomplishments introduced golf to people who knew little about the game, and he motivated those who did play, especially returning GIs. His streak increased attendance at events, which allowed for larger purses and greater winnings for professionals.

Many soldiers believed that sports could be a key to a lasting peace. Representative Samuel Arthur Weiss, a Democrat from Pennsylvania, joined ten other members of Congress for a postwar tour of Europe. He reported,

"Almost to a man, they feel that the possibilities of bringing about a better understanding through athletic competitions should not be neglected. . . . Those kids would like to see the Olympic Games held every two years instead of four, dual track meets between our universities and schools over there, weekly boxing, tennis, golf, swimming and other engagements. Air travel will make this possible."

At the end of World War II, with the economy expanding and leisure time increasing, golf seemed poised for a second boom. Ike would play a starring role in this new era. For comparison, in the 1920s, two million people played the game; by 1950, there were four million golfers. Shortly after he entered the White House, the *New York Times* reported that Ike's love of golf had dampened enthusiasm for other sports, notably tennis. The article quoted an employee at the Forest Hills tennis club in New York who explained, "I remember just as late as last year you couldn't get on these courts without a reservation a couple of days in advance. . . . When President Eisenhower started playing golf it changed the whole sports picture." Mercer Beasley, an area tennis coach, agreed, saying, "Sure, Ike is creating a golf boom. But what is there for us tennis people to do about it except elect Adlai Stevenson next time."

TWO

THE GOLFING GENERAL

I love the game, no matter how badly I play.
—DWIGHT D. EISENHOWER

Fred Corcoran, a golf promoter and eventual PGA Tour manager, once said that Dwight D. Eisenhower's dedication to golf was "the greatest thing that ever happened to the game." Sport was one of the few constants in Eisenhower's life, as he confessed in middle age: "One of my reasons for going to West Point was the hope that I could continue an athletic career. It would be difficult to overemphasize the importance that I attached to participation in sports." Ike played baseball and football as a teenager and young man, until he injured his knee at West Point. Searching for a less strenuous alternative, he first picked up a set of clubs in 1912 and, with the exception of a brief hiatus in the mid-1920s, played throughout the rest of his life. Golfing and the Eisenhower image were inextricably linked in the popular imagination. Golf, for Ike, was more than a sport or a pastime. He deliberated some of the most important decisions of his career on a golf course.

In some ways, Eisenhower's personality was at odds with the gentle manners and relaxed pace generally associated with the game. He had a fierce temper and was widely known for explosive, but short-lived, outbursts. Writing for *Golf Digest*, Peter Andrews remarked, "One of the many reasons for Eisenhower's popularity with the troops was that he was a general who could swear like a sergeant. At Augusta he is remembered as a man of moderate speech on the golf course, except when he missed a short putt." Ike used golf to test himself. Unlike baseball and football, for which he had a natural affinity, golf was a sport at which he was neither temperamentally nor athletically inclined to excel. Yet, he was dogged in his pursuit of improvement. He used it, as so many other presidents have, as a form of relaxation. But it was more than that. Golf constantly tested Ike's composure and helped him endure numerous crises during his two terms in office. It was never merely a sport for Ike; it was a great challenge, and perhaps the one he never truly mastered. ·

Biographers often measure Eisenhower's life against the well-worn Horatio Alger rags-to-riches mythology. He was not born in a log cabin, what one author termed "that supposedly nineteenth-century prerequisite to political success." Nevertheless, his circumstances were modest, making his achievements even more remarkable. Ike's ancestor Hans Nicolas Eisenhauer came with a group of Mennonites from Germany aboard the *Europa* and settled near the banks of the Susquehanna River in Pennsylvania on November 20, 1741. The family name translated into English meant "iron striker," or "iron beater." Ike's ancestors embraced pacifism, yet members of his family in nearly every generation fought in the major American conflicts, from the Revolution to

World War II. Ike's paternal grandfather, Jacob Eisenhower, was a farmer and a leader of the Brethren in Christ (also known as the River Brethren), a pacifist religious sect that migrated from Pennsylvania to Kansas in 1878. Ike's father, David, did not want to follow in his father's footsteps and attended Lane University in Lecompton, Kansas, hoping to become an engineer. There he met Ida Elizabeth Stover, and the two married at the United Brethren Church on September 23, 1885.

Dwight David Eisenhower was born on October 14, 1890, the third of seven sons (one son, Paul, died of diphtheria), in Denison, Texas, and though he rarely lived in the South, he always considered himself a native of the region. (This would prove important in the mid-1950s in the midst of the struggle to desegregate Central High School in Little Rock, Arkansas.) Historian Stephen Ambrose described the family's precarious financial situation in 1890: "At the time of his birth, Dwight Eisenhower's parents owned their clothes, a few household possessions, and one ebony piano. . . . They had three sons and precious few prospects." While Ike was an infant, the Eisenhower family moved to Abilene, Kansas, so David could take a job for $50 a month as a mechanic at the Belle Springs Creamery Company, owned by the River Brethren and run by his brother-in-law, Chris Musser. Money was tight, as evidenced by one story that Ike told about having to wear his mother's high-button shoes to elementary school because the family did not have the resources to buy a new pair to replace the ones that had become worn.

Ike and his brothers grew up at 201 East South Fourth Street on the south side of the Kansas Pacific (later Union Pacific) railroad tracks in a white frame, three-

29

bedroom house, measuring 818 square feet. Later, the construction of a small wing added two more rooms to accommodate Ike's grandfather. The Eisenhower boys grew up with a keen affinity for rural America and the sporting opportunities it afforded. To supplement their income, the family raised chickens, ducks, and rabbits and tended a fair-sized garden. Ike even sold hot tamales—three for five cents—on the street for additional money. Years later, he recalled that his hometown "provided both a healthy outdoor existence and a need to work. These same conditions were responsible for the existence of a society which, more nearly than any other I have encountered, eliminated prejudices based upon wealth, race, or creed and maintained a standard of values that placed a premium upon integrity, decency, and consideration for others." Ike's mother, Ida, taught him to sew and cook, and Ike became responsible for preparing the family's Sunday dinner and was known for his apple pies.

Abilene forever shaped Ike's view of the world. Historian Piers Brendon described the town: "It was a friendly, respectable, tradition-bound world, remote from the more brutal manifestations of emergent industrialism; a moderate, balanced homogenous world, which paid lip service and more to ethical and egalitarian ideals; a narrow, mealy-mouthed, hypocritical world, which preferred ancient prejudices to novel ideas and banished plain speaking along with abrasiveness; but a world of conciliation, compromise, simple verities, and common decency." With some irony, historian Carl Becker observed that "the fundamental characteristic of Kansas individualism is the tendency to conform." Both assessments neatly sum up the values and culture that shaped Ike.

Eisenhower attended Lincoln Grammar School, Garfield Junior High School, and Abilene High School, where he played center field in baseball and defensive end in football. He had a reputation as a fierce but fair competitor. One Saturday the Abilene football team faced an opposing team that had a black player. When Ike's teammates refused to play against him, Ike stepped forward to play center opposite the black player, shaking the young man's hand before and after the game. Years later, he remembered that the "rest of the team was a bit ashamed." Sports defined Ike's high school years and helped him develop his leadership skills. In 1908, he even helped establish the Abilene High School Athletic Association, a group outside of the school system that coordinated games between different schools and clubs. But Eisenhower was far from a one-dimensional student. His 1909 senior yearbook reported, "Dwight is our best historian and mathematician. His interest in history is one of his outstanding traits as a scholar." In Ike's last year, he had a part in the senior class play, a slapstick version of the *Merchant of Venice*. His performance was reviewed in the local paper: "Dwight Eisenhower as [Launcelot] Gobbo won plenty of applause and deserved it. He was the best amateur humorous character seen on the Abilene stage in this generation and gave an impression that many professionals fail to reach." Fortunately, he did not take the praise too seriously and sought other employment after graduating on May 23, 1909.

Following high school, Ike worked at the creamery with his father to help pay for his brother Edgar's tuition at the University of Michigan. In 1910, his last year in Abilene, he was the second engineer or night foreman, which required him to work eighty-four hours a week

31

for $90 a month. He also briefly played center field in a semiprofessional baseball league in Kansas under an assumed name (Wilson), though he rarely talked about it. But Ike had bigger plans, and with the assistance of family friend Everett "Swede" Hazlett Jr., he began to prepare for the United States Naval Academy's entrance exam. Upon learning that he was too old, he changed course and made application to the United States Military Academy at West Point. With the support of Senator Joseph L. Bristow and after passing the entrance examination, Ike—four months shy of his twenty-first birthday and with $5 in his pocket—entered West Point on June 14, 1911, along with 264 other incoming cadets.

In his first year as a plebe, Ike played football for the Cullum Hall team, which was the equivalent of a junior varsity squad. That spring he played baseball with teammate Omar Bradley. By the fall 1912 season, Ike weighed 174 pounds and was selected for the varsity football team. At five feet eleven inches, he played in the backfield, as what was known then as the number two back. He was given the nickname the Kansas Cyclone. The *New York Times* reported that Ike was "one of the most promising backs in Eastern football." Although he excelled at sports, he proved a mediocre student. His 1912 record is riddled with demerits: "Late to gym formation; alcove not in order; dressed improperly in room; failure to execute a right into the line properly; shoes require polishing." Ike was not too concerned. "I enjoyed life at the Academy, had a good time with my pals, and was far from disturbed by an additional demerit or two," he recalled. Academics were not Ike's priority. By the end of his first year, he ranked fifty-seventh out of 212 cadets. In 1915, he graduated sixty-first among 164 cadets. Ike's graduating class, called "the class the stars fell upon," produced fifty-nine officers who eventually reached the rank of general; two of them (Eisenhower and Bradley) achieved five stars.

Ike said his fondest memory of that time was when he tackled Jim Thorpe in a football game between Army and Carlisle on November 9, 1912. Later that season, in a game between Army and Tufts, Ike twisted his left knee. He described the incident years later: "I was plunging, having broken through the line, and a man got his hands on my foot. Although my knee swelled rapidly, the inflammation was accompanied by little pain. I was hospitalized for two or three days waiting for the swelling to disappear. . . . A few days after release from the hospital, I reported to the riding hall. While taking part in 'monkey drill,' I leaped off my horse to vault over him as he jumped a low hurdle. . . . The landing shock to my injured knee was more than I could take. I ended on the ground with my leg twisted behind me. Cartilages and tendons obviously were badly torn." In an era before knee surgery, Ike was sent to bed for a week with a weight to keep his leg straight. The knee healed, but it was never the same again and would plague him on the golf course for the rest of his life.

From 1914 to 1915, Ike coached junior varsity and served as a cheerleader for the football team. In that capacity, he excelled, as Virgil Pinkley noted: "Ike designed black and gold capes to be worn by certain cadets over their gray uniforms. He arranged their seating in the stands in such a way that they spelled out the word Army. His innovation was the model for today's card stunts. His capes also were the forerunners for the World War II Eisenhower battle jacket."

Ike's knee injury did not keep him from active service in the U.S. Army. Upon graduation, he reported to the

33

Nineteenth Infantry Regiment on September 15, 1915, at Fort Sam Houston near San Antonio.

Sports, however, would remain a key part of Ike's life, and he surrounded himself with former athletes. While serving in World War II, he explained, "I had occasion to be on the lookout for natural leaders. Athletes take a certain amount of kidding, especially from those who think it's always brain vs. brawn. But, I noted . . . how well ex-footballers seemed to have leadership qualifications and it wasn't sentiment that made it seem so." Generals MacArthur and Marshall would have agreed. MacArthur, who was the superintendent at West Point, once wrote, "Upon the fields of friendly strife / Are sown the seed / That, upon other fields, on other days / Will bear the fruits of victory." Those words were etched onto a stone archway that leads to the main gym. As Army chief of staff during World War II, Marshall declared, "I want an officer for a secret and dangerous mission. I want a West Point football player." A plaque bearing those words was mounted on the northeast corner of Michie Stadium at West Point.

At Fort Houston, Ike was asked to coach the football team at the local Peacock Military Academy for $150 a season; the next year he was hired to coach at St. Louis College, a Catholic school. This activity kept him involved in the sporting world that he so loved. In October 1915, Ike met Mary "Mamie" Geneva Doud, who happened to be vacationing in Texas. She was the daughter of John Sheldon Doud, who was the U.S. ambassador to Belgium. After a brief courtship, Ike proposed on Valentine's Day 1916. Though they initially intended to wait, the demands of Ike's career expedited the engagement. On July 1, 1916, in Mamie's family's

34

home at 750 Lafayette Street in Denver, Colorado, they were married by a Presbyterian minister. On the day of his wedding, Ike received the rank of first lieutenant. The couple honeymooned at Eldorado Springs, a nearby resort, though there is no evidence that Ike played golf.

From March 1918 to November 1919, Ike was commanding officer at Camp Colt in Gettysburg, Pennsylvania, a training center for the newly established tank corps. He was quickly promoted and in 1920 received a Distinguished Service Medal for his work, with a citation honoring his "unusual zeal, foresight and marked administrative ability in the organization, training and preparation for overseas service of technical troops of the Tank Corps." From 1922 to 1924, Ike served in Panama in the Canal Zone under Brigadier General Fox Conner and began the transient life of an Army officer. Early on Ike realized that he needed to balance his growing responsibilities with building important friendships. Recreation would be the key.

As newlyweds, Ike and Mamie occasionally played tennis together, even though Mamie was a reluctant athlete and had a heart murmur from rheumatic fever. The tennis matches did not last, as Ike was unable to control his temper and often stormed off the court after a poor shot. He finally gave up the game completely in 1936. Over the years, Ike cultivated numerous hobbies that were much less stressful. He loved watching movies and, later, television, hunted periodically, fished at his friend Aksel Nielsen's retreat in Colorado, and often relaxed at home listening to Mamie play the electric organ. In the evenings, he read Western novels by Luke Short and Bliss Lomax and more serious books on American history. He was an avid cook and while

35

in the White House often gathered a small group of friends in the solarium on the White House roof to grill steaks and roast corn. When he was in Denver in the summers, Ike would don an apron and make pancakes, beef stew, and chili for the family and his guests. Vegetable soup that he simmered for three days was one of his specialties. For Ike's 1956 reelection campaign, the Minnesota Citizens for Eisenhower distributed recipe cards for President Eisenhower's Old Fashioned Beef Stew. Writing for the *New York Times*, Joseph A. Loftus explained that Ike was "as vain as any dilettante chef about his own private recipes."

Poker and bridge were his particular favorites, and the games helped forge important friendships throughout his life. As he grew older, Ike played less and less poker, but he remembered that while serving in Europe he had once won $3,900 in a year. He had learned the game from Bob Davis, a local illiterate hunter and guide, in Abilene. Bridge, though, remained a lifelong obsession. He was apt to call a legion of men—including General Alfred Gruenther, George Allen, James Lemon, W. Alton "Pete" Jones, Sigurd Larmon, Barry Leithead, Ambassador John Hay Whitney, Clifford Roberts, William Robinson, Ellis D. Slater, Charles S. Jones, and Clarence Schoo—to join a weekend bridge session at the last minute.

Ike took up painting while at Columbia when his friend British artist Thomas E. Stephens was working on a picture of Mamie. While observing, Ike casually remarked that it looked easy. Surprised, Stephens urged him to try his hand. With an improvised canvas constructed by Sergeant Moaney from a piece of a box and a dustcloth, Ike did just that. The *New York Times* reported, "Using brush and colors borrowed from Stephens, the

General produced what the artist called a 'magnificent primitive portrait head of Mrs. Eisenhower.'" Several days later, Stephens sent Ike a package of paints, brushes, and canvasses. Ike began copying magazine covers and eventually outdoor scenes and portraits of former presidents, such as Abraham Lincoln and George Washington, which he gave as gifts to friends. In a December 14, 1954, letter to Winston Churchill (who was also an amateur painter), Ike asked his old friend, "Would it be an intolerable burden on you to allow an artist friend of mine to visit you long enough to take a few photographs and draw a few hasty color sketches that I could use in such an attempt?" Churchill replied on January 11, 1955, "Should be delighted to see your artist friend and am much honored at the prospect." Ike never took formal lessons and always called himself a "deliberate dauber." He confessed that he had nearly failed drawing while a student at West Point but came to enjoy painting for fifteen or twenty minutes early in the morning or very late at night. The pastime helped him escape from what he called "the incessant contemplation of heavy and weighty problems." Because Mamie used her bedroom in the White House as an office, the small room that Bess Truman and Eleanor Roosevelt had used became a painting studio for Ike.

Golf clubs, though, would become his most constant companions. In August 1925, Ike enrolled in the U.S. Army's Command and General Staff School, the Army's graduate college, at Fort Leavenworth, Kansas. Founded in 1881 by General William T. Sherman to provide advanced training for soldiers with the rank of major or above, the CGSS was a stepping-stone to success in the Army. Like George C. Marshall had done eighteen years earlier, Ike, on June 18, 1926, graduated first in his class (of 245). Any question of his ability as a scholar and military leader was now put to rest. Eisenhower thrived under the pressure and called Leavenworth "a watershed in my life." Just before graduation, he began playing golf again in Kansas. Though in interviews Eisenhower always said it was his first attempt, he had actually played briefly at West Point, a fact noted in his medical records. Regardless of when he actually first picked up a club, he still confessed that he could not then tell the difference between a putter and a pitching wedge. He remembered that "if my progress in academics had been no greater [than that] in golf I would never have gotten through the course." He took to the sport quickly, playing on weekends on the newly built post course. In June 1926, during a family reunion in Abilene, brothers Ike, Roy, Edgar, and Arthur Eisenhower played together for the first time.

By the time Ike graduated first in his class at the Army War College in Washington, D.C., in June 1928, he was regularly shooting in the 80s. Mamie strongly encouraged him to play because she saw how much it helped relieve his stress. Despite the occasional outbursts of ill temper, Eisenhower found golfing a welcome respite from his duties. Their son John, who was born in 1922 (their first son had died the year before), remembered that his father's golf ball "seemed to wind up in the alfalfa an inordinate amount of the time, the air punctuated with certain expletives that I had thought were unknown to adults—only to kids." During this period, Ike met Harry Butcher, who would later become the chief of the Washington bureau of the Columbia Broadcasting System. Ike and Butcher became lifelong friends and frequent golfing partners. Butcher laughingly recalled an incident where Ike tried to launch his golf ball over a stone wall only to have it bounce back at his head "like a rocket."

From 1928 to 1939, Ike, Mamie, and John lived in Paris, Washington, D.C., and Manila, where Eisenhower "studied dramatics" under Douglas MacArthur. After paying Sunday calls to his superior officers, Ike played golf with his friends. While in the Philippines, one of his favorite golfing partners was Marian Huff, the wife of naval officer Sidney Huff, who also worked for MacArthur. A bit jealous of the arrangement, Mamie bought a new pair of golf shoes and joined the group. Ike was delighted, as Mamie later reported: "Yesterday Ike and I went out and played 9 holes of golf and we plan to go out this P.M. and do the same. Ike gave me lots of good pointers yesterday and my game improves. I like it swell." Her enthusiasm for and commitment to the sport was short lived.

Ike and Mamie returned to the United States late in 1939, and, in 1940, at the age of fifty, he became chief of staff of the Third Division. In 1941, Eisenhower was assigned as chief of staff of the Third Army and moved back to Fort Sam Houston, where he would remain for five months and regularly play golf. He was on the base on December 7, 1941, preparing to take a two-week leave when the Japanese bombed Pearl Harbor. In the wake of the crisis, George C. Marshall called him back to Washington. When Ike was named assistant chief of staff in charge of the War Plans Division in February of 1942, the *Washington Post* reported, "Essentially a top-notch tactician, this man—known as 'Ike' to his personal friends—is perhaps the best-read man in the Army, and one of its foremost authorities on military history." On June 9, 1942, Ike was promoted to major

39

general and was named commander of the European Theater of Operations.

Historian Stephen Ambrose made an important observation about Eisenhower that bears repeating: "Eisenhower was destined to be a world figure from June 1942 until January 1961. In those two decades, virtually his every move, decision, habit, friendship, and action were observed and reported. No other public figure in America of this century, not even Franklin Roosevelt, spent so long a time under such close scrutiny; no other public figure, save only Roosevelt, was so popular with the working press; and no other public figure, save the two Roosevelts [Franklin and Theodore], enjoyed such widespread and deep popularity with the American people."

The pressure must have been immense, and his need for recreation increased, while his ability to get any decreased. In 1942, General George Marshall wrote, "Eisenhower, I'm pleased with your progress in building a coordinated allied team, but not with your physical condition. You're working too-long hours. Get more rest and take time away from war for peace of mind and exercise. I want you to ride at least three times a week." Marshall then sent him a box of baseball gloves and balls, ordering him, "Work out every day with your commanders for a half-hour. Then you'll all make the team." Ike had trouble heeding Marshall's advice. In 1943, Ike wrote, "For the past three weeks, I have been getting in some five or six hours a week of rather vigorous riding, which represents the only exercise I have had since the war started. The only difficulty I have at all is sleeping in the later hours of the night." He did periodically find time to play table tennis and badminton.

40

Resettled in London on June 24, 1942, Ike was originally housed in the city's finest hotel, Claridge's, where Lieutenant Commander Harry C. Butcher shared a suite with him. Ike was unaccustomed to its elegance, complaining that the sitting room "looks exactly like a funeral parlor" and the bedroom made him feel "as though I were living in sin." He eventually moved to the Dorchester Hotel, which was closer to his headquarters at 20 Grosvenor Square. His new responsibilities gave Ike little opportunity for recreation, so he quickly looked for a place outside the city to get some fresh air. Butcher found and rented, for $32 a week, the seven-room Telegraph Cottage, in Kingston, Surrey, eleven miles southwest of London. Most importantly, it had a back gate that opened onto Coombe Hill Golf Course and was close to Little Coombe Hill Golf Course as well. Designed by J. F. Abercromby, Coombe Hill was a welcome respite for Ike. His wartime chauffeur, Kay Summersby, recounted how he used the course in her book *Eisenhower Was My Boss*: "The General had no time for a complete round but was to spend many easeful hours playing the several holes nearby. He became an expert on the 13th in particular."

The conditions on Coombe Hill, according to historian John Strenge, were typical for wartime: "The course, like so many around the world, had fallen into disrepair. A herd of twelve goats had joined its grounds crew, grazing at will on the rough, keeping it in check, while also contributing a dozen quarts of milk each day. It was no way to maintain a course, but with the labor shortfall brought on by war, the goats were an acceptable alternative to allowing it to go to seed. Ike didn't mind. He seldom hit his target anyway. Whether it was groomed properly was of no consequence to him in this time and place. It was golf, and it served its purpose by clearing his mind." Eisenhower, reluctant to venture too far from the cottage, often played the eleventh through fifteenth holes with Butcher, giving him enough of a chance to practice his game. Overall, though, Ike had almost no time to practice. The invasion of North Africa, which lasted from November 8, 1942, through May 13, 1943, demanded his undivided attention. In the months leading up to the D-day invasion of occupied France in June 1944, Ike developed chronic wrist pain resulting from bursitis that limited his physical activity even further. But this did not keep him from showing the troops something about farm life. In August 1944, Ike was in the recently liberated village of Jullouville when a group of American soldiers told him that a local villager had presented the unit with a cow. No one knew how to milk her. With a smile on his face, the supreme Allied commander sat down and proceeded to fill the pail with milk.

As the Allies were moving through France toward Germany, Ike established his living quarters in the clubhouse at the Gueux golf course. While he was settled there, the United States and Great Britain declared V-E Day on May 8, 1945. General George C. Marshall telegraphed Ike to congratulate him: "You have completed your mission with the greatest victory in the history of warfare." After the celebration, Ike left Reims and returned to London. Exhausted, he went straight to Telegraph Cottage, pulled his golf clubs out of a closet, and went directly to the thirteenth hole. Upon leaving the presidency in 1961, Ike would look back and say that the day Germany surrendered was the climax of his career, "That's what I was trained for." During the postwar occupation of Germany, Ike was living at Schloss Friedrichshof (Kronberg Castle) near Frankfurt, where golf had been played since 1914.

At the end of the war, Eisenhower was one of the most respected men in the world. But he never lost his modesty. When his hometown of Abilene decided to celebrate Eisenhower Day upon his return from Europe, he sent a telegram that read, "If you folks try to high-hat me and call me by titles, instead of Ike, when I come home, I shall feel like a stranger. The worst part of military rank is the loneliness that prevents comradeship." While he had hoped for a quiet retirement, with time to write, lecture, and play golf, everyone else conspired against him. In July 1945, President Harry Truman told Ike, "General, there is nothing that you may want that I won't try to help you get. That definitely and specifically includes the presidency in 1948." On November 20, 1945, Ike succeeded General George C. Marshall as chief of staff.

The Allies stumbled over themselves to honor Eisenhower. On June 12, 1945, he was named a Freeman of the City of London. On October 3, 1946, Edinburgh and the borough of Maybole bestowed the same honor upon him. That same day, Edinburgh University gave him an honorary doctorate of laws. The Scottish National Trust gave him a lifetime residence at Culzean Castle. A week later, Cambridge University gave him a doctor of laws. Ike was also given the Navy Distinguished Service Medal, the Legion of Merit, the Distinguished Service Medal with four Oak Leaf Clusters, and numerous other awards. France awarded him the Grand Cordon of the Legion of Honor and the Croix de Guerre with two palms. Great Britain gave him the Knight Grand Cross of the Order of the Bath and the Order of Merit.

Awed by these honors and countless others, he was equally humbled by the golf clubs around the world that began granting him memberships, including the Royal and Ancient Golf Club of St. Andrews on November 17, 1945. The honorary life membership was given to Ike in "gratitude to you for your Service to all mankind." In his reply, dated December 21, to Chairman M. E. Lindsay, Ike quipped, "I trust that my performance as a golfer will not be publicized to my Scottish friends as they would disown me at once." He played the Old Course on October 9, 1946, to accept the membership. The first part of the round was described in detail: "Gen. Dwight D. Eisenhower holed an eighteen-foot putt today for a teamwork birdie three on the first hole of the Royal and Ancient Golf Club. The grinning general . . . let club Captain Roger Wethered, his partner, hit the first two shots, a sizzling drive and an approach to within eighteen feet of the pin. Then the general stepped up and sank the putt."

In 1946, while stationed at Fort Myer in Arlington, Virginia (that he once told his son was "a sorry place to land after having commanded a theatre of war"), as chief of staff, Ike and Mamie settled into a more relaxed life, with plenty of time to golf and fish and a yard where Ike could plant flowers. He underwent daily treatment for bursitis in his left arm, which noticeably improved. He told his friend Beetle Smith, "I feel better than I have in many months. I am more refreshed and generally in better tone than I have been since the shooting stopped." On December 7, 1946, five years after the attack on Pearl Harbor, the *Washington Post* announced that Ike would get his first vacation in eleven years. Under doctor's orders, he traveled to Florida for treatment at Pratt General Hospital in Miami for the bursitis, but he was able to play golf and go fishing.

On May 17 and 18, 1947, Ike joined other luminaries for the National Celebrities Golf Tournament, a two-day event held at Columbia Country Club just outside of Washington, D.C. It was one of the few times he played at a public event. General Omar Bradley, Babe Didrikson Zaharias, Jack Dempsey, Gene Tunney, Babe Ruth, Bing Crosby, Gene Sarazen, Glenna Collett Vare, and even Bobby Jones came out to help raise money for the event, which was sponsored by the *Washington Post* on behalf of charities that sought to build recreation facilities for children in an attempt to curb juvenile delinquency. The event attracted 7,500 spectators, including seventy-five amputees from nearby Walter Reed Hospital. Actor Edward Arnold joked that he was there to serve as Ike's caddie. Upon announcing his newly acquired job, Arnold pulled off his coat and revealed a pair of red suspenders, which the *Washington Post* reported "would have done credit to the late Gene Talmadge." Arnold also placed a golf ball on his nose and asked General Ike to tee it from there. Ike ended his round on Saturday with a 97, having to pause periodically during the round to sign autographs. He gave his spot away to Major General Anthony C. McAuliffe on Sunday, because he could not play both days. The event raised more than $10,000. In subsequent years, the organizers created an Eisenhower Presidential Trophy, an award for "old-timers" such as Gene Sarazen, Johnny Farrell, Jim Barns, and Byron Nelson.

45

In 1947, Eisenhower announced that he would step down as chief of staff to become the thirteenth president of Columbia University on June 7, 1948, following Nicholas Murray Butler. Ike had been offered the position by Thomas J. Watson, a Columbia trustee and the president of IBM. Upon hearing the news, poet Carl Sandburg visited the Pentagon to interview Ike. Afterward, Sandburg announced, "Why, Columbia's getting the pick of them all. He's got what the greatest scholars of all time have had—wisdom and humanity." In May 1948, Ike and Mamie reluctantly moved to the university president's house, a four-story Italian Renaissance–style building at 60 Morningside Drive. They had never lived for any length of time in a large city, and Ike admitted that he knew nothing about operating a university, certainly not one with 31,000 students and 3,000 staff and faculty. For their part, the staff and faculty were apprehensive about having a military hero leading one of the nation's premier educational institutions. At a reception, one professor said to Eisenhower, "You know, General, when we heard you were coming here, some of the faculty were downright scared of you." Characteristically, Ike replied, "The faculty would have been reassured to know I was scared to death of them."

In July, he said, "All I want is to be a good president of Columbia University and to break 80 in golf." Ike had taken the job because he believed it would be less demanding than his previous assignments. But he was quickly disabused of that notion. In a letter to his friend Swede Hazlett, he explained, "My schedule of appointments for the first month there has already grown to appalling proportions. If current indications provide any index of what my future life there is to be, I shall quit them cold, and deliberately go to some forsaken spot on the earth's surface and stay until I am fully ready to go back to work." In 1950, however, Ike tried to set aside the weekends for relaxation and a full week out of every month to regain his strength. He played regular rounds of golf, and his physician, Dr. Howard Snyder, reported that the new regimen worked: "His shoulders had broadened and firmed, he could hit a golf ball fifty yards farther by 1950 than he had been able to do in the early years following his return from Europe."

Ike's philosophy about his position at the university was summed up in a short speech he made early in his tenure: "I decided to come to Columbia only after months of discussion and thought. When I accepted finally it was with no illusions that I could contribute anything academically. I did think I could probably learn to run the place efficiently. But, most important, I saw the opportunity to advance education in citizenship, to promote faith in the American way of life among the youth who will be the leaders of America in the near future." One story involving a group of Columbia's staff illustrated Ike's leadership style. Soon after becoming president of the university, he invited all the building-service employees—porters, elevator operators, and the housekeeping staff—to gather in one of the classrooms for an informal discussion. At the end of his talk, he said, "When you see me around, I'll be pleased if you say hello. I ain't hard to recognize—round face, no hair on top, mouthful of teeth. If you have any doubt, just yell—Hey, Ike!"

Ike liked Columbia, though he once grumbled, "I can't get used to this vertical living thing." After he settled in, the pace of academic life allowed him plenty of opportunities to play golf at Blind Brook Country

Club in Westchester County, where William Robinson made him a member. Ike often left campus on Wednesdays and Saturdays to get in a quick afternoon game. A month into his presidency at Columbia and in anticipation of the 1948 elections, he was heavily courted by both parties to run for president. Jim McCord, governor of Tennessee, explained, "I think his nomination would be the answer to all the problems of the South." When the Nashville *Tennessean* polled twenty-seven of the state's forty delegates to the Democratic National Convention, twenty-one confirmed that they would vote for Ike. He declined.

Eisenhower left a mixed record behind during his years at Columbia, but two incidents reflect his approach to the job. He urged the university to offer an honorary doctorate to Ralph Bunche, undersecretary of the United Nations, who helped broker peace in the Middle East. When he invited Dr. Bunche and his wife, both of whom were black, to dinner, one professor asked, "You're not going to have a black man seated beside you, are you?" To which Ike replied, "Yes, he will be seated on my right hand, and Mrs. Bunch on my left. I trust that you and others invited will come to dinner, but if not, I will proceed with the Bunches as my distinguished guests." Ike also introduced Russian language courses to the curriculum and weathered criticism about whether he was trying to "make young minds receptive to communism."

The job at Columbia, however, was not a good fit, and Eisenhower soon became restless. In December 1948, he came to Washington for a few months at Truman's request to advise James Forrestal, the first secretary of defense. Then in 1949, Truman asked him to take a leave from Columbia and serve as the informal chairman of the Joint Chiefs of Staff, but Ike soon found that the position had no real power. Struggling with a stomach ailment diagnosed as chronic ileitis, in the spring of 1949, Ike spent a week in bed, followed by several weeks in Key West at Truman's invitation. On April 12, Ike went to Augusta National Golf Club for a month's rest. Frustrated by the Truman administration, he returned to Columbia full-time, vowing to steer clear of Washington politics. The North Korean invasion of South Korea on June 25, 1950, changed Ike's priorities. In October, Truman appointed him to command the Supreme Headquarters Allied Powers Europe (SHAPE), the group responsible for creating military forces for the North Atlantic Treaty Organization (NATO). He would hold this position until 1952.

Though he wanted to resign, the Columbia University trustees gave him a leave of absence, and in 1951 Eisenhower returned to Europe, this time to Paris. He was the logical person to head SHAPE. As commander of liberating U.S. forces in Europe during World War II, Ike had earned the respect of European nations. He had fifty decorations, including the equivalent of four U.S. Distinguished Service Medals and the USSR's Order of Suvorov and Order of Victory. Eisenhower also held eighteen honorary degrees from universities around the world. The *New York Times* reported, "The mere fact of his presence in Europe has a restorative and inspiring effect." It was a difficult job, especially regarding the situation in Germany, and Ike once again turned to golf, fishing, and bridge to wind down. While in Marnes-la-Coquette, Mamie and Ike lived in a two-story house (called Villa Saint-Pierre) that sat on six acres. Ike had

49

a pond stocked with trout and a vegetable garden that he tended himself. As a surprise for Ike, Mamie had a putting green installed on the lawn.

Golf, however, was difficult for Ike to play in France, so he turned, as the *Washington Post* reported on August 8, 1951, to painting: "The shift to oils from golf, which used to be Ike's favorite way of getting-away-from-it-all, came about because Ike finds the crowds are too great every time he leaves the Petit Trianon Hotel near Versailles, where he lives, for a swing around a French golf course. . . . Seems as if every time he steps out the door of his hotel he is pursued by a mushroom army of admirers and plain gawkers, French style, who march along with him every step of the 18 holes. So just to get a little peace, Ike holes up every weekend now in his hotel room—and paints. Time was when Ike enjoyed a victory at the eighteenth hole about as much as success on the battlefield. Last year when he took a quick trip to Puerto Rico, he talked about his 'battle of the birdie' as if it had been the Battle of the Bulge. 'I feel mighty good when I get two birdies in a season,' he told a friend after his return here and before he took off for Europe. 'But when I made three birdies in two days down in Puerto Rico, I wasn't fit to live with!' "

Without his knowledge, in the summer of 1951, two Eisenhower supporters, Charles Willis and Stanley Rumbaugh, organized Ike Clubs in New Jersey to support his candidacy for president. Inspired by the effort, many of his friends from Augusta National Golf Club, where he had been a member since 1948, began establishing additional Citizens for Eisenhower clubs. By June 1, 1952, the organization had become a powerful political force, growing to nearly eight hundred clubs by early 1953. Clifford Roberts, a broker who had founded Augusta National in the early 1930s with Bobby Jones, financed the effort, along with W. Alton Jones, Sidney Weinberg, John Hay Whitney, and Ellis D. Slater. General Lucius Clay, Paul Hoffman, Walter Williams, Mary Lord, Sigurd Larmon, and Bradshaw Mintener managed the clubs. Ike, however, was lukewarm to the idea, as he had revealed in his diary eighteen months earlier, on January 1, 1950: "I do not want a political career; I do not want to be associated with any political party, although I fervently believe in the two-party system and further believe that, normally, a citizen is by no means performing his civic duty unless he participates in all applicable activities of his party, to include participation in precinct caucuses." His resistance only seemed to fuel the draft-Eisenhower campaigns.

The grassroots Ike Clubs, which remained generally nonpartisan, as Ike had never declared official political allegiance to any party, generated widespread support. Several newspapers, such as the *New York Times*, *New York Herald Tribune*, *Kansas City Star*, and the *Los Angeles Mirror-News*, advocated for an Eisenhower nomination. On February 8, 1951, a midnight Eisenhower-for-President rally that attracted thirty-three thousand people was held at Madison Square Garden and featured the Irving Berlin song "I Like Ike" to generate additional support. Three days later, famed aviatrix Jacqueline Cochran, who helped organize the event, flew to Villa Saint-Pierre to deliver a copy of the film of the rally to Mamie and Ike. That same year, W. G. Clugson published *Eisenhower for President? or, Who Will Get Us Out of the Messes We Are In?* The opening paragraph described the terms in which the Republican Party would cast Eisenhower's candidacy: "On the day when President Truman leaves the White House our Nation may well be facing, or be in the midst of, the greatest crisis in our history. The fate of the country, and perhaps of all humanity, may be in the hands of the man who succeeds him. A word, a nod, a shake of the head by that man, may determine whether civilization is to survive or perish."

The pressure mounted as dozens of business and political leaders visited Ike in Paris, notably Senator Henry Cabot Lodge on September 4, 1951, urging him to consider a presidential nomination. A month later, William Robinson wrote a front-page editorial for the *New York Herald-Tribune* encouraging Ike to run as a Republican. *McCall's* magazine even joined the fray, offering a $40,000 check if he would answer the question, Are you a Republican? In confidence to Robinson, Ike once confessed, "the seeker is never so popular as the sought. People want what they think they can't get." But he finally relented and early in 1952 announced that he would run for president. Doing so meant he had to retire from the Army, because regulations prevented an officer from taking part in political campaigns. He resigned and lost his annual pay of $18,761. On June 1, 1952, Ike returned to America and four days later gave his first nationally televised political speech in Abilene, Kansas.

Eisenhower faced a difficult road for the Republican nomination against Robert Taft, a consummate politician and fellow golfer. Bob Hope often told this revealing story about Ike's opponent: "Ike won the nomination, and shortly after he and Taft had a reconciliation round of golf at Burning Tree. The next day a friend of mine was in the Senate gallery, with his two sons. Down on the floor, engaged in earnest conversation with a couple of other senators, was Robert Taft.

My friend told his sons, 'Look boys, there's Robert Taft, one of the great Americans of all time. He's probably discussing some of the most important issues of the world with those men, issues that will affect all of our lives.' At that moment, Taft pushed the men aside and went into his golf swing."

A week before the Republican National Convention, scheduled to begin on July 5, 1952, Ike and his family went to Denver to stay with his mother-in-law, to sit in a rocking chair, "putter around in Mrs. Doud's flowers," and play some golf. Senator Frank Carlson, a Republican from Kansas, and Thomas Stephens, Ike's appointment secretary, accompanied him on the trip. They fished, while Ike managed to play a few rounds of golf at Cherry Hills Country Club. Then it was off to Chicago, where Ike won the nomination over Taft on the first ballot. A week later, he was back in Denver with a golf club in his hands.

During the 1952 election, journalists were constantly looking for ways to distinguish Illinois Governor Adlai Stevenson from Eisenhower. They were so similar that James Reston, writing for the *New York Times*, exclaimed, "In fact the idea that I can't get out of my head is that both political parties chose excellent candidates but maybe each of them should have nominated the other man." Even so, Reston went on to use golf to make an important distinction: "The general is a remarkably optimistic human being, Stevenson a congenial skeptic. . . . This is part of [Ike's] nature which you see even in the way he plays golf. He's a bad putter, for example, but when he addresses the ball, even if he's 50 feet away from the cup, the thing that is in his mind is that ball curving boldly and triumphantly into the hole. Not Stevenson. He can always see himself

53

missing the 18-inchers, and he frankly cannot believe in that happy world of tolerable coexistence with the Russians." During the election, both Eisenhower and Stevenson consented to having their medical records made public, the first time presidential candidates had made such a disclosure. Dr. Howard Snyder, Ike's physician, reported that his patient exercised an average of eight hours a week, mostly playing golf, but occasionally using a rowing machine and stationary bicycle. Dr. Emmet F. Pearson reported that Stevenson played golf and tennis and was an avid horseback rider.

In the months leading up to the Republican National Convention and during the 1952 campaign, Ike did not have occasion to play much golf, partly because he was again suffering from bursitis. In a letter to Clifford Roberts, he complained, "I have a bad wrist, which you will remember started ailing while you were here. . . . Now I get it baked every morning and have to bind it up every night, and I don't know when it will be before I can take a full golf swing again."

Even though he was temporarily sidelined, Ike enjoyed widespread political support from the sports world. Jack Westland, the 1952 U.S. Amateur Champion and a Republican candidate for Washington's Second District, offered his putter to Eisenhower as a "good luck omen." Maury Luxford, who was in charge of the Bing Crosby Golf Tournament, founded the National Golfers Committee for Ike. A month before the election, the Republican National Committee organized a Sports Committee, which included decathlete Bob Mathias, boxers Gene Tunney, Jack Dempsey, and James J. Jeffries, and baseball star Ty Cobb. Fellow Augusta National member Bobby Jones actively campaigned for him, even though he was a lifelong Democrat and in poor health. Jones helped resolve a dispute between rival Georgia delegations to the Republican National Convention, shifting support to Eisenhower. Oddly, though, the only district that Jones could not influence was Augusta, because a local political leader, Landon Thomas, was an old friend and golfing partner of Taft's.

Jones's assistance helped Eisenhower do something that no Republican had done in a long time—court the southern vote with the intention of breaking the Democratic stronghold on the "solid South." Southern Democrats, who rejected Truman because of his support in 1948 of a civil rights platform, were looking for an alternative. Ike's focus on the South came as a surprise to his advisors, who reminded him that Republicans had not won in the region since Reconstruction. While Hoover carried eight southern states in 1928, he did so only because he was running against Alfred E. Smith, who was Roman Catholic and reviled by the largely Protestant South. Regardless of the facts, Ike insisted, "I'm going south if I have to go alone." He received a hero's welcome in Tampa, Little Rock, Jacksonville, and Miami. But that affection did not translate into votes. The nine states that Ike did not carry were mainly in the South.

Eisenhower won with 55 percent of the popular vote and 442 electoral votes to Stevenson's 89. An elderly woman summed up the nation's sentiment on Election Day, calling Ike "the man God always sends this country in time of need." On November 15, 1952, Eisenhower wrote a formal letter of resignation, effective on January 19, to Frederick Coykendall, chairman of the Columbia University board of trustees. Once elected, dozens of golf clubs from Luxembourg to Leesburg,

Virginia, extended another round of honorary memberships to Ike. The Carlisle Country Club did so in December 1952, with the hope that Ike would play at the eighteen-hole course when he visited his 188-acre farm in nearby Gettysburg, which he and Mamie had purchased on January 15, 1951.

His victory came as little surprise to anyone, and certainly not to Gene Tunney, the former heavyweight boxing champion. The day after Truman defeated Governor Thomas E. Dewey in 1948, Tunney (while playing golf with Eisenhower and Clifford Roberts at Augusta National Golf Club) had predicted that Ike would become the next president. The nation would now have to wait to see what kind of president Ike would become. Before the inauguration, syndicated columnist Henry McLemore made his best guess: "I can picture the changes that will take place at the White House when the Eisenhowers move in. The General will probably build an 18-hole golf course on the lawn and drain the swimming pool for a putting green. And I bet you that the Cabinet will have to wait more than once while the President practices chip shots or tries to improve his swing." McLemore was not far off base.

THREE

OUR FORE FATHERS

*The presidential candidate who can take five of
six bad holes in a row without blowing his stack
is capable of handling the affairs of state.*
—JIMMY DEMARET

On March 14, 2006, the prime minister of South Korea,
Lee Hae-chan, resigned after facing relentless criticism
for playing golf while his country suffered a devastating
railway strike. Though Lee held a largely ceremonial
position (power in South Korea resides with the president), his incessant golfing left the impression that he
was not on the job. On the day in question, Lee joined
several wealthy businessmen at an elite course, and
the press reported that the men wagered $411 among
themselves. Lee may have done well to remember
the simple rule of politics—perception matters. As an
isolated incident, he may have been forgiven, but in
April 2005 he had been roundly criticized for playing
golf while wildfires burned a 1,300-year-old Buddhist
temple. Two weeks before his resignation, Lee began a

golfing vacation, to celebrate a national holiday to mark the 1919 Korean uprising against Japanese colonial rule. To complicate matters, his golfing partners included a businessman who had been fined $3.6 million for rigging flour prices. Even today, zeal for the sport can be a serious political liability. Dwight D. Eisenhower and the men in the White House before him who played golf learned that lesson well.

Bob Hope once said, "Playing golf with America's Presidents is a great denominator. How a President acts in a sand trap is a pretty good barometer of how he would respond if the hotline suddenly lit up." Longtime sports broadcaster Heywood Hale Broun put it another way: "Sports do not build character. They reveal it." Five American presidents before Ike regularly played the royal and ancient game, four of them while they were in the White House. William Howard Taft, Woodrow Wilson, Warren G. Harding, and Calvin Coolidge all used the game to escape from the burdens of the presidency; that they were golfers told the public something important about these enigmatic men. Franklin D. Roosevelt loved the game but was stricken with polio and unable to play during his presidency. The public's perception of the golfing proclivities of Ike's predecessors dramatically shaped the public's view of Eisenhower and his frequent forays onto the golf course.

Throughout his two terms in office, Ike was constantly compared to the other men in the White House who also chose golf as their main form of relaxation. Though he was neither the first nor the last president to play golf, his good-natured obsession with the game and his outgoing personality drew fans to the sport in an unprecedented and unmatched manner. In the 1950s and early 1960s, Ike was so identified as "the golfer in the White House" that John F. Kennedy went to great lengths to deflect attention from his own love of and skill at the game.

In 1995, James Carney, writing for *Time* magazine, declared William Jefferson Clinton the most dogged duffer since Ike. The article recounted an episode that could have been told of Eisenhower forty years earlier: "As usual Mack McLarty was all business when he arrived at the Oval Office for an appointment and was quickly waved inside by Bill Clinton's longtime door-keeper, Nancy Hernreich. But the inner sanctum was empty. 'Where's the President?' asked McLarty, a senior advisor. 'What do you mean?' Hernreich responded with alarm. Before they could panic, McLarty noticed the French door near Clinton's desk was ajar. Picking up the trail, he went outside. There on the South Lawn, about 30 yards from the Oval Office, the President of the United States was standing in shirtsleeves and tie, his hands gripping the shaft of a putter, his eyes fixed on a small white ball at his feet. The President looked up, 'He had this pained look on his face, like, "I guess I've got to go back inside now,"' McLarty recalls of that late-spring afternoon. 'And I said, "Mr. President, it's OK. I just have a checklist. Let's do it here." And so for 15 minutes, as the Commander in Chief practiced his chip shots and short strokes, McLarty tagged along, running down items of business. 'We should do this more often,' McLarty said when he was finished. Replied Clinton hopefully: 'Yeah, it kinda works, doesn't it?' "

Two months earlier, Clinton, who like Eisenhower collected putters, had refurbished the South Lawn putting green. As his predecessor had done, Clinton used Ike's green to practice and often referred to it as his think tank. This allowed him to take time out of his busy schedule to practice without leaving the confines of the White House, something that Ike had realized long ago.

No matter one's popularity, the job of president has always been subject to the fluctuations of the public mood. Ike's predecessor, Truman, referred to 1600 Pennsylvania Avenue as the "Great White Jail." Harding once responded to Senator Frank Brandegee's query about how he liked occupying the highest office with, "Frank, it is hell! No other word can describe it." No wonder Ike turned to golf. Harold Hinton, writing for the *New York Times*, recounted in the spring of 1953, "President Eisenhower's fondness for golf, including practicing iron shots on the White House lawn and last week's outing on the links of Augusta (Georgia) National Golf Club, is the mild sort of revolt all presidents stage against the confinement of their job—now probably the greatest burden placed on any human being in the world. The load has become heavier with the passing years, until it has reached the extreme limit of one man's physical capacity to bear." Hinton went on to argue, "Between the pressure of duty and the strain of the constant surveillance, there develops in every President an intense need for relaxation." Golf had an even more practical and diplomatic purpose. Eisenhower often invited other heads of state to play with him before beginning any type of negotiations. One of Ike's aides explained why: "The President feels that a game of golf with a prime minister is worth [many] hours at the conference table. He doesn't go into conference matters on the course, but he and his visitor get to know one another better and that makes for a better relationship."

Like Ike, past presidents found creative and energetic ways to escape the tension of the Oval Office. George

Washington had to defy the First Continental Congress to justify his love of horseback riding because it passed a resolution in 1774 calling for the colonies to "discountenance and discourage every Species of Extravagance and Dissipation, especially all horse racing, and all kinds of gambling, Cock Fighting, Exhibitions of Shows, Plays, and other expensive Diversions and entertainments." John Quincy Adams regularly swam in the Potomac. One story goes that a female reporter named Anne Royall was granted an exclusive interview with the president only after meeting him at the bank of the river and sitting on his clothes until her request was granted. Andrew Jackson, Martin Van Buren, Woodrow Wilson, Warren G. Harding, and William Howard Taft all rode horses. Theodore Roosevelt, undoubtedly the most athletic president next to Ike, boxed, wrestled, and practiced jujitsu. Wilson coached varsity football at Princeton and served as chairman of the committee on outdoor sports, forerunner to the athletic director. Calvin Coolidge fished (sometimes wearing white kid gloves), rode a mechanical horse, and worked jigsaw puzzles; Harry Truman was an avid walker; Herbert Hoover occasionally fished and played with an eight-pound medicine ball; after his polio diagnosis, Franklin D. Roosevelt swam. The *New York Daily News* even sponsored a campaign to build a pool in the White House for FDR in 1933. A 1954 *Washington Post* editorial compared the leisure activities of the presidents: "George Washington, it is said, liked to go 'to the races'—Lincoln hunted rabbits—'Teddy' Roosevelt carried a 'big stick' (not a golf club) and took long walks and horseback rides—Warren Harding played golf often (his private golf club hangs in the banquet hall at Burning Tree as does President Eisenhower's) and Harry

Truman wasted a lot of Government time practicing the 'Missouri Waltz'—watching Margaret on television and writing personal letters!"

Writing for *Golf Digest*, Peter Andrews put presidential hobbies into perspective: "Every President is criticized to some degree for his choice of hobby no matter what it is. Thomas Jefferson had rather too many French vintages in his wine cellar. Franklin Roosevelt was forever fiddling with his stamp collection. And whenever you needed Harry Truman, he was out on his damned boat." *U.S. News and World Report* kept constant tabs on presidential pastimes, publishing in 1960 a list of work-play vacations, comparing the average of forty days that FDR and Truman spent on holiday to Ike's seventy-three.

Not surprisingly, the public often had something to say about Ike's hobby. Because golf was perceived as an elitist sport associated with wealth and exclusivity, the golfing presidents were scrutinized more than any other White House sportsmen. The nonplaying public has often viewed golf—more than fishing, horseback riding, or hunting—with suspicion. In *Golf and the American Country Club*, historian Richard J. Moss explained that "the country club was an attempt to preserve certain aspects of Victorian culture before they were overrun by new values spawned in the burgeoning industrial city." Members of such clubs were largely Protestant, affluent leaders of the community, whose social status was solidly established. Immigrants, women, African Americans, Jews, and others were generally excluded from participation in the sport through overt restrictions or more subtle persuasion.

Many American presidents tried their hand at one sport or another, though not all could overcome their frustration with golf. Jefferson, who called the presidency a "splendid misery," did not have golf as an option but still advocated exercise. He once said, "You must give two hours a day to exercise. . . . As a species of exercise, I advise the gun. While it gives a moderate exercise to the body it gives boldness, enterprise and independence to the mind. Games played with the ball are too violent for the body and stamp no character on the mind." One newspaper account revealed Ulysses S. Grant's introduction to the game. Though golf did not become popular in the United States until the end of the nineteenth century, it was played widely in Britain. When Grant was visiting Scotland, he decided that he wanted to see how the sport was played. According to the article, "The host teed the ball . . . and waggled the club with all due solemnity, and the general's expectation ran high as he observed these impressive preliminaries. Presently, there was a heavy thud, a flight of turf and the little ball still sat on the tee. Again, and yet again a thud heavier than before, with turf still flying, with ball unmoved and the golfer perspiring and perplexed. Whereupon General Grant gently remarked: 'There seems to be a fair amount of exercise in the game, but I fail to see the use of the ball.'"

In 1899, William McKinley golfed in White Sulpher Springs while convalescing from an illness. On May 1, the *Boston Record* featured a cartoon of McKinley with an accompanying article that asked, "Shall the President or shall he not become a golfer? Shall he allow the thought of a possible lack of dignity to interfere with his restoration to health?" Boston's mayor, Josiah Quincy, made his position clear: "The President of the United States should not make an exhibition of himself for the gratification of the curious." But neither Grant nor McKinley played the game on any regular basis. Theodore Roosevelt, the most sporting of the twentieth-century presidents, disdained it, declaring, "Golf is for the birds." Frank Ahrens, writing for the *Washington Post*, argued, "Golf has clung to the 20th century presidency like an attentive caddie to a touring pro. Introduced to the chief executive's office by the pro-sized William Howard Taft, it has been the companion of most presidents since." Andrew Mutch, the former director of the USGA Museum and Archives, speculated on why golf has been so popular: "The common denominator seems to be the escapist quality of the strolling, pastoral game and its simultaneous appeal to intensely competitive men."

William Howard Taft was the first golfing president, and when he wanted to escape the public eye, he played on the private course owned by Edward Beale McLean. Taft often remarked, "As every man knows who has played the game, it rejuvenates and stretches the span of life." This certainly proved true for Taft, who at more than three hundred pounds was not light on his feet. He is rumored to have become stuck in the White House bathtub on at least one occasion. One popular joke parodied his excessive weight: "If he put a golf ball where he could hit it, he couldn't see it. And if he put the golf ball where he could see it, he couldn't hit it." Another one was similarly revealing: "Taft was the most polite man in Washington. One day he gave up his seat on a streetcar to three women." These jabs, however, obscure the fact that he was a decent player, who shot in the high 90s. When he broke 100 and reportedly won a $1,000 bet at Myopia Hunt Club in 1909, his aide Archie Butt recounted his glee: "I think he showed more pleasure over it than he did over the passage of the tariff bill. Mrs. Taft takes the greatest interest in his game always, and the news that he had made it under a hundred made her most happy. She went up to him and kissed him when she heard it, a mark of great favor from Mrs. Taft, for she is not demonstrative as a rule in public." Taft had a short choppy swing like a baseball player, but his drives averaged 175 yards. He was a good putter and played with a Schenectady model, one that had been banned by the Royal and Ancient Golf Club of St. Andrews in 1904. In fact, he was asked by noted amateur Walter Travis to weigh in on the controversy. In a reply to Travis, Taft gladly declared, "I think putting with a Schenectady putter is sportsmanlike, and gives no undue advantage."

Born in Cincinnati, Ohio, in 1857, Taft had wanted to play football as an undergraduate at Yale University but was discouraged by his father because it was "not a gentleman's sport," so he joined the crew and wrestling teams. He learned to play golf in 1894 while vacationing at his family's summer cottage in Murray Bay, Quebec. Taft played at Chevy Chase Club in Washington, D.C., Cincinnati Country Club in Ohio, and Myopia Hunt Club in Massachusetts while on vacation. Self-taught, he played constantly during the 1908 election, which provided fodder for political satirists. At one point, Theodore Roosevelt wrote in a letter to Taft, "It would seem incredible that anyone would care one way or the other about your playing golf, but I have received literally hundreds of letters from the West protesting about it." A second letter from Roosevelt focused on the same theme: "I myself play tennis, but that game is a little more familiar;

65

besides, you never saw a photograph of me playing tennis. I'm careful about that; photographs on horseback, yes; tennis, no. And golf is fatal."

But Taft went on the defensive. While campaigning in Wolsey, South Dakota, he answered his critics: "They said that I have been playing golf this summer and that it was a rich man's game, and that it indicated that I was out of sympathy with plain people. I want to state my case before the bar of public opinion on the subject of that game of golf. . . . It is a game for people who are not active enough for baseball or tennis, or who have too much weight to carry around to play those games; and yet when a man weighs 295 pounds you have to give him the opportunity to make his legs and muscles move, and golf offers that opportunity." Taft, like those who followed him, needed golf. It helped him survive the campaign trail, a time he later referred to as "one of the most uncomfortable four months of my life." During the 1908 election he reportedly told a California crowd, "I don't know of any game that after a while makes you so ashamed of your profanity. It is a game full of moments of self-abasement, with only a few moments of self-exaltation. And we Americans who are not celebrated for our modesty, may find such a game excellent training." In the end, Taft and his pastime prevailed; he defeated Democratic candidate William Jennings Bryan to become the twenty-seventh president of the United States.

Taft served in the Oval Office from 1909 to 1912, as the Kent professor of constitutional law at Yale Law School from 1913 to 1921, then as the tenth chief justice of the Supreme Court, a position he held until 1930, the year Bobby Jones won the Grand Slam. When the press speculated that Harding would appoint him to the position, Taft wisely retorted, "I'll wait until the golf ball is in the hole." So honored was he by the appointment that he later commented, "I don't remember that I ever was president." And he remained so widely associated with the sport that in 1915 the Pyramid Film Company released a short film, *Taft Playing Golf,* directed by Harry Palmer.

Taft moved into the White House just as American golfers were gaining recognition in the sport. During his first year in office, Tom McNamara placed second in the U.S. Open, giving him the best finish by an American-born golfer in that event. American golfers dominated the U.S. Open from 1911 through 1914: Johnny McDermott (1911, 1912), Francis Ouimet (1913), and Walter Hagen (1914). Ouimet's victory over Harry Vardon and Ted Ray, the best British players of their day, signaled a new era.

Paolo E. Coletta, in *The Presidency of William Howard Taft,* explained that Taft loved "to laugh and to share his laughter with those about him. Rarely critical of others, he had a sense of humor that enabled him to enjoy jokes of which he himself was the butt." But Taft's affability could not hide his competitive streak. William Lyon Phelps told a story of Taft while he was at Yale: "That Spring of 1913 I played golf very often with him; and he was the best of company, though always keen to win. One day, when he was playing in another foursome, he came into the locker room, banged his clubs down on the floor and gave a snort of rage. (He never swore.) I said, 'Why, you feel worse about being beaten at golf than you did on losing the presidency!' He replied, 'Well, I do, *now!*' " Taft played what he called "bumble puppy golf" for most of his adult life; at the age of seventy and down to 260 pounds, he was reported to have played thirty-six holes a day.

As with Eisenhower nearly forty years later, Taft's time on the golf course became a popular topic for the media. Clearly, he preferred the game to some of his official duties. When told by his staff that the president of Chile was on hand for a visit, Taft replied, "I'll be damned if I will give up my game to see this fellow." Taft realized early on what later presidents would come to understand: "The beauty of golf is that you cannot play if you permit yourself to think of anything else." Regardless of the criticism Taft endured, the *New York Times* on June 25, 1909, reported that his love of the game had doubled the number of players at public golf clubs.

In contrast to Taft, Woodrow Wilson was a somewhat reluctant golfer, though he played more often than any other man who had occupied the White House. Wilson had little passion for the game but nevertheless realized its therapeutic value. He once noted, "Men of ordinary physique and discretion cannot be Presidents and live if the strain is not somehow relieved. We shall be obliged always to be picking our chief magistrates from among wise and prudent athletes—a small class." Wilson had played as a professor at Princeton in 1898 but did not take up the sport regularly until after the age of forty at the request of his personal physician, Dr. Cary T. Grayson, in 1914. Wilson was plagued with physical ailments, and Grayson had encouraged him to use calisthenics and golf to help reduce stress. Wilson obliged, but he was a poor athlete and had limited vision. He explained, "My right eye is like a horse's. I can see straight out of it but not sideways. As a result I cannot take a full swing because my nose gets in the way and cuts off my view of the ball. That is the reason I use a short swing." He occasionally had trouble with his right arm and thus played left-handed.

After an early breakfast of two raw eggs in fruit juice, oatmeal, and coffee, Wilson would drive to Columbia Country Club, Chevy Chase Club, or Washington Golf and Country Club for a quick game, often playing just twelve holes. In the summer, he played every day except Sunday. On Saturdays, he would occasionally complete eighteen holes. Golf was not a social event for Wilson; he mainly played with Grayson and later his wife and, unlike Ike, was widely criticized for not inviting more people to play with him. According to Grayson, Wilson "found that most men whom he invited to play with him insisted on introducing public business into the conversation."

Wilson often carried his own bag and rarely played in the afternoons. He once described golf as "an ineffectual attempt to put an elusive ball into an obscure hole with an implement ill-adapted to the purpose." Wilson's only joy came when he realized that Edith Bolling Galt enjoyed the game, making golf part of their courtship. Wilson's first wife, Ellen, died seventeen months after they moved into the White House, and he soon began courting Edith, whom he had met at a White House tea. They often played together and shared a disdain for their scores. It often took Edith more than two hundred strokes to finish eighteen holes. Wilson typically shot between 115 and 120.

Wilson spent so much time on the course that his aides often delivered important messages to him there. He was on the golf course when he was told that the

Lusitania had been sunk, and he had a golf club in his hands when he learned that Lenin had become the Russian premier. But Wilson became sensitive enough about his image on the eve of the U.S. entry into World War I that he was reluctant to play. The diary of Colonel Edward House, one of Wilson's advisors, explained, "Mrs. Wilson spoke of golf and asked whether I thought it would look badly if the President went on the links. I thought the American people would feel that he should not do anything so trivial at such a time. The President at last suggested a game of pool." He did, however, eventually resume his forays onto the links.

In April 1918, a year after the United States entered the war, Wilson burned his right hand when grasping a hot pipe while reviewing a British tank on exhibition in Washington. This, however, did not limit his play, indicated by a letter that Edith Wilson wrote to Colonel House: "Woodrow is becoming the greatest one-arm champion in the world." He also played in the snow; he bundled up in a coat, gloves, and a hat and painted his golf balls red so he could see them.

Although Wilson played more than Taft, the press did not ridicule him for his time away from the office. The affable, and sometimes boisterous, Taft was criticized because he seemed to put golf ahead of his official duties. That could never have been said of the scholarly and solemn Wilson, who treated golf like an unfortunate task to be dispensed with each day. Another explanation for the public's differing perceptions may have stemmed from Wilson's approach to the game—he did not care about his score or improving his performance. He simply played to reduce stress. This unusual prescription worked, but only for a while. On October 2, 1919, while on a cross-country speaking tour to promote the League of Nations, Wilson suffered a severe stroke and never played golf again. In a 1957 *Washington Post* article, Eisenhower was urged to learn from Wilson's example and keep up his exercise program. By the time Ike came into office, though, the game and the nation's opinion of it had altered dramatically. It was no longer seen exclusively as a sport of elites. This had begun during Warren G. Harding's administration, which happened to coincide with Bobby Jones's competitive career.

Harding's golf game reflected the Jazz Age's penchant for leisure and recreation. He is once reported to have said, "I like to go out into the country and bloviate." For Harding, that meant to "loaf around, chat with people, and in general enjoy oneself." (This applied on the golf course and in the Oval Office.) Though not as casual about his score as Wilson was, Harding played two or three times a week, largely for companionship. He would play at Chevy Chase Club, at Washington Golf and Country Club, on the estate of Edward Beale McLean, and, occasionally, at East Potomac Park, a local municipal course. Harding was a betting man who preferred shots over water hazards, upon which he frequently wagered. He often partnered with Will Rogers, Grantland Rice, and Ring Lardner. Urged by his doctor to play to improve his health, Harding nevertheless drank, gambled, and joked on the course. According to Harold Hinton, Harding "was a gambling golfer and contrived to make almost every stroke of a round a separate source of excitement. He liked to play a six-dollar Nassau—six dollars on the outward nine, six on the return nine and six on the eighteen. In addition, he bet every other man in the foursome on low score, and interlarded the play with bets on the individual shots

71

and particular holes." There were plenty of reports of Harding playing for even higher stakes—$25 Nassaus with notable professionals Leo Diegel and Fred McLeod.

Shirley Povich, a veteran of the *Washington Post* sports department, caddied for Harding in the fall of 1922. The reporter recalled years later, "I showed up at the first tee and [Edward McLean] was glad to see me. He turned to the man standing with him and said, 'Mr. President, this is Shirley Povich, the best caddie in America,' which was untrue." As the round progressed, Povich remembered being surprised when waiters appeared on the tee with alcoholic drinks, even though it was the midst of the Prohibition. Harding sometimes took his dog, Laddie Boy, along when he played. Between rounds, at the White House, Harding often spread an old carpet on the South Lawn and teed off from the artificial turf, with the dog shagging balls for him.

Like Taft, Harding loved golf, and he was even listed as an honorary member of the United States Golf Association's executive committee from 1921 to 1923. He was a stickler for the rules, and the strongest part of his game was around the green. At the 1921 U.S. Open at Columbia Country Club in Maryland, Harding was on hand to present Jim Barnes with the trophy. Barnes later said that Harding confessed during the ceremony, "I would give anything to be in your shoes today." Harding donated a trophy to the USGA for the Amateur Public Links championship in 1923.

Walter Hagen played periodically with Harding, enough that he was a regular visitor at the White House and able to claim "my regular place at the table was next to the President with his dog Laddie Boy, sitting on the floor between us." Hagen retold a widely circulated anecdote in his autobiography in which Hagen, the master of gamesmanship, left Harding waiting at the first tee while he was in the clubhouse ostensibly trying to find a matching pair of socks. If Hagen intended for the inconvenience to rile and unsettle his opponent, he miscalculated. The congenial Harding simply bloviated until Hagen appeared. On the course, Harding never forgot his caddie's name and made it a point to ask about the boy's family throughout the round. Every caddie was eventually rewarded with a silver dollar.

Harding approached the game much as Taft did, with a relaxed kind of zeal. Sportswriter Grantland Rice explained that Harding "knows how to take the breaks of the game as they come and he realizes, which many don't, that bunkers are out there for the express purpose of catching all mistakes. All of which makes him an extremely attractive golf companion, one with dignity minus pretense." Harding, who learned to play in 1917 while serving as a senator from Ohio, was a fair player, but he focused more on betting than on practicing. He played in a few tournaments, but he mostly played to socialize. Still, he was dedicated enough to play in foul weather and occasionally took leave of his official duties to slip in a round. In the midst of a disarmament conference in Washington after World War I, Harding and Charles Evans Hughes, his secretary of state, played in a terrible thunderstorm. When called upon to sign the joint congressional resolution terminating the state of war with Germany, Harding was on the golf course. When his staff finally found him two hours later, he walked casually into the room in his golfing togs, read and signed the document, and returned to his round.

Calvin Coolidge ranks among the worst of the presidential golfers, perhaps because he was the stingiest. He hated to spend money and resented the fact that golf was expensive and time-consuming. In 1926, he complained, "You have to dress for golf. . . . Then you have to drive out for some club. . . . It takes three hours to play a round, then you have to undress, take a shower, dress again, and drive back. . . . Callers at the White House might wonder why the President wasn't on the job." Coolidge's complaint about the expense of the game may seem ironic when put in perspective. He was the first U.S. president to be paid an annual salary of $75,000. Coolidge played, not to improve his score, but because he realized the importance of the game in business and politics. A left-handed player, he was introduced to the sport on his honeymoon in 1905. Coolidge was not much of a sportsman—his only other recreation seems to have been a mechanical horse that he reportedly rode three times a day. But golf apparently captured his imagination, at least for a time. According to presidential lore, when he vacated the White House, the only thing he left behind was his golf clubs.

Harding's and Coolidge's tenures in the White House coincided with the first real sports boom in America. Legendary players such as Babe Ruth in baseball, Bill Tilden in tennis, Johnny Weissmuller in swimming, Red Grange in football, and Jack Dempsey in boxing attained the status of celebrities during the 1920s. Atlanta native Bobby Jones dominated the golf scene. No player ever beat him twice in competition. He became and remains the only golfer to achieve the Grand Slam—winning golf's four major championships in a single year. In *Triumphant Journey*, Richard Miller concluded, "In the Golden Age of Sport, his name shone the brightest." Coolidge was occasionally photographed with Jones, but his presidential distaste for athletics contrasted sharply with the era.

While Taft and Harding were criticized for playing too much golf during their tenure in the White House, Coolidge was derided for playing too little. In 1927, the *American Golfer* reported on his vacation in Sioux Falls, South Dakota, claiming "it was too bad the Chief Executive [was not among those] who are given to walloping golf balls all over the thousands of courses throughout the country. For Sioux Falls was equipped and ready to lead him to the scenes of activities of this kind that must surely have pleased him, had he been only of the golfing clan."

The last of the presidents to play golf before Ike was Franklin D. Roosevelt. FDR learned to play by watching his father, James Roosevelt, who, after a business trip to France in 1890, brought home golf clubs and set up an informal course on their estate in Hyde Park. FDR played at Groton, at Harvard, and often at the family retreat on Campobello Island. Between 1913 and 1920, while assistant secretary of the Navy, he played frequently before being diagnosed with polio. FDR usually shot in the high 80s and often partnered with then Senator Warren Harding. Even after he could no longer play, FDR supported the game. During the New Deal, he advocated construction policies that built more than 250 municipal courses. Sportswriter Al Barkow described FDR's golfing talents: "Photographs and old movie footage of Franklin D. Roosevelt playing golf as a young man reveal a well-formed swing; he came close to making his college golf team. FDR was very fond of the game, and he deeply missed playing after he was

75

stricken with polio." During World War II, long after he was able to walk a golf course, he urged the PGA of America to continue the Tour to help boost morale. FDR's enthusiasm for the game was undiminished, even as his physical ability to play waned.

The men in the White House who played golf before Eisenhower influenced the public's perception of the game. Whether they loved it or played it out of a sense of necessity, their constituents were seldom silent on the matter. But none of his predecessors could match Ike's enthusiasm for the game. He was an avid player, spending much of his time in and out of the White House thinking about how to improve it. He constantly analyzed his putting stroke, took innumerable lessons, pored over his scores searching for ways to improve, and was often planning his next round. Ike was, after all, a military man who approached running the country and running around after a golf ball with the same intensity. He had a rigorous practice regime and was dismayed when it was interrupted. Ike expected the same level of commitment from those around him. He once chided Vice President Richard M. Nixon for his poor performance at golf: "You're young, you're strong, and you can do a lot better."

Ike's passion for golf posed a unique problem for the Secret Service. In contrast to Taft, who had only one agent follow him around the course at a modest distance, by the time Ike moved into the White House, security for the president had intensified to the point of obtrusiveness. The Secret Service would visit the course Ike planned to play several hours in advance to search the clubhouse, the grounds, even the ball washer. With a command post set up in the clubhouse, a contingent of agents, dressed in golfing attire, accompanied Ike's party around the course with walkie-talkies and golf bags filled with high-powered rifles. In the nearly eight hundred rounds that Ike played during his presidency, the agents never encountered any notable problems. But they certainly were prepared. They even had a "doomsday briefcase" that contained the codes that could launch a nuclear strike from anywhere in the United States.

Eisenhower's passion encouraged others to play, especially middle-aged Americans. A staff member at a public golf course in Washington noticed a significant change after Ike entered the White House: "People like to follow the leader. The papers keep talking golf. People start talking golf and then they start playing it. I tell you, the President really has given the game a shot in the arm. . . . Ever since he went into the White House, all you hear is golf, golf, golf."

Writing for *Golf Digest* in 1953, John Fitzpatrick noted, "Washington, D.C. has been seized with a golfing fever like never before in history. . . . Golf interest and activity in the Capitol—as reflected by equipment sales, lessons, daily fee play and applications for private club membership—are at an all-time high. On a smaller scale, a similar golf boom is taking place all over the country. Reason for this sudden surge of popularity for the royal and ancient game, of course, is the tremendous publicity it has received as a result of President Eisenhower's great devotion to it. This not only has focused public attention on the links pastime, but has also brought home the therapeutic value of the sport."

But not everyone celebrated the golf boom. Peter Andrews, writing in *Golf Digest*, explained that he was paired with a man from Texas on a crowded course.

77

Exasperated by the slow play, the man said, "God, I sometimes wish Adlai Stevenson had been elected President. Then maybe some of these morons in front of us would be off playing tennis."

In fact, the nation's perception of Ike's golf game changed during his eight years in office. At first, Ike was derided for taking so much time away from the office. After his first heart attack, however, a round of golf became a tangible way for the administration to show that the commander in chief was in good health and thus capable of leading the nation. At times, Ike was criticized for embracing an elitist and exclusionary sport, yet he was simultaneously praised by others for choosing a democratic one that could be enjoyed by men and women, children and the elderly. Golf was a conundrum, beholden to the politics of the moment, for each president who played it. No one worked harder to distance himself from the game than Ike's successor, John F. Kennedy, probably the best presidential golfer. Kennedy was keenly aware of the proliferation of Eisenhower golf jokes, and so he golfed in secret. Jacqueline Kennedy was also a golfer and was mortified when J. Walter Green, an Associated Press photographer, snapped an image of her hitting balls in Newport, Rhode Island. Photographers were banned from the course the next day.

Every president, with the exception of Jimmy Carter, has played golf since Ike. Lyndon B. Johnson was known to take a fair number of mulligans and had difficulty breaking 100. Richard M. Nixon created a three-hole course at his home in San Clemente, California, and called golf "my lifesaver" after his resignation in the face of the Watergate scandal. By the time Gerald Ford came to office in 1974, the stigma of presidential golf had almost completely disappeared. Ford became the first president to compete regularly in public events. In February 1975, he played before forty thousand spectators in a pro-am event for the Jackie Gleason Classic at Inverrary Country Club in Florida. As during Eisenhower's administration, Ford's presidency was often linked in the public consciousness to his fondness for golf. He was a fine player, notwithstanding his several mishaps on the course, including hitting a spectator with a golf ball. Ronald Reagan worked as a caddie as a young boy in Peoria, Illinois, got his handicap as low as 12 while acting in Hollywood, and played once a week in his retirement. George H. W. Bush was an excellent all-around athlete and was known for his speed of play on the golf course. His son, George W. Bush, preferred more active sports, such as mountain biking and running, but was not a stranger to the links.

Bill Clinton, most often photographed jogging, also loved the game. A round of golf with Clinton was much like one with Taft or Harding, casual and leisurely. For Clinton, competition was secondary to camaraderie. A 1993 commentary in *Runners' World* mused about the relationship between a president and a sport: "Several people have suggested that Clinton could do for running what Ike did for golf. Having heard that a number of times, I began to ask myself, What did Ike do for golf? It turns out quite a lot, just as President Kennedy's promoting 50-mile walks helped launch an entire physical fitness movement in this country. A president's interests—be they in sports, music, food or entertainment—become emblematic of an era." Golf, as we shall see, reveals a great deal about the 1950s.

FOUR

GOLF IN THE
AGE OF IKE

*Ben Hogan for president. If we're going to have
a golfer, let's have a good one.*

—BUMPER STICKER

Eisenhower on the golf course sheds new light on 1950s
America. Jacques Barzun once famously said, "Who-
ever wants to know the heart and mind of America
better learn baseball." But it might make more sense
to argue that to understand this decade, one needs to
study golf—and, in particular, Ike's relationship to the
game. During his two terms in the White House, he
played nearly eight hundred rounds. Subtracting the
time he was convalescing from illnesses, that averages
three times a week. Today, a sitting president would
likely be impeached for such behavior. Ike was simultaneously credited with the sudden surge of the sport's
popularity and criticized for running the presidency
from a golf course. He was known for playing at the
most exclusive clubs in America, while tentatively sup-

porting civil rights. By his second term, Ike and his golf game became symbols of social, economic, and political contradictions of the 1950s.

More than any other sport in America, golf resisted change. Jackie Robinson helped desegregate baseball in 1947; Charlie Sifford would not be given that opportunity until 1964, when he became the first African American player to qualify for the PGA Tour. Golf seemed immune to the growing agitation for equality and justice among disenfranchised Americans. Unlike baseball and basketball, the working classes did not embrace golf. With the exception of a handful of Scotsmen, it did not attract new immigrants. Though the USGA supported the creation of public courses to democratize the game, golf was still a comparatively expensive sport. Golfers had to invest in a bag, clubs, balls, and, to be accepted, special clothes and shoes. Perhaps more importantly, they needed money for greens fees. In contrast, a basketball player needed only a basketball and access to a public court equipped with a hoop. Gene Sarazen worried that the expense of golf kept it out of reach of the average player. He argued that greens fees were $7.50 at most Florida courses during the 1950s. Add to that $6 for a caddy fee and tip, and the game becomes pricey. "A fellow playing in a foursome can't go out for a day's fun now without having to shell out $20 or more. What young men can afford that on a steady scale?"

Several editorials printed in *Golfing Magazine* observed, "Those who want to keep the game as the exclusive property of the wealthy who belong to clubs are not carrying out the ancient and honored traditions. In the old country, it is possible for everyone to play and no one has ever objected to this." Even though he was part of the sport's establishment, Eisenhower worked hard to dispel the myth that golf was undemocratic. In a May 1953 letter addressed to "golfers and fellow duffers," Ike wrote to the sponsors of the PGA Championship, scheduled to be held at Birmingham Country Club in July: "While I know that I speak with the partisanship of an enthusiast, golf obviously provides one of our best forms of healthful exercises, accompanied by good fellowship and companionship. It is a sport in which the whole American family can participate— fathers and mothers, sons and daughters alike. It offers healthy respite from daily toil, refreshment of body and mind." In this way, golf became an American symbol of prosperity, even if only a relatively small portion of the population could afford to play. Ike's colleague Jack Westland once said when running for Congress, "Early in the campaign the opposition tried to brand me with the country club stamp. But it didn't hurt. Everybody plays golf nowadays."

At the end of World War II, with the economy expanding and leisure time increasing, golf blossomed in America. *Newsweek* reported on August 31, 1953, "Last week a sampling across the country showed that golf-course attendance, booming before the Inauguration, had since risen as much as 25 per cent in some places; club pros reported that: (a) their junior pupils had more than doubled this season, and (b) an uncommon number of old gaffers were looking into the game for the first time." The *Washington Post* reported that local sales of golf equipment in March 1953, two months into Ike's first term, were robust. A salesman for a local Wilson Sporting Goods store reported, "At one club, they've already sold more equipment in two months than they usually sell in six." Newt Priestly, a Washington representative for A. G. Spalding and Brothers, called Ike "the finest advertisement possible for golf as a competitive, but relaxing game." In the words of professionals Mel Shorey of Indian Spring and Bill Hardy of Chevy Chase, "Everybody's talking golf in the middle of winter, a sure sign that the President's game will have a great impact on sales."

Ike, of course, was not single-handedly responsible for the boom, but he was the most visible figure associated with it. Sports historian Benjamin Rader explained the role of celebrities in this transformation: "In the nation's capital, the new president, Dwight D. Eisenhower, unlike two of his golf-playing predecessors (William Howard Taft and Warren G. Harding) made no secret of his addiction to the game. . . . At the other end of the continent Hollywood celebrities took up golf with equal ardor. Often as part of a gimmick to hawk local real estate, Bing Crosby, Bob Hope, Perry Como, Danny Thomas, Andy Williams, and Jackie Gleason, among others, sponsored new professional tournaments. The association of golf with a popular president and a host of celebrities lent to the sport a glamour perhaps unequalled by any other sport."

With a little help from the United States Golf Association, Ike brought golf to the White House. The minutes of the January 30, 1953, Executive Committee meeting indicate that the USGA approached the president about installing a putting green on the White House lawn. A resolution was passed approving a proposal that the USGA establish a putting green "if desired by the President." A confidential memorandum addressed to the Management Committee of the USGA from April 15, 1954, revealed that Ike was pleased by the suggestion: "The White House has now indicated that it will accept a putting green but only as a gift from an organization such as the United States Golf Association." Al Radko of the USGA was then dispatched to the White House to inspect the site and consider whether installation of the green was "feasible."

The USGA spelled out its role in the project, which consisted of "technical advice and funds for materials up to $1,500." The three-thousand-square-foot green was made of polycross creeping bent grass, a new strain that had been developed by H. B. Musser, an agronomist at the University of Pennsylvania. Aronomink Golf Club in Pennsylvania provided the sod, and the green's apron was sodded with Merion bluegrass. According to the June 1954 issue of the *USGA Journal and Turf Management,* "The green was designed and constructed under the direction of Alexander M. Radko, Northeastern Director of the USGA Green Section, and Richard Watson, turf advisor to the Burning Tree Club, Chevy Chase, Maryland, where President Eisenhower often plays golf. James E. Thomas, golf course superintendent of the Army-Navy Country Club, Arlington, Virginia, and president of the Mid-Atlantic Association of Golf Course Superintendents, assisted. The Mid-Atlantic Association of Golf Course Superintendents and the Golf Course Superintendents Association of America cooperated." The intention was to have golf course superintendents in the Washington, D.C., area maintain the green after it was built. On May 14, 1954, USGA agronomists began constructing a putting green so Ike could practice.

A month later, USGA President Isaac B. Grainger received a letter from the president that read, "Dear Mr. Grainger: I am deeply indebted to you and your associates in the United States Golf Association for the help given to the White House staff in the creation of a putting green on the lawn. As you may know, I enjoy and need the exercise I get from occasional golf practice, and this makes it easy for me to slip out for a half hour or so whenever I find the time. Please convey to all those whose assistance made the green possible the sense of deep appreciation I feel. With warm regard, Sincerely, Dwight D. Eisenhower." The green did not survive subsequent administrations. Years later, George H. W. Bush put down artificial turf and used it primarily as a target for chipping. During the Clinton administration, while Reg Murphy was president of the USGA, Robert Trent Jones Jr. was hired to redesign the green that Eisenhower had so loved. But not everyone liked the idea of the president of the United States golfing on the lawn. In fact, one of Eisenhower's friends suggested that it made the president an easy target for assassins. Never one to shy away from danger, Ike replied, "Point out one of those fellers to me and I'll show you a direct hit at 250 yards."

Celebrities, especially Bob Hope, kept golf in the public eye throughout the 1940s and 1950s. Hope met General Eisenhower in 1943 when he was doing a series of performances for servicemen in Algiers, North Africa. During one rehearsal with Hal Bloch and Frances Langford, Eisenhower's aide came to ask Hope if he could take a break to come meet with the general. Hope recalled the first meeting: "Ike was seated behind a desk in his command post, studying some maps. He got up quickly, walked over to extend his hand. His first words to me were 'How's your golf?' " That initiated, Hope explained, "a beautiful friendship that endured for over a quarter of a century." Hope once quipped, "Ike plays like a General. Every time he strokes a putt, he snaps to attention and barks, 'Fall in.'" According to Hope, "playing golf with Ike is very handy. If you hit a ball into the rough and it stops near a tree, the tree suddenly becomes a Secret Service man and moves away."

In popularizing golf, Ike and his celebrity friends had some help from Tour players. Byron Nelson, who won an amazing eighteen PGA events in 1945, retired in 1946 and occasionally played with the president. He recounted one story right after the 1952 election: "The first day we played, I was chosen to drive his golf cart. He was like a cricket, he moved very quickly. I'd get within 5 to 10 feet of his golf ball and he'd jump out of the cart before the cart even stopped. So I began trying to stop a little quicker and that still didn't work. So I told him, 'Mr. President, I would feel a lot better if you would sit in the cart until I stopped. Because it's going to make great headlines if Byron Nelson throws the President out of the cart and he breaks his leg.' Next time I stopped, he stayed in the cart—and that was the last time. He jumped out the rest of the day."

The 1950s was a golden era for golf, dominated by Sam Snead, Ben Hogan, Jimmy Demaret, Cary Middlecoff, and Arnold Palmer—all of whom played with Eisenhower. Though he had made a name for himself in the 1940s, Snead remained competitive, winning the Vardon Trophy in 1949, 1950, and 1955, having also won it in 1938. He would eventually end up with eighty-one Tour victories, including the PGA Championships in 1949, 1952, and 1954. An exacting player, Snead once said, "Show me a golfer who walks away calmly after topping a drive or missing a kick-in putt, and I'll show you one who is going to lose." No wonder Snead found an ideal partner in Eisenhower.

87

In his book *Golf Anecdotes,* Bob Sommers included an amusing story that was frequently and fondly retold by the Secret Service whenever Ike played with Snead: "Invited to play a round with the President at Burning Tree, Sam Snead kept his thoughts to himself through seventeen holes, but as they walked onto the eighteenth tee he said to the President, 'Mind if I tell you one thing?' Pleased to take such advice from one of the greatest golfers the game has known, Eisenhower said, 'No, not at all.' Snead looked at him in the eyes and said, 'Stick out your fanny, Mr. President.' His fanny in the proper position, Ike then whacked a 220-yard drive that split the fairway." In 1956, Ike played regularly with Snead, who by then was the golf professional at the Greenbrier Hotel in White Sulphur Springs, West Virginia.

One of the best-known golfers of the era, Ben Hogan, also befriended Ike. From 1946 to 1953, Hogan won the U.S. Open four times, the Masters and the PGA Championship twice, and the British Open once. In 1949, his image graced the cover of *Time* magazine. Severely injured in a crash with a Greyhound bus that same year, he came back to win the U.S. Open in 1950 at Merion Golf Club in a play-off with Lloyd Mangrum and George Fazio. In 1953, Hogan had one of the most extraordinary years in the history of golf. He won the Masters, U.S. Open, and British Open. He chose not to play the PGA Championship, the fourth event that makes up the modern, professional Grand Slam, because of the rigors of match play (a format by which a golfer wins or loses by holes rather than by strokes, often resulting in long, arduous matches) on his ailing legs. Had he won, he would have matched Bobby Jones's Grand Slam 1930 record. Upon winning the British Open, Hogan became only the second golfer

(Jones received two during his competitive career) to receive a ticker-tape parade down Broadway.

Hogan played his first round with Ike in 1953, two days after winning the Masters Tournament. Ike arrived the day before, and Clifford Roberts arranged the afternoon foursome (that included Ike, Hogan, Byron Nelson, and Roberts) on April 14. It turned out that Hogan and Ike's first game together came on the same day as Hogan's wedding anniversary. Bobby Jones and Barbara Eisenhower, Ike's daughter-in-law, followed the group around the course in an electric cart. During the round, Ike teased Roberts about Hogan's Masters performance (he had shot a 274 for seventy-two holes): "Ben Hogan made fun of your course, didn't he Cliff?" Ike shot a 94, Roberts an 87, Nelson a 72, and Hogan a 70. Hogan complimented Ike's performance, remarking, "The President shoots a nice game for a man whose job doesn't give him much chance to play or practice." Hogan also thought Ike had a good sense of course management and made wise club selections. That may be why, two years later in June 1955, Hogan sent Ike a set of his own brand of golf clubs.

Though often overshadowed by Snead and Hogan, Jimmy Demaret, Cary Middlecoff, and Lloyd Mangrum were also stars during the 1950s, and Ike played with each of them as well. Demaret won the Masters in 1947 and again in 1950, and he played on the 1951 Ryder Cup team. Though his best years were behind him, he continued to win PGA events throughout the decade. He is probably best remembered for his outrageous clothes and antics on the course. As John Companiotte recounted in his book *Jimmy Demaret: The Swing's the Thing*, Demaret acquired his taste for bright colors from his father, a house painter. In New York in the 1930s, Demaret had shirts and slacks made from fabric that was used for women's clothing, thus launching a "sartorial revolution." He ended his career with thirty-one PGA Tour victories and was a popular commentator with Sarazen on "Shell's Wonderful World of Golf." In 1964, years after he had left the White House, Ike and Arnold Palmer teamed up to play in a charity exhibition match against Demaret and singer Ray Bolger, best known for his portrayal of the Scarecrow in the 1939 film *The Wizard of Oz*.

A former dentist from Memphis, Tennessee, Middlecoff became one of the best players of the decade. In 1951, he won three consecutive events. He won the U.S. Open in 1949 and 1956, competed on three U.S. Ryder Cup teams (1953, 1955, and 1959), won the Masters in 1955, and won the 1956 Vardon Trophy. A regular player with Ike, Middlecoff said after an early round, "The President shoots a lot better golf than I thought he would. He can belt one off the tee and knock it a pretty good chunk from the fairway. . . . He chips exceptionally well." On May 25, 1955, Ike played a round with Byron Nelson and Middlecoff at Burning Tree Club. Both Nelson and Middlecoff shot 68s; Ike's score was not reported. Mangrum, who won a total of thirty-four Tour events, won the 1946 U.S. Open and topped the money list in 1951. He won the Vardon Trophy in both 1951 and 1952. He and Ike played together occasionally, and according to Bob Sommers in *Golf Anecdotes*, "Mangrum survived eleven heart attacks; the twelfth killed him in 1973. While he was recovering from his seventh, President Eisenhower had his second. Thinking he could cheer up the President, Mangrum sent him a telegram. 'Dear Ike,' it read, 'I'm five up on you.' "

Along with Ike, Arnold Palmer, whose star began to rise in the 1950s, was the person most responsible for the second golf boom in the twentieth century. Al Barkow and David Barrett, in their book *Golf Greats*, begin their biographical sketch of Palmer by observing, "It is a rare athlete who achieves a level of popularity that transcends his sport and becomes a national folk hero." Palmer turned professional three months after winning the 1954 U.S. Amateur. He won his first event, the Canadian Open, in 1955 but did not capture the public's imagination until the 1958 Masters, in part because his style and persona came across well on the new medium of television.

In the 1950s, professional golf entered an unprecedented era of prosperity, popularity, and change. Palmer's charisma broadened the fan base. The exposure of golf through television led to increased purses for professional tournaments, made corporate sponsorship an integral part of the sport, and made Snead, Hogan, Demaret, Middlecoff, and Palmer household names. Local television coverage of golf began at the 1947 U.S. Open in St. Louis, but it was not until George S. May's World Championship of Golf at the Tam O'Shanter Golf Club in Chicago was broadcast nationwide in 1953 that the public began to take notice. In addition, the advent of new technologies—such as multiple cameras, color, replay, and slow motion—made spectatorship more appealing. Palmer's dramatic style of play helped build "Arnie's Army," cadres of hard-core fans that followed Palmer's every move. Because television coverage so effectively showcased his unique playing style and personality, Palmer became a hero, even among Americans who had little or no interest in golf.

91

Of all the Tour players, Palmer was probably Ike's closest friend. Ike once said, "How I admired that man. He lived the kind of life everyone dreams of. It always stirred me to play in his group, and those days always will rank among my fondest memories." The depth of their friendship is illustrated by an event after Ike left the White House. For Palmer's thirty-seventh birthday, on September 10, 1966, Palmer's wife, Winnie, arranged a surprise visit from Ike and Mamie. Throughout the day, Winnie worked hard to keep Arnold occupied with tasks about the house, to keep him out of his workshop (where his assistant, Doc Griffin, was setting up a command center for the Secret Service). Unbeknownst to him, Winnie sent Arnold's new airplane to pick up the president. A few minutes after the plane landed, there was a knock at the Palmers' door. When Arnold opened it, Ike stood with a small overnight bag and asked, "You wouldn't have room to put up an old man for the night, would you?" For a birthday gift, Ike had painted a rural scene of Pennsylvania for Palmer, a painting that still hangs in a hallway in the Palmers' home, between the kitchen and living room. In his book *Arnold Palmer: Memories, Stories and Memorabilia*, Palmer reflected, "Of all the people I've met and befriended over the years, the most special to me was America's thirty-fourth president. Other than my father, no man had a bigger impact on my life than President Dwight David Eisenhower, whom I feel fortunate to have known and whose time with me I will always cherish."

Another group of Tour professionals helped popularize golf in the 1950s, and their presence also helped democratize the game. In 1950, the Ladies Professional Golf Association (LPGA) was officially chartered, though there had been other organizations for women as early as 1944. The year Ike was first elected president, the LPGA boasted twenty-one events. Babe Didrikson Zaharias, Patty Berg, Betty Jameson, Betsy Rawls, Louise Suggs, and others became household names. The Bauer sisters, Marlene and Alice, were a main attraction of the fledgling women's Tour. In 1950, Zaharias was named the Associated Press's Woman Athlete of the Year for her victories in the Titleholders, the Western Open, and the U.S. Women's Open. In 1953, she was diagnosed with colon cancer and underwent surgery, but she managed to return to the LPGA for the 1954 season. Like Hogan in 1950, Zaharias's comeback drew intense interest. She would win the U.S. Women's Open at Salem Country Club by twelve strokes, and her triumph put golf on the front page of newspapers around the nation.

Though they were friends, Ike never had a chance to play with Zaharias. He did, however, participate in activities that helped raise money for cancer research. When she visited him at the White House to launch an American Cancer Society campaign, Ike used the sword that symbolized the organization as a golf club to get a lesson from Zaharias. At an event for the same organization in 1954, Zaharias shelved her speech on her battle with cancer and decided to chat with the president about his golf game. When she asked about his golf, Ike replied, "Well, it could be a lot better. But as long as I've got people like you to emulate, I'll be all right."

The Babe's extraordinary feats, though, did not help average women on the golf course. In 1956, the *Washington Post* began an article on women by intoning, "Pity the poor woman who wants to learn golf," and then detailed how difficult it is for women to play. Samuel Rauworth, a teaching professional in Chicago who specialized in teaching women the game, explained, "Out on the fairway, it's downright dangerous the way men will blast their drives through women players." Women athletes would eventually enjoy increased access with the passage of Title IX of the Education Amendments Act in 1972, passed during Nixon's administration.

As women slowly gained access to the links and faced a certain measure of disrespect, they still fared better than African American players. After the war, football, basketball, and baseball were transformed by black athletes who had been restricted from these sports for most of their history. More often than not, gaining access to fields of athletic endeavor required extensive legal battles. Throughout the 1950s, African Americans were barred from nearly all golf courses in the United States, save a handful of public courses. It would only be after Ike left the Oval Office—and largely the result of the Civil Rights Act of 1964—that golf became more accessible for African Americans. Yet, many of the decisions that Ike made during his presidency regarding public accommodations paved the way for these changes.

In his book *American Sports: From the Age of Folk Games to the Age of Televised Sports*, Benjamin Rader explained that despite a few experiments with integration—baseball in the 1880s and a handful of college football and track teams in the North—sports reflected the Jim Crow policies of the nation that separated "whites and blacks in ballparks, beaches, churches, trains, toilets, schools, and even water fountains." From bicycling to baseball, most sports adopted "whites-only" rules for competition. The only sport where African

American players enjoyed some degree of fairness was prizefighting. Jack Johnson held the world heavyweight title from 1908 to 1915. But black athletes would not be widely accepted until after World War II.

On April 9, 1947, Branch Rickey, general manager of the Brooklyn Dodgers, released a short statement that would forever change American sports: "Brooklyn announces the purchase of the contract of Jack Roosevelt Robinson." In an article published forty years later, George Will claimed that Jackie Robinson and Rosa Parks were the two most important blacks in American history. Football, not baseball, however, was the first major sport to desegregate. A year before Rickey's announcement, the National Football League's Los Angeles Rams and the All-America Football Conference's Cleveland Browns had black players. In 1949, the American Bowling Congress was desegregated. A year later, two black players joined the National Basketball Association (NBA). Rader explained that these swift changes "arose from a combination of pressures: increasing agitation by blacks from outside the world of sports, assertions of black political power, international circumstances, shifting attitudes of whites toward blacks, and quests for additional profits by sports entrepreneurs."

Golf did not formally desegregate until 1961, Ike's last year in the White House. Even so, black men and women had played the game for decades. African American golfer John Shippen and Native American golfer Oscar Bunn qualified for the second U.S. Open in 1896, won by James Foulis at Shinnecock Hills Golf Club. When other players complained about their presence, USGA President Theodore F. Havemeyer remarked, "We're going to play this thing today even if Shippen and Bunn are the only people in it." But the rest of the sport did not embrace Havemeyer's position. As historian Richard Moss described segregation in golf, "Young blacks could learn the game and earn money as caddies, but if they wished to continue in the game, they were pushed into the margins. The few African Americans who carved out a place for themselves did so at a tiny number of black clubs and public courses."

Restricted from tournaments sponsored by the USGA and PGA, whether formally or informally, black players resigned themselves to compete in all-black tournaments sponsored by the United Golf Association (UGA), a loosely organized tour for black golfers founded in 1928. Ted Rhodes, Charlie Sifford, and Pete Brown competed on these circuits. Rhodes won more than 150 tournaments on the UGA Tour but never captured a major title. In 1934, the PGA of America added an article to its constitution (Article III, Section I): "Professional golfers of the Caucasian Race, over the age of eighteen (18) years, residing in North or South America, who can qualify under the terms and conditions hereinafter specified, shall be eligible for membership."

Sifford, who broke racial barriers in the 1940s and 1950s and turned pro in 1946, was denied access to most professional tournaments. Agitation for change occurred decades before the game was formally desegregated, but it was not until 1964 that Sifford became the first black player on the pro Tour. Still, he remained a token. In 1975, Lee Elder became the first black player to qualify for the Masters. Althea Gibson and Renee Powell were the first two black members of the LPGA, in 1963 and 1967, respectively. Not until 1990 and the PGA of America's battle with Shoal Creek, the site of the PGA Championship, did Augusta National accept a black member. Even today, Tiger Woods remains the only black Masters champion. In his book, *Just Let Me Play*, Sifford argues that it is not reasonable to compare him to Jackie Robinson because it implies that golf, like baseball, has been fully integrated.

During the 1950s, then, golf remained entrenched as a sport dominated by wealthy white men. Yet, Ike somehow made it an acceptable game for middle-class families, even while he personally embraced and benefited from its elitism. A year after Ike was elected to his first term, dozens of magazine and newspaper articles began celebrating his obsession. In one titled "President's Drives Send Golf in Capital Over Par," one writer remarked, "Activity on the tees, fairways and greens of this city's golf courses has been over par this year. . . . Golf authorities here are unanimous in agreeing that one of the city's residents—Dwight D. Eisenhower of 1600 Pennsylvania Avenue, N.W.—has done more to stimulate interest in the game than any other person in the country." Ike's enthusiasm was infectious. Bob Hope once joked, "By the time Ike was elected President in 1952, his devotion to golf had become legendary. No administration ever had more suntanned Secret Service men. You could always find his farm at Gettysburg because it was the one completely surrounded by divots. Ike's neighbors didn't know he had moved in until Mamie knocked on their door and asked to borrow a cup of golf balls."

Golf came to function in the 1950s as a dual symbol of progress and provincialism. On one hand, it symbolized prosperity and vitality. It was seen as a democratic sport that grandfathers and granddaughters could play. At the same time, it was a troubling symbol of white privilege for a nation just awakening to a national civil rights struggle. It was, above all, the sport of a president who was a reluctant supporter of the changing times. Golf, then, becomes a lens in which to understand the decade's social tensions and the president who guided the nation through it.

Elite golf clubs such as Burning Tree and Augusta National became havens for Ike, safely removing him from the turmoil of the outside world. But that turmoil was just outside the gates. In 1951, after Ike joined Augusta, four black men 180 miles away in Atlanta changed golf history. On July 19, Dr. Hamilton Holmes Sr., Alfred "Tup" Holmes, Reverend Oliver Wendell Holmes, and Charles Bell arrived at the Bobby Jones Golf Course, at 384 Woodward Way, "ready, willing and able to pay all lawful, uniform fees." Bill Wilson, the club's manager, who cited a city law that prohibited African Americans from using the park, refused the men admittance.

This refusal came as no surprise. A series of Jim Crow laws enacted in the 1890s sanctioned the segregation of public facilities in most southern cities, including Atlanta. The fact that the city accepted Springvale Park in 1893 "with the condition that blacks be prohibited from using it dramatically demonstrates the changing tone of race in Atlanta during the 1890s." By 1890, East Lake provided a lake with boating, fishing, and swimming and permitted "reputable persons" (that is, whites) to swim. East Lake was also home to the Atlanta Athletic Club's East Lake golf course, where Bobby Jones learned to play. Throughout the 1890s, black and white communities were segregated legally on streetcars, railroad sleeping cars, and waiting rooms and informally in public libraries and white churches. In 1910, the city segregated its eating establishments. In 1913 and 1916, the city of Atlanta passed measures that provided separate blocks for black and white residences in order to "promote the general welfare." Residential zoning laws with classifications based on race were further codified in the 1920s. With the exception of domestic servants, blacks and whites were not permitted to reside in the same districts. This pattern of segregation was not successfully challenged in Atlanta or most of the South until Eisenhower's second term. Although the black community petitioned for separate parks, Atlanta did not deliver. The desire for recreational facilities encouraged the development of private initiatives in racially segregated neighborhoods. One of the most visible responses was the establishment of an all-black country club.

Lincoln Country Club, at 2405 Simpson Road in northwest Atlanta, was chartered by Alonzo Fisher, James Ivey, Theodore Grimes, and A. W. Parks. When it opened in 1927, it served as the only golf club for blacks in Atlanta. Because blacks could not play on municipal courses, Fisher's nine-hole, thirty-three-acre course trained many of the South's African American golfers, including many of the men who later caddied at East Lake, Peachtree Golf Club, and Augusta National. In 1937, in the midst of the Great Depression, the club was reorganized as the New Lincoln Country Club. Poor course maintenance, along with the mounting frustration over Atlanta's refusal to desegregate, prompted four black men to try their luck in 1951 at the public Bobby Jones Golf Course, which had opened in Atlanta in 1931. They chose the course for its symbolic value. Jones was one of the world's most famous golfers who had helped popularize the sport among Americans of every race and class. He was a close friend of President

Eisenhower, who would ultimately have to guide the nation through desegregation of public facilities, just as he had with the armed forces. The course that bore Jones's name would be the perfect testing ground.

When the four black men were not permitted to play, an Atlanta Golf Committee was organized and the services of Roscoe Edwin Thomas were retained to fight the city. It would take four years and a series of lawsuits before the city's public courses would be formally desegregated. On December 24, 1955, the *New York Times* reported, "Five Negroes took their places in line with the usual weekend crowd of white golfers at Atlanta's North Fulton Course today and played without incident." Despite a few threatening phone calls, Tup Holmes, Oliver Wendell Holmes, Charles Bell, T. D. Hawkins, and E. J. Peterson teed off in two groups. Thomas kept score. When asked about the historic moment, Hank Whitfield, the assistant pro at North Fulton, said they "just came out, paid their fees and teed off." Though there is no record that Dwight D. Eisenhower followed the reports of the lengthy battle as it was covered in many of the major newspapers, it certainly foreshadowed how the South would respond to desegregation.

Georgia Governor Marvin Griffin termed the *Holmes* decision "regrettable" but declared that the state had no jurisdiction in the matter. As he explained, "All attempts to mix races, whether they be in the classroom, on the playgrounds, in public conveyances, or in any other area of close personal contact, constitute the gravest peril to harmonious race relations in Georgia and the South. I am opposed to any breakdown in such barriers, no matter how slight, for no one can, in good conscience, condone this in one instance and be opposed to it in another." The governor was frustrated by city leaders' refusal to sell the courses to private companies and individuals as an alternative to integration. Griffin's statement was but a glimmer of what Ike would face from Governor Orval Faubus in 1957 in Little Rock, Arkansas, over the desegregation of Central High School. Until then, Ike's South was viewed from a terrace overlooking Magnolia Lane at Augusta National.

FIVE

IKE'S FABULOUS AND FRETFUL FIFTIES

My first day at the president's desk. Plenty of worries and difficult problems.
—DWIGHT D. EISENHOWER

Dwight D. Eisenhower was the last U.S. president born in the nineteenth century, and this fact, perhaps more than any other, explained the difficulties he faced when trying to reconcile his private and public lives. Ike and his golf game became symbols of the contradictory nature of the 1950s—a decade remembered both for conservative political culture and the emerging civil rights movement. In Ike's first term, he was viewed as an athletic, congenial president who balanced the intense pressures of the office with his love of sports. Toward the end of his second term, however, he was increasingly seen as a golfer who sequestered himself from the opportunities, challenges, and perils of the atomic age. Consumerism, suburbanization, McCarthyism, and the space race shaped daily life in the United States, as well as Eisenhower's evolving views of the nation's future.

Like the decade he came to represent, Eisenhower was an enigma. During World War II, he was a modest general surrounded by gruff egotists Winston Churchill and Charles de Gaulle and flamboyant generals Bernard Montgomery, George S. Patton, and Douglas MacArthur. Like contemporary actors Jimmy Stewart and Henry Fonda, Ike possessed a charismatic appeal that drew strength from his commonness. Like many Americans, Ike struggled with the contradictions of war and peace during the 1940s and 1950s. He was a career soldier who abhorred war. He believed in fairness but could not articulate or commit to a clear civil rights policy. He advocated peace at the height of the Cold War while engaging in precipitous brinkmanship with the Soviet Union. He was a strong supporter of the armed forces but warned against the "unwarranted influence, whether sought or unsought, by the military industrial complex." He was liberal in international affairs and human relations but conservative in domestic policy and obsessive about balancing the budget. (His critics jokingly characterized his fiscal policies as "better dead than in the red.")

Ike's golf outings at exclusive clubs in the presence of wealthy businessmen gave the nation the impression that he was not fully committed to the presidency; yet he won reelection in a landslide in 1956, with the largest popular-vote margin up to that point. Toward the end of his second term, Democrats reflected back on "eight long years of golfing and goofing, of puttering and putting." In *Ike: His Life and Times*, British historian Piers Brendon declared, "Eisenhower's negative and unimaginative presidency seemed an altogether apt reflection of the tawdry decade of the 1950s." In the same book, though, Brendon argued that in comparison to the 1970s, plagued by Watergate and the energy crisis, "Eisenhower's administration appeared moderate, honorable and wise." Most historians who have assessed Ike's legacy conclude that this enigmatic man was often "underestimated."

On November 4, 1952, at the age of sixty-two, Dwight D. Eisenhower was elected the thirty-fourth president of the United States. The phrase "Peace and Prosperity" dominated his tenure in the White House. Americans elected Ike twice because they saw him as a symbol of stability. Samuel Lubell, a 1950s political reporter, commented, "Rarely in American history has the craving for tranquility and moderation commanded more general public support." Tranquility and moderation, however, were slow in coming. The specter of nuclear annihilation and a global war against Communism cast long shadows across the decade. In addition, there was a widespread perception that juvenile delinquency was on the rise (perhaps best symbolized by James Dean's character in the 1955 film *Rebel Without a Cause*), spies were everywhere (a middle-class couple, Ethel and Julius Rosenberg, were executed in 1953), and a new voice of discontent was emerging from the margins of society (Allen Ginsberg published his controversial poem "Howl"). It was a time of enormous social change that was simultaneously hopeful and unsettling.

For the most part, however, Americans during the 1950s embraced middle-class values and had confidence in a president who typified middle-class virtues. Even Ike's hobbies—painting, cooking, golf, and fishing—were perceived as solidly middle-class, though

105

art had decidedly bohemian roots and golf was, a generation earlier, seen as elitist. At the beginning of the decade, the nation's population was 151,684,000. The life expectancy for women was seventy-one and for men sixty-six. Car sales averaged 6,665,800 a year, and the typical salary was $2,992. (In this context, the $380 in annual dues plus additional fees that Ike paid at Burning Tree suggests that country club golf was still very expensive.) A loaf of bread cost fourteen cents; a gallon of gasoline was twice that. The gross national product was $285 billion in 1950 and $485 billion in 1959. Consumer food products boomed, revolutionizing dinner tables across the United States. In 1953, C. A. Swanson and Sons introduced the first TV dinner. Kentucky Fried Chicken opened in 1954, and by the time Ike left the White House, five hundred restaurants dotted the American landscape. The next year, Ray Kroc signed a franchise deal with brothers Maurice and Richard McDonald to peddle hamburgers, French fries, and milkshakes. By 1958, Hershey's Instant Cocoa and Kraft Jet-Puffed Marshmallows were available in grocery stores.

Americans entered into an era of modern, credit-based mass consumerism. The introduction of credit cards (initially, Diners Club) and the GI bill (which helped educate sixteen million veterans) offered a new world of possibilities. From 1948 to 1958, thirteen million new homes were built, all but two million in the suburbs. In 1954, the United States had 6 percent of the world's population but owned 60 percent of the world's automobiles and 45 percent of its radios. In addition, twenty-nine million homes could boast at least one television set. Consumerism became a ubiquitous secular religion. Beacon Wax celebrated the explosion of a second hydrogen bomb in March 1954 with a newspaper advertisement that read, "The bomb's brilliant gleam reminds me of the brilliant gleam Beacon Wax gives to floors. It's a scientific marvel." The future seemed so promising that, in 1959, Ike was named *Time's* Man of the Year for "the political miracle of making the economy popular."

It was a decade of explosive growth—in wages, in home ownership, in college attendance, and in golf. As Charles Price, writing for *Golf Digest* in 1989, explained, "Indeed, you can measure the ups and downs of golf in America by the state of the economy. The game took permanent root here during the tax-free Gay Nineties and grew its fastest during the Roaring Twenties, when there was nothing more than newspapers and newsreels to explain to the great unwashed who Bobby Jones and Walter Hagen were. Only during the Great Depression of the 1930s did golf wilt. And the population of the U.S. then was only half what it is now. Golf boomed during Eisenhower's years in the White House because of the unprecedented prosperity his administration brought with him, not by his charisma, considerable though it was."

Golf's growth was directly linked to growing prosperity and the rise of the interstate highway system, both essential for suburbanization. Developing a uniform system of roads began with the Federal-Aid Road Act of 1916 and the Federal-Aid Highway Act of 1925. Before cars became widely available, carriages, streetcars, bicycles, and railroads were the main forms of transportation. By 1941, FDR had appointed a National Interregional Highway Committee to investigate the need for a limited system of national highways. The most significant effort, under Truman's Federal-Aid Highway Act of

1952, was the first to authorize funds on a fifty-fifty basis between state and federal governments, but the allocation ($25 million) was inadequate. When Eisenhower took office in 1953, only six thousand miles nationwide were completed. Eisenhower's principal contribution was to convince Americans that the task belonged to the federal government. Ike worked with Congress to pass the Federal-Aid Highway Act of 1954, but it was not as comprehensive as he wanted. Over the next two years, he and other political leaders worked to pass the the Federal-Aid Highway Act of 1956, with a provision that funding would come from gasoline taxes and user fees. Eisenhower signed the legislation on June 29, 1956, from Walter Reed Hospital, where he was recovering from ileitis. It was the largest public works project since fifty thousand miles of roads had been built in the Roman Empire. To honor this feat, on July 29, 1993, the nation's highways were renamed the Eisenhower Highway System. Few could have anticipated the impact of the far-reaching legislation on urban, suburban, and rural America. The American Society of Civil Engineers called the highway system one of the "Seven Wonders of the United States."

To showcase the nation's efforts, Ike invited Soviet Premier Nikita Khrushchev in September 1959, eight months before the U-2 spy plane debacle, to tour the city of Washington, first in a Lincoln convertible to view historic sites, then in a helicopter because Ike wanted "Khrushchev to see all those middle-class homes, and all those automobiles rushing out of Washington in the late afternoon to get to them."

The growing abundance and affordability of automobiles and the building of safe highways encouraged mostly white, middle-class Americans to move out of

city centers in search of land, fresh air, affordable housing, and recreation. Levittown became a symbol of
this new age. Though not the first planned community, it was the largest and most influential. In 1946,
the building firm Levitt and Sons, headed by William
Levitt and his brother, Alfred, developed a model for
mass-produced housing that would indelibly change
the American landscape. Levitt transformed home construction by using Henry Ford's assembly line approach
to expedite and reduce the cost of manufacturing. With
sixteen million service men and women returning from
the war, the nation needed a quick and affordable solu-
tion for the pending housing crisis; hence, Levittown
on Long Island, New York, was born. Opened in 1947,
the homes were constructed from preassembled sections and placed a mere sixty feet apart. It would eventually grow to include more than seventeen thousand
units. Before Levittown, the majority of homebuild-
ers were mainly small-scale operations, with builders
typically constructing fewer than five houses per year.
Highly skilled craftsmen and their small crews moved
from task to task on the job at a cost that placed home
ownership beyond the reach of most Americans. Levitt
developed a new model by dividing home construction
into twenty-seven discrete steps, which made construction and the training of new workers more efficient.

The first home, the Levittowner, was situated on a
lot seventy by one hundred feet. Eventually, residents
could choose from the Jubilee, the Rancher, the Colonial, the Pennsylvanian, and the Country Clubber, with
prices ranging from $8,000 to $16,000. Targeting veterans, Levitt signed 1,400 contracts on the first day the
office opened for business in March 1949. Each family
was provided with landscaping (averaging 2.3 trees per

109

lot) as well as the latest amenities—a washing machine, stove, and refrigerator. Despite the democratizing of home ownership that Levitt promised, the subdivisions had specific restrictions, the most unfortunate of which was a Caucasian race clause that was printed in capital letters on the buyer's contract. Though being Jewish himself and acutely aware of discrimination, Levitt nonetheless justified the decision by claiming, "We can solve a housing problem, or we can try to solve a racial problem, but we cannot combine the two." The racial clause was eventually dropped, but even today, nearly 95 percent of Levittown's residents are white.

Traveling the ever-growing distances between work, the golf club, and the suburbs required a new automobile, and the big three manufacturers in Detroit were willing to oblige. The Cadillac became the standard against which all other cars were measured. Eisenhower rode in a Cadillac to his 1953 inauguration, and Elvis Presley owned several, including a 1955 model painted pink for his mother, though she never drove it. Cadillac became a symbol of both prosperity and fame. Writing for *Fortune* magazine, Lucian K. Truscott IV reflected on what the Cadillac symbolized: "I grew up in an Army family during the '50s and '60s, and my early understanding of car culture had a distinctly military cast. Lieutenants and captains drove '55 Chevys, or '49 Fords carefully coaxed into middle age. Majors drove two-year-old Oldsmobiles or, more likely, Plymouths or Dodges. Lieutenant colonels . . . could afford to drive Buicks. Generals . . . were more circumspect and could be seen . . . behind the wheel of an aging Mercedes. . . . Terminally ambitious colonels drove Cadillacs. . . . Cadillac had been around since 1902, but only after the [second world] war did its cars achieve a precise fit with the upwardly mobile business class. As Americans embraced postwar prosperity, all they had to do was flip the pages of *Life* or turn on the box in the corner with the glowing nine-inch screen to see that Cadillac had become the Hollywood glamour car." The top model line, the Eldorado, had a sticker price of $7,750 in 1955—almost the cost of the cheapest home in Levittown.

Upwardly mobile suburbanites could also choose from the new Ford Thunderbird (base price $2,695) or Chevrolet Corvette (base price $2,909) or settle for a less expensive Dodge (for about $1,500). Imported automobiles were making their first inroads to the domestic market, and adventuresome Americans could acquire an Austin-Healey, a Jaguar, or a Porsche. During the 1950s, the number of cars in the United States nearly doubled from 0.3 to 0.5 per person.

Suburban housing developments and automobiles had wide-ranging effects on American families. Historian David Halberstam argued, "It would change the very nature of American society; families often became less connected to their relatives and seldom shared living space with them as they had in the past. The move to the suburbs also temporarily interrupted the progress women had been making before the war in the workplace . . . leaving them, at least for a while, isolated in a world of other mothers, children, and station wagons." The decade was particularly promising if you were white, native born, and male; for African Americans, immigrants, and women, it could feel like a step backward. Middle- and working-class women who willingly became war workers in factories were told at the end of the war that they were better suited as Betty

Crocker, perfecting their culinary skills in suburban kitchens outfitted with shiny new appliances, than as Rosie the Riveter. Magazines, newspapers, and television told women that their job was to stay home and stay married. A mere nine in one thousand marriages ended in divorce.

Mamie Eisenhower was the perfect embodiment of this ideal. She once said that women's lives "revolve around our men, and that is the way it should be." Women's worth was often measured by their skill in the kitchen. The ability to master Mamie Eisenhower's favorite desserts—prune whip, frosted mint delight, and floating island—became symbols of achievement. With the growing independence fostered by the two-car family, women found ways to lighten the burden of housework. New laborsaving appliances, such as the dishwasher and frost-free refrigerator, were heralded as the answer to the busy housewife's prayers. Casseroles were touted as easy-to-prepare meals. Yet, as the decade progressed, it became clear that a woman's place was still in the home. *Ladies' Home Journal* advertisements promising quick, nutritious meals of Campbell's soup during the war gave way to elaborate four-course meals that were intended to impress the husband's boss.

Mamie's fashion sense was also an expression of the decade's rededication to a conservative, feminine ethos. She wore closely cropped bangs, color-coordinated stockings, and charm bracelets. Long gone were Rosie's overalls; in their place, women like Mamie wore tight-waisted dresses and high heels. Ann Whitman, Ike's personal secretary, revealed in a diary entry how strongly some young women resisted this ideal. While visiting New York, she had dinner at Trader Vic's and reported, "I have never felt so much like a hick and never have been so astounded at the shortness of dresses and the absolute different look (I guess the Brigitte Bardot look) of some of the females on the street." It was a time of contradiction; respectable women were expected to appear demure, with hats and white gloves, in public. For their husbands in private, they were expected to mimic the increasingly sexualized images of women shown in *Life* and the *Saturday Evening Post*.

The media reinforced stereotypical gender roles through the new medium of television. Sitcoms such as "Father Knows Best" (1954–60), "I Love Lucy" (1951–57), "The Adventures of Ozzie and Harriet" (1952–66), and even "The Honeymooners" (1955–56) and variety shows like "The Milton Berle Show" (1948–56), "Ted Mack's Original Amateur Hour" (1948–70), and "The Colgate Comedy Hour" (1950–55) reinforced the middle-class ideal, often through humor. "Guiding Light," which began as a radio serial in 1937 and then moved to CBS television in 1952, offered housewives romanticized versions of daily life. But women, no matter how conservatively they dressed or how much they consumed comedies reinforcing the status quo, did not conform blindly. Nine years after the end of the war, one in three American women worked outside the home, compared to one in five in 1940. In 1952, women became a political force to be reckoned with, casting 52 percent of the vote that put Ike into office.

Recognizing the changing times, Ike appointed Clare Boothe Luce as ambassador to Italy and Oveta Culp Hobby to his cabinet. Though not the first female cabinet member (Frances Perkins had been appointed in 1933 by Franklin D. Roosevelt), Hobby's position was important. She had enjoyed a distinguished career with the Women's Army Corps and played a key role in the national Democrats for Eisenhower movement. Eisenhower first appointed her chairman of the Federal Security Agency; then, on April 11, 1953, she became the first secretary of the new Department of Health, Education and Welfare. While Ike made it a point to socialize and play golf with members of his cabinet, there is no evidence that he ever invited Hobby onto the links. Even if she did play, she would not have been likely to receive an invitation to Burning Tree or Augusta National, largely male-only enclaves. She would have to exert her influence in other ways.

Among other issues, Hobby's agency tapped into the general interest in sports and physical fitness. In 1953, the American Management Association reported that more than 450 large corporations in the United States and Canada had executive health programs for their top managers. Time off from work, in the form of coffee breaks and vacations, was widely supported to help combat mental fatigue. Country club memberships became coveted benefits for middle and upper management. Ike supported these trends and went as far as to insist that his staff members take half days off during the week for exercise. Even Nikita Khruschev lent a hand, observing, "You Americans use your cars too much. You don't walk enough. You should walk to be fit. I don't play golf, myself, but President Eisenhower's intense interest in golf seems very sensible to me. It gives him good exercise."

114

Ike embraced the philosophy that leisure was the key to happiness. Believing that a strong body contributed to a strong nation, on September 27 and 28, 1955, he convened 139 sports figures and top educators at a conference on youth physical fitness. As one reporter noted, "The President has expressed concern that lack of such participation [in athletics] is responsible in part for increasing juvenile delinquency, and for failure of so many young people to measure up to selective service requirements." Gene Tunney of boxing, Bobby Jones of golf, Rogers Hornsby of baseball, and Kenneth L. Wilson, the president of the United States Olympic Committee, joined the meetings to debate how American children could remain competitive in sports. On July 16, 1956, the President's Council on Youth Fitness was established. John F. Kennedy would later change the name to the President's Council on Physical Fitness to reflect the organization's role in promoting health and exercise for all Americans.

In the area of fitness, Ike also set an important example, especially when he suffered ill health. Norman Palmer, the golf professional at Cherry Hills in Denver, where Ike played, reflected on Ike's impact on sport: "By his courage in returning to the golf course after his series of illnesses—heart attack, ileitis, and mild stroke—Mr. Eisenhower showed the sickly and handicapped they could play golf—and play it well. He also showed what a tonic golf can be for the busy executive or professional man, burdened with the problems and pressures of a busy, active life."

Americans had numerous ways to spend their free time. One million went to Disneyland in Anaheim, California, in the first two months after its July 1955 opening. Anyone could now pick up a copy of *Sports Illustrated*, which began publication in 1954. At first, the magazine focused on yachting and polo, but it quickly changed to cover spectator sports like baseball. Television was also a popular leisure-time activity, one particularly suited to golf. Historian Benjamin Rader

115

explained that "even when the nation was blanketed with snow, viewers could be transported to sylvan, semi-tropical sites." In fact, many who tuned in had never played golf or had no intention of taking up the game. Televised golf helped change that. The U.S. Open was the first televised golf championship, though only available locally on KSD-TV in 1947 in St. Louis, Missouri. A national broadcast of the event would not happen until 1954. That same year, Arnold Palmer won the U.S. Amateur and turned professional three months later. Tournament broadcasts were not the only way Americans saw golf on television. Three-time Masters champion Jimmy Demaret made a guest appearance on the May 17, 1954, episode of "I Love Lucy," in the show's third season.

Ike was, as UN ambassador Henry Cabot Lodge urged him to be, the "first great television president." Just as FDR had utilized radio to cultivate his image and promote his message, Ike and his advisors realized that television would allow the president to speak directly to the American people. With actor Robert Montgomery enlisted as a consultant, it worked. Arthur Krock, writing for the *New York Times*, commented on the experiment: "Never was there a more winning personality projected to the American people. Never was there a more engaging smile and grin in politics . . . and nature threw in a graceful bearing and strong physique for good measure."

The mythology of a "Leave It to Beaver" decade—filled with obedient children, complacent domestic goddesses, and gray-suited suburban fathers—obscured the complexity of the 1950s. It was, in many ways, an age of anxiety, as the Cold War, the Soviet Union, and the bomb loomed large. At his 1953 inauguration on January 20, Ike did not make a reassuring appeal to the nation; instead, he warned, "science seems ready to confer upon us, as its final gift, the power to erase human life from the planet." When Ike entered the White House, only the United States, Britain, and the Soviets possessed nuclear weapons, but this still generated plenty of fear.

On November 1, 1952, a few days before Ike was elected, the United States exploded a ten-megaton hydrogen bomb, code-named MIKE. It proved much more powerful than either "Fat Man" or "Little Boy," the two atomic bombs that were dropped on Japan during the war. On March 1, 1954, the United States exploded a second bomb, on Bikini Island in the Pacific. Not to be left behind, the Soviets exploded their own bomb on August 12, 1953, and the first true hydrogen bomb on November 22, 1955. These developments dramatically shaped Ike's foreign policy. His administration argued that Soviet atomic capability threatened to lead to a third world war, whether the world was ready or not.

The possibility of nuclear annihilation had a profound impact on American life and popular culture. Bomb shelter plans, such as the government pamphlet *You Can Survive*, became widely available. In 1951, the Federal Civil Defense Administration released *Duck and Cover*, an informational cartoon directed at children. But not everyone took the threat seriously. In 1954, Oklahoma A&M College asked students to list their greatest fear, to which they answered, not "finding a parking space." In the summer of 1959, *Life* magazine reported on a young couple who planned to spend their honeymoon in their eight-by-eleven bomb shelter, declaring, "fallout can be fun."

117

Hollywood contributed to the fear with films like *Atomic Kid* (1954), *The Day the World Ended* (1955), and *On the Beach* (1959). Such uncertainty about the future was not entirely misplaced; Russia successfully tested the R-7, the first intercontinental ballistic missile, in August 1957. Recognizing that the stakes had changed, Ike announced, during a golf outing at Augusta National in 1959, that America would change its policy. On December 28, after coming to Augusta following an eleven-nation tour of Europe and meeting with top administrators, he announced that the United States would end its voluntary moratorium on further testing of atomic bombs.

The 1950s were a time of extraordinary scientific discovery, offering hope that science could eradicate disease and social ills. The birth control pill was perfected; DuPont began producing polyester; Harvard physicians completed the first successful human kidney transplant; Texas Instruments announced the first silicon transistor; and Bell Laboratories announced the development of solar power. The celebration of American innovations, though, was short-lived. While Ike was mired in the Little Rock crisis in the fall of 1957, the Soviet Union launched *Sputnik* on October 4, taking the United States completely by surprise. The 183-pound satellite, which could circle the globe in ninety-six minutes at a speed of eighteen thousand miles per hour, brought America's military and scientific superiority into question. Secretary of Commerce Sinclair Weeks said in 1958 that *Sputnik* was responsible for the recession because Americans were "nervous" and thus putting "their money in socks for a while." Although for the first half of the decade American scientists had claimed superiority over all other nations, *Sputnik* was a powerful blow. A few years earlier, when Jonas Salk announced that he had discovered a polio vaccine, the world rejoiced. Such celebration would pale in comparison to the missile gap that *Sputnik* exposed. Ike would immediately turn his attention to stressing science and defense in American education. In 1958, he supported the National Defense Education Bill to strengthen American schools.

In the wake of *Sputnik*, critics declared that the antiquated American educational system and rampant consumerism were to blame for the United States falling behind the Soviet Union in the space race. Ike's close friend and Augusta National member William Robinson wondered, "Is there any justification for a *Sputnik* to create a cacophony of petulant and frantic voices which are intent on substituting fear, terror and dissension for the nation's natural values?" One political cartoon, titled "The Race," originally published in the Nashville *Tennessean*, took an overt jab at Ike by portraying *Sputnik* flying past a golf ball. The immediate attempts of the United States to catch up failed. On December 6, 1957, the U.S. *Vanguard* satellite exploded above the launching pad. Finally, on January 31, 1958, *Explorer I* went into orbit but by that year Russia had three satellites in space, one as heavy as 2,925 pounds. *Explorer V*, the American satellite, weighed 37.16 pounds (approximately the size of a Cadillac fender). On July 29, 1958, Eisenhower signed the National Aeronautics and Space Act, which established NASA and stipulated that "all activities in space should be devoted to peaceful purposes for the benefit of mankind."

Russia was not Ike's only concern. Recently, historians and journalists have assessed Ike for what he did

119

not do. During his entire eight years in office, he kept America out of armed conflict, boasting, "The United States never lost a soldier or a foot of ground in my administration." He had plenty of opportunity with Iran (1953), Guatemala (1954), Indochina (1954), Quemoy and Matsu (1955), Hungary (1956), Suez (1956), Lebanon (1958), Berlin, Germany (1959), and Cuba (1959). In their book *Reevaluating Eisenhower*, Richard A. Melanson and David Mayers contended, "Eisenhower's natural caution and good sense enabled the United States to maneuver through these crises without palpable damage to itself, and by 1961 American armies were nowhere engaged in combat—a considerable achievement, apologists argue, especially when compared with Truman and with Eisenhower's successors."

On the domestic front, what Eisenhower did not do as president eclipsed many of his accomplishments. Ike did virtually nothing to control the excesses of congressional fearmongers like Wisconsin Senator Joseph McCarthy, despite his contempt for them and despite repeated calls from moderate supporters. Although rabid anticommunism and the unwarranted suspicion of intellectuals and ordinary Americans were most often associated with McCarthy, his was not the only voice. William Jenner of Indiana, William Knowland of California, Karl Mundt of South Dakota, and even Ike's occasional golfing partner, Robert Taft, supported the anticommunist crusade. As chair of the Senate Investigating Subcommittee, McCarthy had a four-year spree of accusations, capitalizing on the political anxieties of the day. His accusations resulted in the investigation of six million Americans, only a tiny fraction of whom were convicted of anything.

The most regrettable incident involved Eisenhower's failure to defend his close friend and mentor George C. Marshall from accusations of disloyalty by McCarthy, who called Marshall "the dupe of traitors." Loathing McCarthy as Eisenhower did, he had intended, in a speech to be delivered in Milwaukee, to defend his friend but allowed himself to be dissuaded by others who feared losing votes in Wisconsin. He never spoke out against McCarthy during his entire career and refused to mention him in his memoirs *The White House Years*, despite his son's recommendation to address it. Public opinion eventually turned against McCarthy, largely aided by the March 1954 broadcast of a special entitled "A Report on Senator Joseph P. McCarthy" by CBS newsman Edward R. Murrow and producer Fred Friendly, as well as the nationally televised Army-McCarthy hearings that year—both of which showed the Wisconsin senator in a negative light. The Senate finally removed his chairmanship and later censured him, a year before his death in 1957.

Ike's second domestic failure involved race relations. Despite some halting efforts, Ike also did little to promote the welfare of African Americans after the Supreme Court's decision in 1954 in *Brown v. Board of Education* and the subsequent southern resistance to desegregation. A glance through a 1954 issue of *Life* magazine reveals the uneasy tensions between harmonious social life and the unequal treatment of blacks in America. Interspersed with articles on Little League baseball and the booming stock market is a series of stories on racial violence. The October 11 issue widely criticized the town of Milford, Delaware, for the town's response to the admission of eleven black students to the

121

public schools. The editors cast the segregationist position, just as Eisenhower would during his presidency, as fuel for Communist propaganda. But whites saw it as a regional issue. Historian Pete Daniel wrote, "Many white southerners flinched at integration. Respectability depended on their claim to whiteness, or so they had been coached. Removing the color line would devalue that badge of superiority. Mrs. L. G. Baker, of Pine Bluff, Arkansas, grandmother, asked President Dwight D. Eisenhower in May 1954 if he understood that respectable married Christian white women 'deeply resent the insult handed down by the U.S. Supreme Court's decision on segregation.' A white woman, who had legitimate children, she explained, would now be 'classed with a negress who has children out of marriage, some negroes some half white." On this issue, Ike equivocated and let segregationists take the offensive.

Two recessions, one in Ike's first term (1954) and one in the second (1958), counter the impression that the nation was awash in prosperity. On September 25, 1953, Ike's cabinet warned about a looming economic downturn partially as a result of the drop in military spending for the Korean War (1950–53), and Ike's golf became an easy target. Even children criticized him, but only to a point. When a group of Future Farmers of America were asked to "state in one sentence what you think has been good or bad about the Eisenhower Administration to date," they answered that he "plays too darned much golf but since he's a Texan I'm for him." In the second recession, Ike's golf game again became a magnet for criticism. In 1958, Senator William Proxmire, a Democrat from Wisconsin, said that all the president had done to fight the recession was to "rise like a spring crocus" and hit golf balls on the White House lawn.

In the midst of the first recession, Ike wanted to set a good example for the nation. He would not give up golf, but he was happy to scuttle the presidential yacht, the USS *Williamsburg*, which he had inherited from Harry Truman. It required a crew of 150 men at an annual cost of $600,000. Another, unpublished, reason was that Ike could not play golf aboard a yacht. So, in July 1953, he decommissioned it and turned to Camp David as his primary source of recreation. He turned it into much more of a retreat, adding air-conditioning and taking furniture from the *Williamsburg* to outfit the cabins.

The image of the happy and prosperous 1950s that Ike so embodied was for many an illusion that was exposed through popular culture, mainly film. Along with the top-billed romances, comedies, and Westerns that Ike so loved that celebrated the nation's values and superiority, Hollywood offered a not so subtle critique of American society as well. Film noir features such as *Sunset Boulevard* (1950), *Clash by Night* (1952), *Edge of Doom* (1950), *Niagara* (1953), and *Strangers on a Train* (1951) projected "downbeat stories of murder and passion, of ordinary lives gone hopelessly astray, of evil women casting their net and fatally contaminating the American male," according to film historian Foster Hirsch. Film noir had a nightmarish quality, with shadowed scenes usually photographed in black and white and frantic pacing. For some, the films reflected what was happening to America as it emerged from World War II; many who did not prosper grew disillusioned with traditional American values. Even as the United

123

States was exerting its role as a superpower in places such as Korea, Indochina, and Greece, there was a sense that something was terribly wrong.

Youthful discontent with the apparent complacency of the 1950s also became obvious in such films as *The Wild Ones* in 1954, which featured Marlon Brando and a motorcycle gang terrorizing a California town. James Dean's *Rebel Without a Cause* was released in 1955 a month after he was killed in an automobile accident at the age of twenty-four. The distance between these films and Ike's favorite Westerns was striking. The palpable anxiety was not limited to the silver screen. J. D. Salinger's publication of *The Catcher in the Rye* in 1951 showed that even wealthy, urbane, prep school–educated young men such as Holden Caulfield were at risk. In 1956, at the Six Gallery in San Francisco, Allen Ginsberg first performed his poem "Howl." The next year, Jack Kerouac published *On the Road*. The beat generation was born, but even Jack liked Ike. So, apparently, did nearly everyone else. James Reston, in a September 1955 *New York Times* column, wrote, "The popularity of President Eisenhower has got beyond the bounds of reasonable calculation and will have to be put down as a national phenomenon, like baseball. The thing is no longer just a remarkable political fact but a kind of national love affair, which cannot be analyzed satisfactorily by the political scientists and will probably have to be turned over to the head shrinkers."

Journalist Merriman Smith told a story that revealed how Ike was perceived by everyday people: "A man was driving by the Tamarisk Country Club golf course at Palm Springs, California, while Ike was there and a high-riding hooked ball zoomed through the window of his car and conked him on the side of the head. Dazed by the great pain, the man pulled to the side of the road, and as he slumped over the wheel, a caddie who raced up to the side of the automobile to offer his assistance heard the motorist mutter, 'Thank you, Mr. President.' " Historian Thomas Bailey offered his own assessment: "The experts probably would give President Eisenhower a higher ranking today if he had only made more enemies. Everybody seemed to 'like Ike,' even those who did not like him well enough to vote for him. If great Presidents make many powerful enemies, Eisenhower is not marked for greatness." As decades of scholarship and debate have revealed, this measurement may not be the best test.

SIX

IKE at AUGUSTA

If I go anywhere it will be to Augusta, I feel so much more at home there.

—MAMIE EISENHOWER

Two decades before Ike and Mamie Eisenhower first drove down Magnolia Lane, Augusta had grown into a teeming resort, attracting celebrities and wealthy vacationers. Several presidents visited the "Garden City" before, during, and after leaving office. In 1781, when Augusta served as the Georgia state capital, George Washington inspected students at Richmond Academy. One local story holds that one of his dogs, Cornwallis, died during the visit and was buried in town. Washington was the first of many presidents who came south. James Monroe came to Augusta in 1819 to inspect the city's defenses. In 1849, Martin Van Buren stayed in Augusta; he was followed by Zachary Taylor in 1850, Millard Fillmore in 1854, Ulysses S. Grant in 1880, Rutherford B. Hayes in 1891, and William McKinley in 1898. Woodrow Wilson lived on Seventh Street from 1858 to 1870 as a child during the Civil War and

Reconstruction and attended Augusta's First Presbyterian Church.

By the turn of the century, Augusta had established a reputation as a wealthy retreat, complete with resort hotels and golf courses. The city, called alternately the "Best All-Winter Resort in the South" and the "Winter Golf Capital of America," attracted the attention of William Howard Taft, who built a winter home at the intersection of Milledge and Cumming roads near the Bon Air Hotel. Before his inauguration in March 1909, Taft vacationed for a month in Augusta. According to the *Augusta Chronicle*, he played his best round of golf at the Bon Air Golf Club earlier that year. At a public address on January 20, Taft said, "I am not quite certain today whether I would rather have [shot 88] or have been elected president of the United States."

The city's popularity was due mostly to the warm winter climate, made accessible by comfortable, regular railroad service. As early as 1888, seventy-two trains came in and out of Augusta daily on seven railroads. By April 1923, when Warren Harding visited, tourism was on the wane, because new railroad lines already extended into Florida. Franklin Roosevelt is reported to have made one visit during his presidency, but he remained in his presidential railcar. Lyndon Johnson received a lukewarm welcome in 1964 when he was campaigning against Barry Goldwater; and Jimmy Carter visited just before moving into the White House. Augusta, though, would always be associated with Ike.

The first golf course laid out in Augusta was the Bon Air Golf Club in 1897, built to accommodate the hotel's guests and winter residents. The Bon Air Hotel opened on New Year's Day in 1889, burned in 1921, and was eventually rebuilt. Famous visitors included Presidents

128

Taft and Harding, but also John D. Rockefeller, F. Scott Fitzgerald, and Winston Churchill. The golf course later was called the Country Club of Augusta and then Augusta Country Club. As Stan Burdy explained in his book *Augusta and Aiken in Golf's Golden Age*, "By the time Bobby Jones was born on St. Patrick's Day, 1902, Augusta was well established as a winter haven for the nation's golf elite." The Bon Air Golf Club attracted the likes of Harry Vardon in 1900 and hosted the Southeastern Open at Forrest Hills, where Jones played before beginning his quest for the Grand Slam, in 1930.

Augusta National Golf Club (ANGC) was founded the year after Jones retired from competitive golf. The club was located on a 365-acre plot with a rich horticultural history on the west side of town. In 1854, Dennis Redmond established an indigo plantation on the site and constructed the large two-story house that is Augusta National's clubhouse. When the business failed a couple of years later, he sold the land to Belgian nobleman Louis Matheiu Edouard Berckmans. Baron Berckmans and his son, Prosper Jules Alphonse, formed P. J. Berckmans Company in 1857 and began operating Fruitland Nurseries. The nursery grew many varieties of exotic fruit trees, flowering shrubs, and flowers for distribution around the country. But Prosper Berckmans died in 1910, and Fruitland had foundered by 1918. In 1925, the land was sold to a Miami developer named Commodore J. Perry Stotz, who hoped to turn the nursery into a golf resort—until he went bankrupt. When Jones and Clifford Roberts inspected the property in 1930, it had not been used for more than a decade.

In 1931, the property where Augusta National now stands was purchased for $70,000, and an organizational committee of five men, including Jones and Rob-

129

erts, assembled to build the golf club. Jones selected Dr. Alister MacKenzie as the architect. An English surgeon with Scottish lineage who served in the Boer War and World War I, MacKenzie began his career as a golf course architect in 1907 and designed some famous courses, including Cypress Point in California. His layouts were patterned after the great Scottish and English courses, which meant that they emphasized natural advantages and minimized artificiality. MacKenzie first visited Augusta National in July 1931 to explore the property and stake out the tees and greens. He returned that fall and stayed for two months to oversee work on the course, which opened in December 1932 with a limited amount of member play. A formal opening took place from January 12 to 16, 1933. After a brief illness, MacKenzie died suddenly on January 6, 1934, two months before the first Augusta National Invitational Tournament, which would be renamed the Masters in 1939.

ANGC had to work hard to survive in the early years of the Depression, trading mainly on Jones's fame. The city gave the club a tax advantage and helped promote the early Masters Tournaments, but securing members in the 1930s proved difficult. It was equally difficult to garner the attention of the club professionals, who could often make more money playing in exhibition matches than in the Masters. Al Barkow explained, "From the first year through the 1942 tournament, by which time the depression was easing off and a number of Tour events had gotten up to an average of $7,500 total purse, the Masters paid out only $5,000."

Augusta, in the 1940s, was still largely what Lester S. Moody, secretary of the local chamber of commerce, called an "agricultural and industrial town." The veterans hospital expanded, and Bush Field became a training ground for the Army Air Force. In 1948, the U.S. Army moved the Signal Training Center and Military Police School to Camp Gordon. That same year, the Clarks Hill Reservoir was constructed to supply the burgeoning city with hydroelectric power. In the early 1950s, the population of Augusta increased by 50,000, mainly because of the new Atomic Energy Commission's Savannah River plant, a plutonium production facility. The population in 1950 was 108,876; three years later it had blossomed to 160,000, making it the second largest city in Georgia after Atlanta.

In the spring of 1948, as he was completing his manuscript for *Crusade in Europe*, Eisenhower vacationed for the first time as William Robinson's guest at Augusta National Golf Club. The two men had met four years earlier, when Robinson was in Paris working to resume the publication of the *New York Herald Tribune*'s European edition. It would be Ike's first vacation in a decade; he would later call it "the best two weeks I have had in many years." He had recently completed a two-year position as the Army's chief of staff and just accepted the presidency of Columbia University. He needed rest. No surprise that he would select Augusta National as the spot; it had everything—golf, warm weather, and like-minded friends. Robinson flew Ike and Mamie to Augusta in the *Herald Tribune*'s Lockheed Lodestar, and Ike stayed for eleven days. The men he befriended on this trip indelibly shaped Ike's future.

Robinson, vice president and later publisher of the *New York Herald Tribune*, convinced Ike to write *Crusade in Europe*, a memoir of his service in Europe during World War II. But Ike was initially reluctant to under-

131

take the project. Years later, Eisenhower recounted how Douglas Black of Doubleday and Company and Robinson persuaded him: "You owe it to yourself, to the country, and to history, to tell the personal story of your European campaigns on a factual basis, annotating the book as well as you can. It can serve as a better picture of what was done in your theater and by your headquarters than other, sometimes biased or prejudiced, reports." Ike's book was later serialized in Robinson's newspaper, which became the unofficial organ of the Republican Party in the eastern United States. Eisenhower would eventually pocket nearly half a million dollars from the project.

When Ike and Mamie arrived in Augusta on April 13, 1948, they found the streets from Daniel Field to Augusta National lined with cheering crowds. The couple stayed in Bobby Jones's cottage, though they did not have a chance to meet the famed golfer. During Ike's stay, Roberts hired guards from the Pinkerton National Detective Agency, the same firm he used to manage crowds during the Masters. Ike played golf every day and took lessons from club professional Ed Dudley, who had played on three U.S. Ryder Cup Teams (1929, 1933, and 1937), had served as president of the PGA of America (1942–48), and was a fifteen-time winner on the PGA Tour. Dudley often remarked on the president's energy, "He's tireless. Never saw anything like it. It is the President's remarkable stamina which seems to awe his golfing pals more than anything else."

At the end of the year, Ike wired Roberts a message: "The best thing that happened to Mamie and me during 1948 was the new and wonderful friendships we were privileged to make. Among these friends you have a very special and warm spot in our hearts. [We] hope that

132

1949 will permit us to see you with maximum frequency and growing intimacy." Roberts said that Mamie appreciated Augusta because she "liked the sound of a golf club better than a hunting camp or a fishing lodge."

Ike's telegram to Roberts began an enduring friendship between two men with similar backgrounds but vastly different temperaments. Roberts, the second of five children, was born on March 6, 1894, in Morning Sun, Iowa. His family moved often during his childhood, and as a boy he dug potatoes for money to buy schoolbooks, worked at an oyster house, and helped care for his siblings and his mother. Roberts first played golf as a child in California, where he and his brother caddied for fifteen cents a round. In 1918, Roberts first came to Augusta for training as a private in the Signal Corps at Camp Hancock. He would eventually serve briefly in World War I. Roberts moved to New York City and, in 1922, became the principal in the investment firm Roberts & Company. In 1941, he joined the Reynolds Company and became its ninth general partner. Roberts met Bobby Jones in the mid-1920s, and they developed a strong friendship and successful partnership. Byron Nelson once remarked of Roberts's love of ANGC, "This place was his bride."

Roberts served as chairman of Augusta National from 1931 to 1976 and was named chairman in memoriam after his death on September 29, 1977. He was chairman of the Masters Tournament from 1934 through 1976. Under Roberts's direction, the Masters made numerous innovations to facilitate spectatorship that are now commonplace in golf. He changed the mound locations to give the gallery better viewing. He was the first to use a series of leaderboards throughout the course. He also

133

devised a system for showing the cumulative score of each player—red numbers for under par, a green zero for par, and green numbers for over par.

Roberts, as did most of the Augusta membership, liked Ike and from the beginning hoped he would become a member. On April 18, 1948, five days into the general's first trip, Roberts wrote a letter to a fellow ANGC member from Florida in which he revealed his plan: "During the past week we have had a distinguished visitor in the person of General Eisenhower and I don't mind telling you in confidence, there's some prospects of him becoming affiliated with this club." Upon leaving the club after eleven days, Ike asked if he could take a photograph in one of the members' jackets near the eighteenth tee to send to Bobby Jones, whom he had not yet met. The photograph was inscribed to Mr. Jones and to Cliff, "who did so much to make our visit to Augusta National the most delightful vacation of our lives." Twenty years later, in an interview with a researcher at Columbia University, Roberts reflected on that first visit: "I very quickly discovered that both the General and Mamie were the sort of folks that if they liked you, they liked you a lot, in a hurry."

Ike was not one to stand on ceremony, and before he could be invited to join ANGC, he made the mistake of asking if he could become a member, which was often a fatal error. Yet, Roberts, Jones, and the rest of the membership overlooked the general's faux pas and asked him to become part of the club in October 1948. As there are no honorary members at Augusta, Ike had to pay dues just like everyone else.

Ike's admiration for Bobby Jones was the main reason he wanted to join Augusta. Jones had served under Ike's command during World War II, but they would not meet until after Ike's visit with Robinson in 1948. They became friends, though Jones was not part of "the gang" of Augusta businessmen who were associated with Ike. Jones and Ike maintained a friendship built on mutual respect, not intimacy. In 1951, Jones sent Ike his personal set of clubs, including a 5-wood, a set of irons, a sand wedge, and a putter. Ike was delighted and carried them in a red and black golf bag that today is on display at the Smithsonian Institution. In 1959, Jones sent rose bushes for Mamie's birthday. A year later, Jones sent Ike the first copy of his new book, which Ike acknowledged in a letter dated October 10: "I came over from lunch today determined to concentrate on my television press conference (with the ladies!) tonight, but instead I found it much more enjoyable to read—and try to understand—the various suggestions for improvement of my distressed golf game to be found in *Golf Is My Game.*" To reflect Ike's esteem for the retired champion, he kept, among several other items—some personal (photographs of his mother, wife, and son's family) and others essential (four pens, two phones, and a clock)—a photograph of himself with Jones.

By the time they became friends, Jones could no longer play golf because he was suffering from the effects of syringomyelia, a degenerative spinal disease. Yet, the two men corresponded frequently, and their wives became friends. Mary Jones decorated the Eisenhower cabin for Mamie, using the First Lady's favorite shade of light green. The two women exchanged numerous letters about the interior design. In one dated May 19, 1953, Mamie wrote, "I do think you are very generous with your time to do all of this for me, and I know what an attractive little house it will be. Your idea as to the twin beds with carved headboards is fine, and it's quite all right to go ahead with them."

On January 31, 1953, less than a month after Ike's inauguration, the United States Golf Association (USGA) unveiled a portrait of Jones painted by Thomas E. Stephens to be hung at Golf House, the association's headquarters and museum. The portrait was donated to the USGA by the members of Augusta National Golf Club and presented by Clifford Roberts. At the ceremony, Totten Heffelfinger, the USGA president, read a letter from President Eisenhower: "You all must be as proud as I am to have Bob's portrait hanging in Golf House. Those who have been fortunate enough to know him realize that his fame as a golfer is transcended by his inestimable qualities as a human being." Ike liked the painting so much that he made a copy and signed it, "Bob— by his friend, D. D. E., 1953." When Ike was finished with the work, he presented it to Jones at a small ceremony at Augusta National Golf Club. When Jones first saw the painting, he commented, "I don't blame Stephens for being jealous." He later joked, "I'm glad you didn't take up golf when I was winning tournaments."

The friends that Eisenhower made at Augusta, notably Robinson and Roberts, became his closest confidants. Historian Stephen Ambrose described the group as "all millionaires whose great passions were playing golf and bridge, and talking politics. With one exception, they were all Republicans. They were also united by their hero-worship of General Ike. For his part, Eisenhower was impressed by the gang's business success, appreciated the members' devotion to him, and enjoyed their easy banter, nonstop flow of jokes, and their eagerness to play golf and bridge with him. He sought their advice on politics, economics, and finance, both in general and with regard to his personal fortunes. He accepted from them many gifts, services, free trips, etc. To the end of his life he spent as much time with the gang as he could possibly spare; when they were separated he carried on extensive correspondence with the members. With them, he could relax as he could with no one else." Robinson, who introduced Ike to Augusta, could not have been more different from the general. The effusive Irishman was a master salesman and helped manage Ike's political campaign. More than any other member, though, Roberts shaped Ike's daily life and fortunes, serving as his financial and political advisor. A letter from before the election dated July 23, 1952, showed the depth of Roberts's influence. In it, he detailed how to finance the election campaign, urged Ike to join a church to appeal to evangelical Protestants in the South, described the investments he made for John and Barbara Eisenhower, and outlined the kinds of speeches that Ike needed to make. Roberts would remain involved at this level throughout Ike's presidency.

Various members of the gang stayed close to Ike throughout his presidency and often intervened in the affairs of state. In 1958 Roberts wrote to Ike, urging him to fire Sherman Adams because the White House chief of staff had improperly accepted several expensive gifts, including an overcoat and Oriental rug from Boston textile manufacturer Bernie Goldman. Ann Whitman, Ike's personal secretary, always believed that Roberts's letter, more than the advice of Ike's official advisors, helped him make his decision to accept Adams's resignation. So frequent did Ike and Roberts consult that Ike

137

urged Roberts to keep a toothbrush and pair of pajamas in the Red Room at the White House, effectively reserving it for his friend and trusted advisor.

Robinson and Roberts led this informal group of Augusta members, who were "bound by golf, money in at least seven figures, and a devotion to the political career of Dwight David Eisenhower," as Peter Andrews put it. Roberts proposed the idea of a gang in a series of letters at the end of 1951 and detailed how the group would be assembled. They were to be men who could give Eisenhower "a little coaching" and "trusted counsel." The initial list was made of men who "are entirely free of ambitions of the sort that would prevent them from giving you their unbiased judgment." Over the next several months, the list was modified and ended up including W. Alton "Pete" Jones (president of Cities Service Company and a member from 1933–62), who often carried $50,000 in cash in his pants pocket and offered to finance Ike's political campaign. Other members included Robert Woodruff (chairman of the board at Coca-Cola and a member from 1935–72), Ellis "Slats" Slater (president of Frankfort Distilleries and a member from 1935–83), Edward J. Bermingham (a broker and a member from 1950–58), Lewis B. "Bud" Maytag (president of the Maytag Company and a member from 1932–62), Albert Bradley (chairman of General Motors and a member from 1951–71), Alfred S. Bourne (heir to the Singer Sewing Machine fortune and a member from 1932–56), and George M. Humphrey (secretary of the Treasury and a member from 1958–64). While Ike was president of Columbia University, many of these men visited his home in New York City to play bridge. They sponsored his honorary membership at Blind Brook Country Club in Westchester County and Deep-dale Golf Club, where Clifford Roberts was a member, on Long Island. The gang also helped raise money for Columbia while Ike was president there, as much as $50,800 during one of Ike's birthday parties.

The gang became, more than anything, constant companions for Ike. They were men with whom he could relax. Slats Slater recounts what it was like to play golf with them: "On Saturday when the President's foursome played, I took George Humphrey in my electric cart, and we followed around the first nine. There was a great deal of banter and kidding about not minding constructive criticism—not the hair-curling kind. When the boss made a particularly good shot, we blew our little cart horns." In 1959, the *Washington Post* reported that Ike called Pete Jones and William Robinson at three in the morning asking them to come to Scotland to play golf. The following day, the two men were on the links with the president.

The gang's most important unstated rule was that they rarely discussed politics with Ike. They certainly, however, discussed it amongst themselves. Woodruff said in a 1950 interview, "Some of us want to see him make president. We sent him overseas [to Paris, as the chief military officer of postwar Allied forces] to give him an international flair, then we made him president of Columbia so the eggheads would like him." Woodruff had long admired Eisenhower and was delighted that as supreme Allied commander in Europe he had insisted "the men would fight for Coke, a wholesome symbol of the American way," and ordered three million bottles on an early convoy in June 1943.

But talk of an Eisenhower presidency in the late 1940s and early 1950s was hushed. Historian Piers Brendon explained that members of the Republican Party

139

assumed that Ike might "succumb to the importunities of friends, to a draft, or to the call of duty." The gang's main role, therefore, was to subtly encourage Ike by helping supplement his income with travel and gifts, and, most importantly, joining his foursome for golf at Augusta. Ike described his Augusta friends in *Mandate for Change, 1953–56: The White House Years*: "These were men of discretion, men who, already successful, made no attempt to profit by our association. It is almost impossible for me to describe how valuable their friendship was to me. Any person enjoys his or her friends; a President needs them, perhaps more intensely at times than anything else."

Though the gang and dozens of other political leaders in both the Democratic and Republican parties pressured Ike to run for president in 1948, he steadfastly refused and kept his commitment to Columbia. Eisenhower even wrote a letter to the editor of the Manchester (New Hampshire) *Evening Leader* stating that he "could not accept nomination even under the remote circumstances that it were tendered to me." He would, however, be unable to refuse four years later, and the gang played a significant role in making Ike's presidency a reality. As an active Army officer, Ike could not, by law, run for public office. Ohio Senator Robert Taft was signing up delegates for the Republican convention, so the gang had to begin campaigning for Ike, helping to keep his candidacy in the public eye until he was ready to leave the Army and run.

On election night, Clifford Roberts was in New York with Ike at the Commodore Hotel and made it possible for Ike to get a brief nap before making his victory speech. The next day, Ike won what he may have considered the real prize—a vacation in Augusta. This would be his sixth visit. Because he was president-elect, it was supposed to be a secret. On November 6, two chartered Eastern Air Lines planes left from LaGuardia Field in New York for the three-hour nonstop flight to Augusta, Georgia. Accompanied by Roberts and Robinson, Ike and Mamie arrived for their ten-day vacation at 5:22 P.M. When Ike got off the plane and walked through the airport, numerous well-wishers called out, "Congratulations, Mr. President," which he ignored. Not until someone yelled, "Congratulations, Ike," did he turn his head and smile. The Eisenhowers were met by 250,000 cheering fans in a city that only had 100,000 inhabitants. Roberts recalled the scene: "It's close to 20 miles' drive, possibly a little more, from Augusta Airport to the Augusta National Golf Club and the road was lined all the way on both sides from two deep to as many as 15 in spots." Ike was well protected on this visit. Four Secret Service men stood sentry outside the cottage, while others were spread throughout the course.

After a strenuous campaign in which he had traversed fifty-one thousand miles, Ike declared that he was ready for a "rest-golf-fishing-no-visitors" holiday. At 2:00 A.M., Secret Service agents took their posts guarding Ike and his family, and the general reportedly slept until 8:00. On the first full day in Augusta, Ike fielded questions about an invitation extended to him by President Harry Truman. Ike agreed to meet with Truman the week of November 18, the first time an incoming president had ever met with an outgoing one before the inauguration. When Herbert Hoover offered to meet with his successor, Franklin D. Roosevelt, he was turned down. Ike took a different approach with Truman: "Thanks for your telegram. I am gratified by your suggestion that we have a personal meeting in the interests of an orderly transition."

Afterward, the *New York Times* reported that "the General took to the links on the Augusta National Course. He wore gray trousers, a short-sleeved tan shirt, a tan cloth hat with the brim turned down in front, and dark brown spiked golf shoes." Throughout the round, Ike joked with photographers, who posed him in a bunker near the ninth hole and on the green as he lined up a six-foot putt. One photographer quipped, "I hope your golf score is not as high as the vote you got." As the president stepped up to the tee, he turned to the press corps and said, "By golly, I hope you fellows carry insurance." He spent much of his time in Augusta considering cabinet nominations. They would later be referred to as "eight millionaires and a plumber."

Ike admitted that during the campaign he had only played six times in the past year and was "a bit off." Bobby Jones was not on hand to greet the new president; he was in Atlanta recuperating from a serious heart attack. But Ike did describe the telegram he received from his old friend immediately after the election, which read, "You sure put that little white pellet right in the bottom of the cup."

During the visit to Augusta, Ike and Mamie once again stayed in Jones's cabin. They had their breakfast and lunch sent to the cabin but ate dinner in the clubhouse Trophy Room. Next door, Mrs. J. S. Doud, Mamie's mother, was staying with Ike's personal physician, Dr. Howard Snyder, and his wife. A third cabin housed Mrs. John Eisenhower, the wife of Ike's son, and their three children, David (age four), Barbara Anne (three), and Susan (nine months). Their father, Major John Eisenhower, was serving in the Third Infantry

142

Division in Korea. Additional members of the party included Ike's appointment secretary, Thomas E. Stephens, and press secretary, James C. Hagerty.

Ike spent a fair amount of time during that visit responding to congratulatory letters, including notes from King Haakon of Norway; Lord Tedder, former chief air marshal of Great Britain; and Winston Churchill, who had just won reelection as the British prime minister in 1951 after having been defeated following World War II. Pope Pius XII cabled, "On the occasion of your election as President of the United States of America, we express to your excellency our cordial felicitations invoking divine blessings upon yourself and your administration of the American people."

Having Ike on the grounds of ANGC posed new challenges, ones that the members were happy to tackle. To ensure Ike's privacy and safety, Roberts requested that the two hundred members, thirty of whom were from Augusta, refrain from bringing guests while the president was on site. Reporters were not permitted on the course. Secret Service agents accompanied Ike during each round of golf, carrying golf bags outfitted with Thompson submachine guns. One tense moment arose in 1952, shortly after Ike had been elected president. While playing in a match with Roberts, Dudley, and Jerome Franklin, Ike's shot on the twelfth hole landed short of the green on a sandbar next to the water. With Roberts's encouragement, the president decided to play off the sandbar. As soon as he stepped onto the bank, he quickly sank to his knees in quicksand. Two Secret Service agents had to rescue him, and the foursome had to wait while Ike returned to his cottage to change clothes. In 1953, the club heeded a Secret Service suggestion and built a chain-link fence around the course.

143

Additionally, the club extended the west wing of the clubhouse to expand the golf shop and built a suite of offices for the president, though Cliff Roberts had the good sense to ask Ike's permission first. Ike spent many hours above the pro shop in that room (measuring ten by twelve feet), writing State of the Union addresses, holding meetings, and making national policy decisions. On November 26, 1954, the *Washington Post* reported that before heading out for a round at Augusta National on the Thanksgiving weekend, he was entertaining Field Marshal Viscount Montgomery. "He sent telegrams to the parents and wives of 13 Americans sentenced to prison by the Chinese Communists, assuring them that the Government is 'using every feasible means' to gain their release." The press and the public saw that national policy was often made on the golf course. In spite of these significant decisions and with all of this attention, former ANGC chairman Hord Hardin remembered, "He never acted like a President. There was no ceremony. At the first tee, we'd throw up four balls and the two closest were partners, the way we did with everyone else."

Ike made twenty-nine trips to ANGC during his two terms as president. His first began in February 1953 and lasted for four days. He spent his first Christmas in office at Augusta, staying for ten days. Upon leaving the White House, he remarked, "Nothing can get me mad today. Anything that will get me away from *this* place!" That year, he bought his grandson, David, his first set of golf clubs, including a 3-wood, a driver, and several irons. Though Ike loved the friendships Augusta brought him, he came to Augusta to play golf. Clifford Roberts remembered Ike's impatience: "The

General was always ready to start swinging the minute he set foot on the club grounds." Augusta became, during Ike's presidency, the second most famous city in America: "Within 24 hours of his sweeping victory in November 1952 President-Elect Eisenhower returned to a tumultuous welcome and established the city as a nerve center of the world, where the great and nearly great joined him in making far reaching decisions. It was in Augusta that Eisenhower reaffirmed his campaign promise to go to Korea and it was here that the preparations for the trip, made in December of 1953, were begun. Gov. Thomas E. Dewey of New York sat with Eisenhower on a bench overlooking the Augusta National Golf course and told him that he would be available as an advisor during his administration but would not accept a cabinet post. The selection of his first cabinet began here and plans for his first administration were developed. From Augusta Eisenhower flew to Washington for his first official talks with President Truman since the election."

As president, Ike often had to travel with sixty aides and security guards. Yet, the White House staff did not share Ike's fondness for the city, largely because they stayed at the aging Bon Air Hotel instead of at the fabled Augusta National. Ann Whitman, Ike's personal secretary, said Augusta was "a town about which I can find absolutely nothing favorable to say." On New Year's Day in 1954, she wrote, "We have fought, for instance, a losing battle trying to turn the heat off in our rooms . . . one of the girls has a bathroom that gives only hot water (red hot water) from both spigots. The food is completely vile. Room service is nonexistent. It seems that the smart people who want breakfast in their rooms stand in the corridor and if a waiter comes along with a tray, slip him a $5 and make off with the tray." Ike, Mamie, their friends, and their family had a much different experience.

During his visits, Ike and Ed Dudley would often play as a twosome, so Ike could concentrate on his game. William Frank Perteet, one of the club's longest-serving caddies, who began with the club in 1936, started carrying Ike's bag in 1948. Given the nickname Cemetery by Ike, he quickly became Ike's favorite caddie. Others called him Dead Man because in 1922, as Roberts explained, "Somebody stabbed him full of holes and he was taken to the funeral parlor. They were getting ready to fill him with embalming fluid when he got up and objected." According to Dudley, Perteet was habitually late, mainly because he was the leader of a local jazz band that played at clubs along Sand Bar Ferry Road late into the evening. Ike would caution him, "If you're late again tomorrow, you've lost your job." Perteet never wavered, and Ike liked him so much that he tolerated his tardiness. Cemetery would often say of Ike's game, "He don't pray over the ball. He just walks up and hits it, and off it goes." Perteet rarely caddied during the Masters, as the club gave him a week off to rest up for Ike's post-Masters visit. Ike paid Perteet $10, with an extra dollar on Sundays for church. During one ten-day visit, Ike said to his caddie, "My word, Cemetery, if this keeps up I'll be working for you."

Eventually, the club had to assign Ike a new caddie, because the aging Cemetery could not keep up with his rapid pace. Perteet did not take the decision personally. One joke of the time held that if you want to know about a man, ask his caddie. Perteet always said that he would vote for Ike. It was unlikely, however, that before the passage of the Voting Rights Act of 1964, an African

American man such as Perteet in a southern town had the opportunity to do so.

In 1953, Ike began a crusade to break 90 at Augusta National. On his first trip outside of Washington since becoming president, on February 26, Ike flew into Augusta for a three-day vacation, with that single goal in mind. The *New York Times* reported, "Only the most serious national problems will be called to the President's attention during his stay here, and advance word from the White House was that the trip would make no big news." From late January through most of February, Ike had tried to break 90 at Burning Tree Club, to no avail. His best score was a 91. Augusta was his best hope. Ike and Mamie traveled south with Stephens, Hagerty, and Whitman, as well as family members. Air Force aide Major William G. Draper flew the party south, and Roberts and Robinson met them. In addition, two old Army friends who had served with him during the war were on hand to meet Ike: Lieutenant General Alexander R. Bolling (commanding general of the Third Army, which was headquartered in Atlanta) and Brigadier General Frank Allen (the commandant at Camp Gordon).

As soon as the plane landed at 4:46 P.M. and the group was ferried to the club, Ike changed into his golfing attire and hit balls on the practice tee as the sun began to set. Instead of coming in, he managed to play seven holes that evening before darkness descended. During the trip, Roberts confirmed that the club was in the process of constructing the Eisenhower Cottage. Though he had a good vacation, Ike left disappointed, having failed in his quest for a round under 90.

In March, the *New York Times* published a short piece entitled "Break That Ninety!" commiserating

147

with Ike: "There are several million of us who know just how the President feels. Some of us are still waiting to crack the hundred. Golf is at once one of the world's great relaxations and the greatest exasperations. We are glad that the President has the will and the opportunity to relax. We are glad also that he can take out his exasperation on a niblick and a scorecard. We could wish, profoundly, that he would never have to meet any hazard worse than a sand trap. Meanwhile, more power to his swing, and more direction to his putts."

On April 14, 1953, the day after Ben Hogan won the Masters with a score of 274, Ike and his family returned to Augusta. He would hereafter make this an annual tradition, occasionally filling out his foursome with players who had competed in the Masters. Ike was so anxious to play that he is pictured disembarking from the plane with his golf shoes covered in green cloth bags in his hands. Upon his arrival, he met Hogan on the practice tee. Representative Jack Westland, a Republican from Washington, joined Ike for an afternoon round. The next day, Ike played with Hogan and Byron Nelson in his quest to break 90, again without luck. On the weekend, Ike sent his presidential plane to Charlotte, North Carolina, to bring Ohio Senator Robert Taft (who had challenged Ike for the 1952 Republican nomination) to Augusta. Taft was no stranger to the city; when he was a child, his father, William Howard Taft, brought him there to vacation.

148

Taft proved to be the good luck charm Ike needed. On April 20, 1953, Eisenhower reached his goal. But he did not want to publicize it and asked his press secretary, James C. Hagerty, to conceal the news. The next day, however, Bobby Jones broke the silence and announced that Ike had shot an 86, beating Senator Taft in a dollar

Nassau. He said Taft's score was much higher but did not reveal the actual number. On April 21, Ike shot an 88. He was so excited that he allowed the press to watch and photograph part of the game, the first time since the inauguration. Reflecting on the round, Ed Dudley said that the president "played the best golf of the year today." He added that seven putts that should have dropped did not. Had they, Ike would have carded an 81. Eisenhower and Taft played with Sherman Adams and Clarence J. Shoo, a box manufacturer from Springfield, Massachusetts. Bobby Jones, who was no longer able to play, rode in an electric cart called an autoette. Eisenhower's five-year-old grandson, David, rode with Jones.

At Clifford Roberts's suggestion, Ike never participated in any activities outside the club. Roberts feared that if he accepted one invitation, an avalanche of social obligations would follow. So he remained sequestered behind the gates at Augusta and was found either on the golf course or at the bridge table. An avid bridge player, he found a willing partner in Roberts and various members of the gang. Roberts described Ike's spirited playing style: "In bridge, as in golf, the President plays a hard, competitive game. He plays to win, but his friends say the stakes, as in golf, are nominal—never more than a tenth of a cent a point in bridge, or a dollar Nassau in golf, which means you can't lose more than $3 in an 18-hole round."

Augusta National became more than a retreat for Ike and Mamie. After Ike left West Point, he and Mamie had moved dozens of times and had to make homes out of officer's quarters, hotels, and European villas. Their frequent moves made it difficult to make lasting friendships. This all changed at Augusta. Mamie's Cabin, as it came to be known, was a gift from the ANGC membership. For the first five years of Ike's membership at Augusta, Bobby Jones gave his cottage over to the Eisenhowers when they visited. A year after the 1952 election, several members raised money to build a cabin for Ike a hundred yards from the clubhouse near the tenth tee. But building a home for a sitting president posed problems. The structure he occupied had to meet presidential security requirements and needed enough space to house his Secret Service contingent. On April 8, 1953, ANGC announced that Augusta architects Eve and Stulb would design the cottage, with construction overseen by another local firm, Claussen and Webster. The white painted brick cottage cost $150,000 to build and was available for use in the fall of that year. The second-floor dormers allowed for observation posts for Secret Service marksmen. Roberts reported that the design "was approved by Mrs. Dwight D. Eisenhower." Ike accepted it on the condition that other members could use it. The cottage, which even today features a gold presidential seal over the front porch, became known as the Little White House.

The house, which still comfortably sleeps eight, was described as a "green-shuttered brick cottage" with two large living rooms, one on the main floor and a second on the top floor. The living room on the top floor featured a portrait of David Eisenhower addressing a golf ball that Ike had painted from a photograph. The rest of the living room, furnished in French provincial, featured pictures of the eighteen homes in which the Eisenhowers had lived before moving into the White House; it was a gift from Roberts and the Air Corps. Bedrooms flanked the living room. There was no formal dining room and only a small kitchen. According to family friend Slats Slater, Mamie believed that the cottage should be kept "on the simple side—and not cluttered" and decorated to accommodate the other Augusta members who would be using it. The company that manufactured the paint wanted to call the color she chose Mamie Eisenhower Green. She declined but allowed them to name a hue of soft pink First Lady, instead. When the cabin was completed, the city of Augusta presented the first family with a silver tea service as a housewarming gift, and it was often used for birthday, Thanksgiving, and Christmas celebrations.

When asked about the new cabin, Ike commented, "It is a beautiful place. As a matter of fact, I didn't imagine they could make anything so nice." Right after they moved in, Slater reported, "The Eisenhowers' joy in being in their own home with their children and grandchild is gratifying and heartwarming." On May 6, 1961—after he left the White House—Ike hosted a Special Improvements Group Reunion Dinner for the members of ANGC who contributed to the building of Mamie's Cabin to formally thank them. He had not known their identities while he was president. After Ike's death, Mamie continued visiting Augusta National, spending most of her winters in their cabin.

Augusta also became a place where the Eisenhowers could feel a sense of normalcy. Ike and Mamie remained within the confines of the club, except when they ventured out to church. The president's visits were not always announced, but locals could tell that he was coming. The police presence was increased, orange cones were placed on the streets, and Secret Service men appeared everywhere. When they were in town, they worshipped at Reid Memorial Presbyterian Church,

151

located at 2261 Walton Way. Large crowds gathered outside the church, and people jostled to shake hands or have their photographs taken with Ike and Mamie. The clergy at the church were so accommodating to their most famous member that when he visited, they often held a special 8:45 A.M. service to allow him to play golf afterward. The typical sermon began at 11:15 A.M. Some locals called the church "St. Ike's on the Hill."

On Easter Sunday, April 18, 1954, Eisenhower laid the cornerstone using two silver trowels for the new church at Reid Memorial. When complimented on his ability, he joked, "I used to do this down on the farm." After the brief ceremony and a tour of the partially completed building, Ike returned to ANGC to take advantage of the spring weather and play a round of golf with his son, John. The new church was completed and dedicated on November 6, 1955. Even after Ike's death in 1969, Mamie continued to worship at Reid Memorial during her winter visits. She would outlive her husband by ten years.

Today, visitors to the church can sit in the Eisenhower pew, the third from the front on the right side of the sanctuary. It bears a small bronze plaque that was dedicated on February 6, 1972, in "loving memory" of the former president. At the other end of the sanctuary is the "Redemption Window," in the balcony adjacent to Walton Way. It was also dedicated to Ike and has an accompanying plaque that features his 1953 Inaugural Prayer. If you turn your head to the right, you can see a stained glass window bearing Ike's resemblance. The story, according to longtime members Phillip and Helen Christman and historian Jim Davis, is that Owen Cheatham, chairman of the building committee, and William D. Eve, the architect, arranged a tongue-in-cheek tribute to Ike by making him one of the three wise men. For years, a large magnolia tree stood outside the window, obstructing the image, so nobody noticed. When the tree was removed in 2001, however, the sunlight began streaming through, revealing Ike's bald head and familiar grin leaning over the Virgin Mary and baby Jesus.

When he was elected president, Ike's membership at Augusta National put the Masters Tournament in the spotlight. The *New York Times* reported that for the 1953 tournament, "officials are preparing for a tremendous crowd, far above the 15,000 that attended the tournament last year, even with an admission charge for the final day of $7.50. Their predictions are based on the steady flow of tourists and golfers who happen to be driving by, who have asked to see and perhaps photograph the cottage where President Eisenhower stayed, and the golf course that brings him all the way down from Washington." Ike especially loved the Masters. But he never attended because he thought his presence was a distraction for the staff and the players. He also did not want to negotiate the huge crowds on the grounds. Instead, he began a tradition of flying to Augusta the Monday after the Masters Tournament to play with the members and occasionally the new Masters champion. In 1954, Ike and Ben Hogan were paired with Roberts and Byron Nelson. Ike insisted that the round not be publicized; only his daughter-in-law was permitted to watch. Ike and Hogan won the match, seven holes to four. In 1960, Ike played with a thirty-year-old Arnold Palmer, fresh from claiming his second Green Jacket. Palmer quipped during the round that he was not sure whether he was more nervous in the final round of the Masters or during the round with Ike.

153

Eisenhower left his imprint on Augusta. In addition to the cabin, there is a pond, tree, and cracker barrel in the clubhouse named for him. During his second visit to Augusta, after the war, Ike suggested to Clifford Roberts that he build a dam to create a pond on the eastern edge of the club's land. In 1949, the club, after consulting with an engineer who agreed with Ike's assessment, paid $7,000 for a spring-fed pond on three acres that is today surrounded by the eighth and ninth holes of the par-3 course. The club stocked it with brim, bream, and bass. Thrilled by the addition, Ike often fished there after playing golf, and it has long been known as Ike's Pond. Still a part of the course, the pond is popular among golfers; Johnny Miller, Jerry Pate, Billy Andrade, Bruce Lietzke, and David Duval have all fished in it.

Every spring at the Masters, visitors can see a tree that continues to occupy the left center of the fairway on the seventeenth hole. Its mere presence suggests that even the president could not sway Augusta National. While in Walter Reed Hospital, Ike wrote his longtime friend and golfing partner, Charlie Yates in Atlanta, to complain about the tree: "If you've read the same Resolution I have you can understand what's going to happen to that misbegotten tree on 17—I note that Cliff says I have to *chop* the damn thing down—but with the leeway he has given me he'll find that I'm sneaky enough to find a bit of use for about one half stick of TNT." Bob Sommers recounted how the issue with the tree was finally resolved: "Recovering from a heart attack, Mr. Eisenhower attended a membership meeting at which Clifford Roberts, the club chairman, rose and said, 'Mr. President, we're so pleased to have you back, we'll make any change to the golf course you'd like.' Face alight with the prospect he'd finally have his way, Eisenhower cried, 'Cut down that tree on seventeen.' Nonplussed, Roberts calmly replied, 'I'm sorry, Mr. President, but we can't do that.' And it kept on growing." When Roberts told the story, he added, "I quickly adjourned the meeting to prevent a mutiny in the club's ranks." The exchange revealed that, while Augusta had an active board of governors, the club was controlled by Roberts. When Ike was asked in 1958 to serve on the board, he wrote to Charlie Yates that he was happy to accept and added a postscript: "Like all the others, I shall merely vote 'aye.' "

Years later, Augusta National was worried that the seventeenth hole was not as challenging as it should be. So, in 1999, the tee box was moved twenty-five yards back, bringing the Eisenhower tree back into play. The players in that year's field, including Tiger Woods, Mark O'Meara, John Daly, and David Duval, faced Ike's formidable obstacle. When asked about it, O'Meara (who had birdied 17 and 18 to win in 1998) answered, "I probably can't hit over the Eisenhower tree now. I probably have to work around it."

Despite the club's refusal to cut down the loblolly pine tree, ANGC's affection for Ike was boundless. The members showered him with gifts while he was a member of the club. During his presidency at Columbia University, Truman asked him to go to Paris to command NATO. At a send-off party at the Park Lane Hotel in New York City, the members at Augusta presented him with a globe with a clock that showed the time at any spot in the world; he kept it in his White House office. During his second term, they became more creative, offering the Eisenhower Cracker Barrel, which was made from wood that had been part of the White

155

House roof. It was presented to Ike on November 18, 1957, by George M. Humphrey, former secretary of the Treasury, who had just become a member of the club. Humphrey was a Cleveland businessman who spent the winters in Thomasville, Georgia, and frequently played golf with Ike. Made of pine, the barrel was a symbol of "free political discussions in the spirit of the old country store." The only condition of the gift was that Clifford Roberts had to keep it filled with crackers. (Even today it sits in the pro shop at Augusta National, stocked with crackers.) Roberts noted that over the years, the club had turned down golf libraries, halls of fame, and museum artifacts but declared that the "cracker barrel is something we can enthusiastically embrace, because we understand it and like it and everything it implies." Humphrey joked with the members that he hoped that the barrel would "solve the world's ills."

On the day the barrel was presented, Ike spent the morning at Reid Memorial Presbyterian Church listening to the minister's sermon, "How to Weather a Crisis." Charles H. Gibboney prayed, "Give [the leaders of our land] strength of purpose. Unite us as a people in goodwill and understanding in a nation where equals of all races may find trust and hope." The sermon was an indirect reference to the recent desegregation battle over Central High School in Little Rock, Arkansas, and Ike's showdown with Governor Orval Faubus that would ultimately strain the president's relationship with the South.

Even after Ike left the White House, Augusta National remained a refuge for him; he and Mamie made eleven trips to the club after his presidency. The first came in May 1961, and he received a warm welcome. The Richmond Academy Band and local dignitaries met him at Daniel Field. The band gave Eisenhower his first salute; President Kennedy had restored his title General of the Army a few days earlier. The most memorable visit he paid to Augusta came in the fall of 1965, when he had his second heart attack. Ike was taken immediately to the hospital at Fort Gordon. He remained there until he was taken to Walter Reed Hospital in Washington. The *Augusta Chronicle* reported, "Top names from the national and international news media flocked to the city to relay thousands of words on his condition. On Saturday, November 13, Western Union and Southern Bell Telephone Co. reported over 60,000 words were filed on Eisenhower's condition marking the second largest day of news covering coming out of the city's history. It rivaled only the coverage of the Masters' Golf Tournament the same year when a record 100,000 words were filed in a single day."

Each time Ike visited the city, the hospital implemented what they called Operation Ike. *Atlanta Journal* columnist Paul Hemphill explained how it worked: "If Ike were in town, the VIP Suite at the hospital would be vacated. Medical people would be on alert. Ambulance personnel would be available." Harry Harper Jr., who trained with Ike's personal cardiologist, Paul Dudley White, served as the president's cardiologist when he was in Augusta. While Ike was recuperating at Fort Gordon in November 1965, he was visited by Dr. Harper and his son Harry Harper III, then a medical student. The younger man recalled, "It was easy to see how he was so popular. He was a people person. He spent most of his time asking about my plans." Ike's last visit to the city and the golf club he so loved came in October 1967.

157

During his lifetime, the city of Augusta embraced Ike and his family and looked for various ways to honor him. The first attempt failed. On the day of his 1953 inauguration, the *New York Times* reported that a local baseball team, previously known as the Tigers, had named themselves the Augusta Ikes and would enter the South Atlantic League in the spring. The club directors voted to honor the president who, as a member of ANGC, was expected to vacation in the city often. Four years earlier, Eisenhower, who played baseball in school, had been a spectator at one of Augusta's minor league games. Drawing from a list of 183 names sent in by newspaper readers, the team selected the top six and asked the sports editor of the *Augusta Chronicle* to choose. Al Glass, a local fan, submitted the name the Ikes and won season tickets to the games at Jennings Stadium. An *Augusta Chronicle* columnist reported two days later that none of the players were such avowed Democrats that "they would balk at playing for the Ikes." But the name was short-lived, and the local paper reported that the directors of the baseball club "charged themselves with the first error of the 1953 season" and elected to change the name again. Apparently, the fans were overwhelmingly against naming the club for the new president. "Fans didn't like the Ikes," explained Bob Tarleton, the general manager. "The reaction I got was about 15–1 against it. And, since the fans are the bosses of this ball club, we'll just have to change the name." The remaining choices were the Rams, Jets, Bombers, Bob Cats, or Hornets. Objections came from all sides, including a newspaper in Montgomery, Alabama, that ruled that using the nickname Ike was not suitably dignified for the newly elected president. In the final tally, the name Rams was selected in a surprise upset to those favoring the Bombers. Today, the minor league team is called the Green Jackets. There is an Eisenhower Park, a facility that includes ball fields and playgrounds, at 1488 Eisenhower Drive near Augusta National that was named for Ike in the 1960s.

Recognition would come after his death. On March 18, 1971, the *Augusta Chronicle* reported that the new hospital at Fort Gordon was to be named the Dwight D. Eisenhower U.S. Army Hospital. Leading the naming effort were local business and military leaders, including Major General John C. F. Tillson II, the commander at Fort Gordon; Charles Presley, president of the Atlanta Chamber of Commerce; and Louis C. Harris, the editor of the *Chronicle*. The Army agreed and broke with tradition, as medical facilities are traditionally named for deceased members of the Army Medical Department. The ground breaking, with a keynote address by General William C. Westmoreland, Chief of Staff, U.S. Army, took place on April 23, 1971. Ike had visited the old hospital at Fort Gordon twice. The original facility, the Camp Gordon Station Hospital, was built in 1941 and housed nearly 1,600 patients during World War II. In 1946, the station hospital was closed and, by 1947, the eighty-acre facility was nearly empty. During and after the Korean War, the hospital expanded to three hundred beds, and it was still about that size when Ike visited during his presidency.

In January 1961, just before Kennedy's inauguration, Ike came to Fort Gordon to say farewell to the Army as commander in chief. At the event, he remarked wistfully, "This is the last review I shall ever receive in my life. I have been a part of many such ceremonies during this half century but none has been more meaningful than this one." Afterward, he went to Augusta National

159

to play golf there for what would be his last time. The new medical complex named for Eisenhower was completed in 1974 and intended to "serve military personnel and their dependents from the entire southeast, Central and South America." A memorial to Eisenhower, in the form of an engraved granite block that included portions of his 1961 Farewell Address, stood for more than thirty years at the main entrance, second-floor foyer, of the hospital. The monument, which was moved to Freedom Park at Fort Gordon on January 10, 1999, was paid for by donations from Augusta companies and individuals, including nickels and dimes from Richmond County schoolchildren.

Today, Augusta National has a modest memorial to Ike, but one that is not open to the public. On the second floor of the clubhouse, there is a library with bookshelves and cabinets holding artifacts from the club's past, including memorabilia related to Bobby Jones, Clifford Roberts, and Eisenhower. The display includes a portrait of Roberts painted by Eisenhower. Off to the side is a desk, a phone, and a chair that, for most of the invited guests and some of the younger members, seems rather innocuous. A small exhibition panel explains that it was the furniture that Ike used in his office at the club. Like most things at Augusta, it stands as a simple tribute to a complex man.

SEVEN

DON'T ASK WHAT I SHOT

*Some of us worship in churches, some in syna-
gogues, some on golf courses.*

—Adlai Stevenson

A young cosmetician's outburst during a September 1954 episode of "Name That Tune" indicates the extent to which Ike's golf game had become part of 1950s popular culture. That night, emcee Bill Cullen played "Hail to the Chief" and waited for the two contestants to identify the song. Upon hearing the first few notes, the male waiter leapt up, only to absently declare, "It slipped my mind." Cullen tried to prompt him by asking, "What do they play when President Eisenhower goes some place?" The waiter answered incorrectly, "The Missouri Waltz." Cullen then turned to the cosmetician to give her a chance to answer the same question. She shouted, "Golf!"

Upon winning the 1952 election, Ike confided to his friend Virgil Pinkley that he wished someone had written a book entitled *How to Be President of the United States*. Without such advice, he began his eight years in the White House with his golf clubs in tow. As had presidents before him, Ike faced a series of crises and decisions, as well as a barrage of more mundane duties, that placed endless demands on his time. Ike received an average of 1,400 letters daily (compared to Abraham Lincoln's thirty). One was written by a young girl who told him that she was planning a surprise party for her mother and was inviting her closest friends: "the President, Mrs. Eisenhower, the Queen of England—and Lassie!" Golf would not, for those years, be simply leisure. It served as an essential escape valve.

Though Ike was an avid golfer, he called himself an "ordinary duffer." His record shows that he was better than that. Throughout his presidency and afterward, he maintained a handicap between 14 and 18. He broke 80 at least four times, shooting 79s at Augusta National, Burning Tree, and Gettysburg Country Club. In 1954, he enjoyed one of his best years. During an eight-week "work-and-play" vacation in the fall, he shot a 77 at Cherry Hills. At Glen Arven in Thomasville, Georgia, he shot an 81. Though he struggled with his putting, Bobby Jones once said of Ike, "He can make enough good shots to have fun."

In March 1953, Ike had a few poor rounds at Augusta and lamented, "There ought to be a law against asking a person what he shot." This remark prompted a sympathetic *Golf Digest* to print thousands of buttons that read, "Don't Ask What I Shot." The magazine sent copies of the button to Ike during his trip after the Masters that year, and the story made front-page news across the globe. The slogan became an answer on television quiz shows, and *Golf Digest* began forming Secret Shooter Societies using the "official" badge. Within a matter of weeks, more than fifteen thousand buttons had been distributed. A newspaper in Lisbon, Portugal, rather unfortunately translated the button to read, "Don't Ask What I Killed," and one in Mexico City read, "¡No preguntes lo que tire!" which translated to mean, "Don't Ask What I Threw." The golf editor of the *Louisville Courier-Journal* even got into the act, making his own button that read, "Don't Tell Me What YOU Shot." Not to be outdone, a columnist for the *Chicago Sun-Times* urged readers not to confuse Ike's button with one that he imagined could be sponsored by the city's criminals: "Don't Ask WHO I Shot."

Four days after taking the oath of office, Ike was on the White House lawn practicing his iron shots from a small tee. He was aimed at the ornamental pool and White House fountain, and it was Sergeant John Moaney's task to shag the balls. Mamie once said, "I'll bet there are a lot of golf balls in those White House fountains." After the public and the press caught on to what Ike was doing, he moved to a gymnasium on the ground floor of the West Wing to hit into a special net. Soon, however, he returned to the South Lawn to practice his chipping and iron shots, to the dismay of the White House gardeners, who had to repair the numerous divots Ike took with his 8-iron and pitching wedge. There was some debate as to whether visitors who stopped to watch the president's progress were in any danger. Democratic congressman Omar Burleson was sent to investigate and, after seeing far how Ike was driving the ball, reported back to his colleagues that the public was safe.

While there was little doubt where Ike would play golf when on vacation, there was much speculation as to which Washington-area club he would call home. The

163

January 2, 1953, issue of *Golf World* reprinted part of an article by Andrew Tulley: "Strange as it may seem, the local country clubs are not falling over one another trying to get Ike Eisenhower to use their golf courses when he moves into the White House. It seems a President actually is a pest on a golf course. The Secret Service gets awful nervous when he's playing; won't let anybody too near him and makes all the other members stand aside until the President plays through." Ike, like his predecessors in the White House, looked to Burning Tree.

As the Army chief of staff, Ike had joined Burning Tree in 1946 and made it his home club while he was in Washington. The staff hung a five-star flag from the rafters in the locker room and added a caricature of him in the club's gallery. Max Elbin became the head professional at the club just about the time Ike joined, and Ike occasionally asked him for advice on improving his game. The course was ten miles from the White House, and before becoming president, Ike was often on the links between four and five times a week. Roger Kahn described its appeal to Ike: "The club is selective rather than exclusive. Membership is limited to 250 people, but it includes newspapermen—for example—in addition to Senators and cabinet members." Applications had to be sponsored by two members, and letters of recommendation were required from others. A potential member's name was posted on a bulletin board for thirty days; if there were no objections, the member would be asked to pay $1,000 for initiation and $380 in annual dues.

The clubhouse was small and unimposing. One member quipped, "With a half-pint of kerosene and a match, you could burn down this place in 30 minutes."

There was no formal dining room; members simply ate at two long tables that could accommodate fourteen people each. Two waiters and two locker room attendants were enough to serve the membership. According to Kahn, "The uncarpeted floor bears the scars of 30 years of spiked-shoe traffic. The furniture is worn. The pale green walls in the clubhouse are ornamented with a moose head, a few trophies and clubs used by earlier Presidential golfers: William Howard Taft, Woodrow Wilson, Warren Harding and Franklin Delano Roosevelt, who played sporadically before polio condemned him to a wheelchair." During Ike's time at the club, the members dressed casually and allowed themselves a mulligan off the first tee. The course periodically organized member-guest events but not tournaments or championships. Ben Hogan and Cary Middlecoff occasionally played at Burning Tree with Ike. Women and political discussion were strictly barred from the club, which appealed to Ike.

The course was incorporated on December 8, 1922, and opened two years later. As the story goes, four men (Isaac T. Mann, Marshall T. Whitlach, John H. Clapp, and William M. Ritter) felt frustrated by the crowds at Chevy Chase Club. To solve the problem, they elected to begin a new club that had a more limited membership. The land that made up the course was purchased from a family named Wetzel and from Walter Tuckerman. Charter members contributed $10,000 each, and the club hired the Scottish firm of Colt, MacKenzie, and Allison to design the par-72 course. In the words of the *New York Times*, "The perfectly groomed, natural course is 'tight' for the first fourteen holes. It is tree-lined on both sides with roller-coasting—but not overtaxing—fairways. It is not heavily trapped, nor is

165

the rough rugged. The greens are of the postage-stamp variety, and are fast, for the most part. But there is not an unfair shot on the course." The name came from a tree that stood on the course's highest point that each year bloomed with bright red blossoms. Supposedly, it had been a gathering place for Algonquin tribes.

At Burning Tree, Ike stored his clothes in a modest locker (No. 85) that bore a nameplate with "Mr. President" and a small American flag pasted on the door by one of the attendants. The club had rules regarding Ike's presence: he had to be greeted as "Mr. President," nobody was permitted to begin a conversation with him, greens fees went up from $5 to $10 on Ike's playing days, he was to be allowed to play through, and his golf scores had to remain a secret. One reason Ike liked the club so much was because he could play it quickly— on Wednesdays and Saturdays, he could finish in two and a half hours. Ike mostly played in a threesome; his favorite partners were George Allen and Tom Belshe. He was allowed to use a cart to help him speed up his game. Depending on his schedule, he would play a quick round and then eat lunch at the common table, stay for a rubber of bridge, or stop at the nineteenth hole to chat with members. Toward the end of Ike's term, Burning Tree created the Eisenhower golf fellowship, which allowed a member of the armed forces in Washington below the rank of general officer to have an honorary membership for no more than three years. Ike named his son, John, the first recipient.

Most of his fellow golfers took Ike's membership in stride, but Merriman Smith recounts one humorous anecdote: "An aspect of the President's golf which seldom gets in the news is the dilemma of some people when they meet the chief executive for the first time—without his clothes on. I know of a couple of instances at Burning Tree. One involves a former Midwestern Senator who had known Ike fairly well before he became President. The Senator was soaping himself one Wednesday afternoon in the shower at Burning Tree and noticed that a soapy fellow next to him appeared somewhat familiar. As the Senator rinsed the suds from his eyes, he was taken aback to discover that his shower neighbor was the President. Although he knew Ike, the Senator did not speak, but quickly shut off the shower and beat it back to his locker. As he explained to friends, 'What in the world can you say to the President of the United States if you're standing there buck naked—and so is he?' "

At Burning Tree, Ike recorded his first eagle (two strokes under par). In a letter dated June 18, 1954, to Clifford Roberts, he described his excitement: "This eagle might not be important to anyone else, but it is my first—and it came on a hole where one day I had an eagle in my grasp and just kicked it out the window by means of a completely inexcusable putt. . . . I was hitting the ball fairly long and straight the other day and on Burning Tree's #10 banged my second one about six feet from the pin (on the former occasion I was twenty inches away). This time I decided to take no chances so I shut my eyes, gave it a prayerful stab—and sure enough there it was."

Allen "Napoleon" Whitehead was Ike's favorite caddie at Burning Tree. During one round, Whitehead bet his caddie fee on the president, who was not playing well. By the sixteenth green, he was exasperated and implored, "For Christ's sake, Mr. President, hit it!" Bob Sommers recalled, "President Eisenhower took occasional license with the rules of golf. During his

167

presidency he played Burning Tree Club every Wednesday he could, quickly becoming known for his novel method of identifying his ball. Rather than stoop over for a closer look, he would use a club and roll his ball over until the trademark became visible. If his ball moved into a better lie, well, Ike *was* the President. One afternoon Eisenhower's ball settled in the rough. When he tried to roll it over, it lodged against a rock. Startled, the President glared at his caddie and snapped, 'What happened?' The caddie answered, 'Mr. President, I'm afraid you have over-identified your ball.' " The caddies, upon learning that the president would play the next day, would line up the night before to be first in line to go along with Ike's foursome because he always gave two golf balls stamped with the words "Mr. President" and a $5 tip.

Bob Hope played with Ike at Burning Tree in a round against General Omar Bradley and Senator Stuart Symington. On the first tee during the discussion over the wager, Ike said, "I just loaned Bolivia $2 million. I'll play for a dollar Nassau." Hope played badly and the twosome lost. The next day, Hope teamed with Senator Prescott Bush against Ike and Bradley. Hope shot a 75. As Ike was paying the $4 winning bet, he turned to Hope and said, "Why didn't you play this well yesterday?"

168

When Ike wanted to get a short distance from Washington, he traveled with his staff and friends to Camp David in Maryland's Catoctin Mountains. The facility covered five hundred acres and had a rustic main building that included a living room, four bedrooms and bathrooms, a kitchen, a butler's pantry, and a sunroom. Roosevelt had called it Shangri-la, but Ike renamed it

Camp David for his grandson. In the summer of 1954, Navy personnel built an elevated tee about fifty yards from a putting green to allow Ike to practice his game. Before it was built, he would sometimes travel to a small nine-hole course in nearby Thurmont, but he had to manage the crowds. His friend Slats Slater described the practice area at Camp David: "It is a nice green, with quite a lot of rough, and protected from two sides by a large trap. The game is to play the green from different positions and distances. We use a wedge, a nine iron, and when you get back into what is known as the 'slot,' you can use even a four or a five to reach the green. Each of us get five shots at the green from each position. From the short positions you must land on the green; from the tees a little farther back all you have to do is end up on the green—for each miss you are penalized $1.00. After playing from the seven positions, including a wedge shot out of the trap and five putts, your score is computed. Actually, it is a good way of getting in a little practice."

Ike's three favorite places to play outside of Washington were Augusta National, Newport Country Club in Rhode Island, and Cherry Hills in Denver, Mamie's hometown. Ike vacationed in Denver in 1953, 1954, and 1955, and it was easy to tell when he was there—the standard-issue flag that flew over Lowry Air Force Base was replaced with one that measured sixty feet long and ten feet high. The office Ike used on the base was about half the size of the Oval Office and was spartanly furnished with a green metal desk and several chairs. A picture of a military jet plane and three photographs of the Rockies adorned the walls. While Ike was in residence, the switchboard operators (who were overwhelmed by three thousand calls a day) would answer

"White House–Denver." Encoded messages were sent over a Teletype machine. Mail, in the form of as many as five hundred letters or packages a day, was brought from Washington three times a week in locked pouches by a commercial plane.

Ike took one of his longest vacations, six weeks, in Denver during the late summer and early fall of 1953. While there, he played nearly three hundred holes of golf and spent ten days fishing. He would typically work for several hours at the base and then drive to Cherry Hills Country Club for a daily round of golf, which was relaxed and informal. Ike would often phone ahead to Ralph "Rip" Arnold, the club's professional, and would simply join three other members on the course for the first nine holes and then join another group for the second nine. He regularly played with Denver businessman Aksel Nielsen, Governor Dan Thornton, rancher Bal F. Swan, *Denver Post* publisher Palmer Hoyt, insurance executive John Culbreath, and oil executive Fred Manning. Thornton often said of Ike's desire to win even the smallest of bets, "If he takes care of the national budget like he watches his pennies in golf we should be in pretty good hands." Ike and Mamie stayed with her mother at 750 Lafayette Street, but Ike would entertain friends in a suite on the eighth floor at the Brown Palace Hotel. Evenings at the hotel began at seven with drinks and lively conversation, dinner was served at eight, and the rest of the night was spent playing bridge.

In August 1955, Ike was on his way to Denver when his plane was briefly delayed at Washington National Airport. Reporters began to speculate that something serious had happened. Just as they were beginning to make inquiries, John Moaney, Ike's valet, came running toward the plane with the president's golf clubs. During that lengthy vacation, newspaper editorials began to wonder if "the country club could be run without the President."

On September 23, 1955, Ike played twenty-seven holes at Cherry Hills. At 2:45 local time the next morning, he suffered a heart attack, the first of three major illnesses during his presidency. The event shook the nation. On the following Monday, the Dow Jones stock index fell by thirty points, the largest decline since 1929. Ike recuperated in Denver and did not get back on the golf course for five months. Members of the 124th Air Transport Group sent Ike an arrangement of flowers in the shape of a golf club. A group of newspaper reporters sent him a pair of bright red pajamas for his sixty-fifth birthday on October 14 with five stars and the words "Much Better, Thanks" embroidered on the pocket. Merriman Smith and Laurence H. Burd of the *Chicago Tribune* also sent a shiny black Western tie with silver sequins that had cost thirty-nine cents. The president wore them both with glee, and he was featured on the cover of *Life* magazine that week. Most surprisingly, a group of prisoners in Siberia smuggled out wishes for his recovery through West Germany's first chancellor, Konrad Adenauer.

Ike left the hospital after nearly seven weeks and returned to Washington and then to his home in Gettysburg to complete his convalescence. The inactivity during his recovery, though, had a profound effect on Ike and, probably more than anything else, revealed that he was not ready to retire and could weather a second term. In *Eisenhower: The Inside Story*, Robert Donovan described Ike's state of mind: "For Eisenhower, Gettysburg came close to being five weeks of torment. His

171

morale slumped. His spirits were low. He fretted over Government affairs. . . . He was tense and nervous and stalked about the house with a golf club for a cane."

Even though cardiologists in the early 1950s warned heart attack patients to avoid vigorous exercise, Ike ignored them. He believed that a regular fitness regimen helped control his weight and lighten his mood. His personal physician, Dr. Howard Snyder, agreed and gave Ike a specific prescription: "The doctor said that I should resume my favorite exercise before too long. This was good news. Golf had kept my muscles in good shape and was partly responsible for the good chances of a full recovery." Ike was urged to keep his weight below 170 pounds and to do more vigorous exercise, such as swimming or cycling. He swung his clubs in the fall of 1955 and played nine holes in Thomasville, Georgia, on February 17, 1956, his first round of golf since the heart attack. Remarking on the round, he joked, "You're going to hear a heck of a lot of laughter today. My doctor has given me orders that if I don't start laughing instead of cussing when I miss those shots, he's going to stop me from playing golf. So every time I miss a shot, you're going to hear haw-haw-haw." Ike's one concession was to give up golf in Denver because of the altitude; he simply turned to Rhode Island or California for his next vacation.

During his presidency, Ike suffered two additional illnesses. On June 6, 1956, he was diagnosed with ileitis, and he had a mild stroke on November 25, 1957. In each case, his golf game became the barometer by which the nation measured his recovery. Snyder said, "Golf is a tonic for the President. I say he should play whenever he gets a chance. He doesn't get away from the office nearly as much as I'd like him to." In the spring of 1959, John

Moaney, who for years had been shagging golf balls for the president, surprised him by putting more than five hundred of them in Ike's dressing room. Historian Clarence Lasby told the story: "The president was surprised that so many had been spread around the house and kept for so long. Indeed, he had received many of them immediately after his heart attack, and they still bore the imprint 'Get Well Ike.' He spent fifteen minutes looking over the accumulation—'pawed them over like a miser counting his gold'—and then took several dozen to put in his practice kit. For many years golf had been his addiction, setting forth its prospect for recreation and joy; now it was his doctor's prescription, holding forth a promise of 'stay well, Ike.' "

After Ike's first heart attack, *U.S. News and World Report* analyzed his proclivity for golf. The magazine calculated that he played 64, 85, and 61 times in his first three years as president. In 1956, he played 72 times. In his second term, Ike played 97 rounds in 1957, 95 in 1958, 122 in 1959, and 116 in 1960. In addition to playing full rounds, he practiced on at least 363 occasions. The USGA's magazine *Golf Journal* computed that Ike's monthly average while he was president rose from 5.3 rounds his first year to 8.4 in the fifth. After 1955, Ike's cardiologist Dr. Paul Dudley White suggested that Ike start using a golf cart. The cofounder of E-Z-Go golf carts in Augusta, Bev Dolan, remarked, "It legitimized them. If a president was using it, everyone could use it. The clubs became more lenient and realized the potential for raising money for the club."

When they wanted to stay on the East Coast and when Augusta National was closed from May to October, Ike and Mamie vacationed in Newport, Rhode Island.

While he was president, Ike played forty-five rounds at Newport Country Club, averaging between 86 and 90 a round. They spent their annual vacation there in 1957 and 1958. But Ike had no love for the 6,655-yard course. Upon first playing it he exclaimed, "There are more darn sand traps on this course that I have ever seen any place in my life, and I've been in almost all of them." He was right; the course had 132 sand bunkers, or 7.3 bunkers a hole, which was twice as many as the average course at the time. Ike and Mamie stayed in 1957, not in the fashionable part of town, but in a twelve-room, four-bath white stone house typically occupied by the base commander, Rear Admiral Henry Cromelin, on Narragansett Bay Isle, home to the Coasters Harbor Island Naval Base and the Naval War College. The course, which provided some measure of privacy, was five minutes from the house by car, ten minutes by boat. But that, apparently, was not close enough. In 1958 and 1960, the couple stayed in a twenty-room house at Fort Adams, which was even more convenient to the first tee. The summer home of New York's premier social list, the fabled Four Hundred, Newport was accustomed to public scrutiny, so most took little notice of Ike. The year-round residents loved having the president, however; one restaurant added "Welcome Mr. President" to a sign advertising steamed clams for eighty-five cents.

174

Ike regularly played with Newport's golf professional who, like Ed Dudley at Augusta National and Max Elbin at Burning Tree, often gave him advice about how to improve his game. Norman Palmer commented on Ike during his 1957 vacation, "For a man of his age (he was sixty-six at the time) he had a full swing. It was amazing to see how far he got his back turned toward the hole, got the weight shifted back to the right side, and how well he moved into the ball. He was much stronger in his swing than I anticipated." But Palmer, as with Ike's other teaching professionals, noted that the president struggled with his putting and his short irons, mainly because he hit behind the ball.

Ike began his vacation in September 1957 at Newport with a phrase that he would later come to regret: "I assure you that no vacation has started more auspiciously." While he was in Newport, one of the most significant crises of his presidency—the desegregation fight over Central High School in Little Rock—unfolded. He did not, however, let it interrupt his golf schedule. Between telegrams, phone calls, and meetings, he golfed incessantly, even inviting a group of young boys who were sponsored by the Chamber of Commerce to play with him on September 19.

Eisenhower's game improved in 1958. Club professional Norman Palmer explained that during that year, "I don't recall seeing a card with an Eisenhower score over 100." During his 1958 vacation in Rhode Island, Sherman Adams visited Ike at Newport before delivering his resignation speech. If Ike was affected by the Adams scandal, it did not show. The day before Adams's visit, Ike shot an 82. Palmer played regularly with Ike and often tore up the president's scorecard after the round to protect his privacy. Palmer often said of Ike's ability, "He was one of the strongest starters I have ever seen. The first year, for instance, he birdied the first hole at Newport seven times in 22 rounds. He rarely bogeyed the hole. His tremendous ability on this hole often demoralized our opponents. I began to think that they'd probably send up a railroad car and shovel up the first fairway and hole and transplant it on the White House lawn. The President played it like he owned it."

Gettysburg, Pennsylvania, became another place where Ike regularly played golf, but few knew that he was breaking the law. In 1794, Pennsylvania declared that sport or any diversion whatsoever was illegal on Sundays, with a penalty of $4 or a six-day jail sentence. The law was not repealed until 1960, long after Ike and Mamie had bought their farm, three miles from the center of town. It was a logical place for them to settle; they had deep roots in the area, and Ike's brothers Earl and Milton lived nearby. The Eisenhowers renovated the two-hundred-year-old structure, creating an eight-bedroom, seven-bath home. The property originally cost slightly more than $40,000; they did more than $150,000 in renovations, including building a small pond stocked with bass and bluegill.

The Professional Golfers Association of America even helped Ike set up a green at the farmhouse, measuring sixty by forty feet. That was not the only gift he would accept. While president, he was given four hundred nut trees, fifty-five head of cattle, most of the home's furnishings and appliances, a pony, a stallion, a $4,000 tractor that had a radio and cigarette lighter, and various other farm implements. Ike was given so much that he and Mamie had to store the extra appliances in the garage. In 1954, for their thirty-eighth wedding anniversary, the couple received an antique mantel that had been in the White House during Chester A. Arthur's administration.

Ike often golfed at nearby courses, including Blue Ridge Summit and Gettysburg Country Club, a nine-hole 35-par layout. In 1952, Carlisle Country Club, about twenty-five miles from Gettysburg, sent Ike an honorary membership. But they were not championship courses, and both tended to dry out during the summer months. Even so, they were convenient, and he enjoyed a fair amount of privacy in town and on the golf course, where he tooled around on a baby blue electric cart. In 1955, the *Washington Post* reported, "The President's total gallery on the last green consisted of three women and one little girl who wandered down from the swimming pool in their bathing suits." Eisenhower's golf was often interrupted by his official duties. Even his health intervened. During one round, on June 14, 1958, he had to stop after nine holes to receive a smallpox vaccination. To minimize distractions, Gettysburg Country Club found Ike a small, private office of six by twelve feet at one end of the locker room, furnished with a desk, a chair, a grass rug, a locker, and two shower stalls.

Ike played at dozens of other courses, and Merriman Smith explained how much work went into preparing for him: "When Ike visited South Dakota in June, 1953, the advance party that went out ten days ahead to set up headquarters for a brief stay at Custer State Park heard about a golf course sixty miles away. It was at Lead, South Dakota, and the President's hosts thought he might want to run over one morning for a quick game. Telephone service was limited, so the Signal Corps installed special facilities at the clubhouse. This involved stringing phone wire eight miles over the mountains from the golf course to the town of Lead— just in case the President visited for a few hours and had to make a call or be called while he was there."

Whether he was in Washington or on vacation, golf was never far from Ike's consciousness. The White House had rules about information that could be leaked regarding Ike's game. His score and club selection were not to be discussed or printed. *Golf* magazine once declared, "Ike's golf score, like the age of Zsa Zsa Gabor, remains a mystery number, hidden even from spies." Sports reporters were sympathetic to his desire for privacy. *Golf World* reported on March 6, 1953, "A Washington golfer whose address is 1600 Pennsylvania Avenue has struck a sympathetic chord with thousands and thousands of hackers. Flying back to Washington after a weekend at Augusta National, President Eisenhower said that unless his golf improves he will try to make it illegal for anybody to ask his score. Many a duffer after a bad round has thought there ought to be a law against curiosity about it."

Unlike Woodrow Wilson or Warren Harding, Ike was deadly serious about his game and pursued lower scores with a kind of religious zeal. Even when he made a bad shot, he never gave up. During a round at the Ottawa Hunt Club in Canada, a local journalist caddied for him and reported, "He got into a difficult trap on the par-4 third hole and took an eight. The sand was hard, more like baked earth, and he banged at it four times before he got to the green. After the second shot he turned and said: 'I'm hitting it as hard as I can. I just can't get the club through.' Then, after he holed out, he returned to the trap and took a couple of practice swings. 'For the future,' he explained."

Ike even went as far as to have his shoes blessed in 1955, with help from his friend and longtime Augusta National member Charlie Yates. Vic Benveniste owned a shoe repair shop on Peachtree Street in Atlanta and became well known for blessing the shoes of famous golfers. He did it for Bobby Jones before the amateur left for England in 1930 on his quest to win the Grand Slam. He blessed shoes for Louise Suggs, a founding member of the LPGA, and also for Yates, who won the 1938 British Amateur. Benveniste asked Yates if he could work on Eisenhower's shoes, and Yates told the following story: "The president and I were playing at Augusta, and Ike wasn't having a good round. I said to him. 'Chief, you need my friend Benveniste to fix your shoes. You'll be surprised how much it helps your game.' " Benveniste blessed the shoes (and received a second pair from Ike for his informal museum), but there is no indication that the blessing worked.

He would have to try a less supernatural strategy. Improving one's golf game requires total concentration, which may be why the sport appealed to Ike. He had an uncanny ability to apply himself completely to the task at hand, whether it was his official duties, golf, or bridge. Ike's longtime friend Slats Slater noted it while visiting the White House on March 7, 1953: "So Cliff Roberts and I left at 9:30. When we got to Bob Schulz's office we could see Ike hitting golf balls on the back lawn and wandered over to see him practice. He was hitting them pretty well, well enough so that he would have scored well in a real game. But as usual, there were comments after each shot—'What did I do right that time?'—'That's good enough for me.' A running line of conversation which indicates his intense concentration on whatever he is doing. . . . When doing anything, golf, bridge, conversation, it's evident he has an ability to completely lose himself in whatever happens to be the thing of the moment. I've often thought that's what enables him to get so much done—and at the same time, it is also what gives him relaxation—relief from his daily tensions."

Yet, Ike was an impatient golfer. He played quickly and rested only briefly after nine holes for a glass of

179

orange juice. A joke widely told in the 1950s has Ike at Burning Tree approaching a foursome in front of him, requesting to play through. When the foursome asked, "What's your hurry?" Ike is said to have replied, "The Russians have just bombed New York." Max Elbin at Burning Tree always gave advice to Ike's new playing partners, "I would tell them one thing. 'If you're riding with Ike, be sure and get into the cart quickly because he's not going to wait for you.' Hell, he'd hit his ball and you'd hit yours, and if you weren't back in the cart he'd damn near take off without you. Now that's a little exaggerated. But he didn't fiddle around and wait for somebody." He could play eighteen holes in a little more than two hours, helped in part by Secret Service men who scouted for his ball. Like so many golfers, Ike was an affable partner who told jokes when he was playing well; when he was not, he became quickly frustrated.

Ike was known to bend the rules a bit, and most of his rounds included a few mulligans. While playing for the first time after his 1955 heart attack, Ike hit three drives in a row that went off to the left. Before his fourth attempt, he said, "I'll be darned if I'm going to start off with a ball like that." Those first three attempts never made it onto his scorecard. In 1956, while playing at Gettysburg Country Club, Ike faced another rules violation, but this one had four legs. At 9:30 on the morning of May 26, a tan and white dog ran onto the course on the second hole and grabbed Ike's ball from the fairway. The Secret Service immediately moved to action but could not retrieve the ball. There is no record of Ike replacing his ball without penalty, under the outside agency rule set out by the United States Golf Association. A third incident occurred in August 1962 at Sunningdale when Eisenhower mistakenly played the ball of Sir James Gault, his playing partner, on the eighteenth hole.

Regardless of his occasional rules violations, Ike played golf because he needed the game. James C. Hagerty, Ike's White House press secretary, explained, "I think the President plays golf for three reasons. First, he's wildly enthusiastic about the game. Second, he needs the exercise. You know, the Presidency is the kind of job where you sit behind a desk all day, never getting up from it except to shake hands. Golf gives him a chance to move around. Third, he finds it relaxing. I've seen days when he left the White House utterly weary, played a round and then came back to work just as fresh as if he'd just gotten up." Without golf, Ike was moody and temperamental. He may have learned his lesson about relaxation from J. P. Morgan, who after the age of sixty would take three months a year away from Wall Street. He used to say that he could do a year's worth of work in nine months, but not in a year.

As he had been on the gridiron at West Point, Ike was a fierce competitor on the golf course, and his temper showed when he played badly. He would, as one partner said, turn red and unleash a "five-star profanity" when he played a bad shot. Bob Hope told a story in *Confessions of a Hooker* about one round in California. When playing at Eldorado Country Club, Ike repeatedly hit his ball into groves of grapefruit trees. At the end of the round he roared, "When I get back to the White House, anyone who serves me grapefruit is fired!" Like most golfers, he was never satisfied. Breaking 90 only made him want to break 80.

Ike usually played with a set of Spalding clubs given to him by Bobby Jones and a putter that was stamped

"Grand Old Putter." Augusta National golf professional Ed Dudley had them duplicated and the irons engraved with five stars, so he could keep one set at Augusta and one in Washington. According to Roger Kahn, "Mr. Eisenhower uses a regular shaft of medium flexibility. The shafts are three-eighths of an inch longer than standard—43⅜ inches for his driver and 39 inches for his two-iron. The swing weight of his driver is slightly less than average." In 1955, retired Air Force Colonel Robert W. Kenworthy of New York sent Ike a set of "B-36" golf balls that would reportedly travel between thirty and forty yards farther than regular balls. Although he may have tried them, Eisenhower preferred Spalding Dot golf balls, embossed with the words "Mr. President."

Ike's handicap vacillated between 14 and 18; he was capable of 225-yard drives, though he averaged 175. A strong man known for his one-arm chin-ups at West Point, he could be heard muttering over a tee shot, "Lord, just give me the strength to hit this thing easy." On the tenth hole at Augusta, he once drove 260 yards, passing Byron Nelson's drive. As Ed Dudley remembered, "Both of them were surprised." Ike was what one of his partners called a "congenital slicer," made more pronounced by a knee injury he suffered playing football at West Point. Ike's brother Edgar, who was an accomplished golfer, observed, "He has a good fundamental swing but he does not shift his weight correctly. He over-pivots a bit, takes too long a back-swing and can't quite get into position to hit the ball solidly. He has a good grip but he has not developed a grooved swing. Dwight is fully capable of getting 7 or 8 pars in 9 holes but he is also capable of getting an occasional 8 or 9 on any hole. His short game is weaker than his long and he has a little trouble on the greens."

In 1954, Ike began using a device that measured the timing of a golf swing, the impact of the club on the ball, and the distance the ball would have traveled. The inventor, Dr. Luis Alvarez of the University of California at Berkeley and a future Nobel Prize winner in physics, gave Ike a prototype of the device before it was offered to the public. Ike worked hard to master the 8-iron, 9-iron, and pitching wedge—the clubs he used most often to practice on the White House lawn. His Achilles heel was his putting. Ike took lessons, changed his grip and equipment, but never could master reading the greens. As James Reston of the *New York Times* reasoned, "If you cannot putt, you cannot learn to putt, even if you're President."

Ike had a distinctive style on the golf course; he was always well dressed. He favored muted colors and comfortable clothes and was admired by none other than Walter Hagen, who said, "I was the first and only golfer to be named to the list of the ten best dressed men . . . at least, I was the only one until our famous golfing President, General Dwight D. Eisenhower, took that away from me." In winter, he wore gray or brown flannel slacks; in the summer, he wore light brown or gray gabardine trousers. For shoes, he alternated between rubber-bottomed golf shoes or spikes. He often wore sunglasses and a cap to protect him from the sun. In 1955, Ike sparked a brief fashion fad when he donned a pink sport shirt and pink-visored cap that Gettysburg Country Club golf professional Dick Sleichter gave him from the pro shop. After playing a round, he was met on the eighteenth hole by "a whole bevy of lady members of the club and their small daughters" who were "wearing cool cotton summer dresses of the same pale, dusty pink of the Eisenhower cap and shirt ensemble."

183

Despite his impatience with his game and the pace of play, Ike was an affable playing partner. Ben Hogan once said, "He has the trick of making you feel at ease. He convinces you, without saying so, that he likes the game as much as you do." Not surprisingly, Eisenhower had many golfing companions, including Senator Taft, General Omar Bradley, Bob Hope, amateur Billy Jo Patton, Ben Hogan, and Byron Nelson. He sometimes played with his pilot, Lieutenant Colonel William G. Draper; his son, John; or his brothers, Edgar and Milton. Edgar, who began playing at the age of thirty-five, was an accomplished competitor, having won the Senior Northern Golf Association Title at the age of sixty-nine and the Washington State Senior Championship four times. In 1958, Edgar shot a 67 at the Tacoma Golf and Country Club and was given an award by *Golf Digest* for shooting under his age. When David, Ike's grandson, became old enough, he often joined Ike on the course, sometimes driving the golf cart and earning a tip of fifty cents. George Allen once quipped that he would have to report the wages to Dave Beck, the head of the Teamsters Union.

Ike saw golf as a practical way to build alliances and frequently invited men from both sides of the aisle in Congress, especially those he was trying to influence, for a friendly round. He would not discuss politics but used the round to size up his opponent. Democratic Congressmen J. William Fulbright and Stuart Symington were as likely to be invited as Republican Senator Robert Taft and Representative Jack Westland. Foreign leaders were put to the same test. Ike used golf as a political instrument, though often guided by an invisible hand. In 1954, he huddled with Victor Andrade, the Bolivian ambassador, to discuss golf at a dinner for the diplomatic corps. Andrade proved to be a good match for Ike, as both regularly played in the 80s to low 90s; but Andrade played in La Paz, where a golf course is fourteen thousand feet above sea level, making the ball go much farther. That same year, the Japanese ambassador expressed an interest in playing with Eisenhower. In 1955, Eisenhower entertained the prime minister of Thailand at Burning Tree; in March of 1956, he played golf with John A. Costello, the Irish prime minister, and later that year, he played with Louis S. St. Laurent, the Canadian prime minister. In 1957, he played with Japanese Prime Minister Nobusuke Kishi. Ike made his decision about whether to appoint Charles E. Bohlen to be the Russian ambassador only after they had played a round of golf in 1953. Anyone in world politics who wanted to negotiate with Ike was smart to buy a set of clubs.

At an April 30, 1954, cabinet meeting, Vice President Richard Nixon reported that a game of golf had a "beneficial effect" on a Republican senator who had not proven particularly cooperative. Playing with Ike sometimes had a political price, as Republican Senator Andrew F. Schoeppel from Kansas learned. Ike invited him for a round at Burning Tree because the senator had been waffling on an important farm bill. After the round, Ike gave Schoeppel a golf ball marked "Mr. President." Schoeppel voted for the bill and was later criticized by his Kansas farm constituents for having "sold their birthright for one golf ball." Little surprise, then, that in 1953 a *Washington Post* columnist would ask for a list of Ike's golfing partners. He justified his request by explaining, "those who golf or visit with the President in Augusta or at Burning Tree Club in Washington can vitally influence national policy."

185

Ike even strongly encouraged the men around him to embrace the game. Nixon had first played in 1951 in Sea Island, Georgia, after taking a few lessons. In 1952, while running on Ike's ticket and carrying out his responsibilities as a senator, Nixon played a total of five rounds, which explained why his score was often close to 120. After accepting the nomination for vice president, Nixon told Ike that he was not good enough to join him on the links: "I'd just spoil the round for a good golfer, so I don't try to play them." The *Washington Post* confirmed Nixon's assessment: "Frankly, Nixon is a dub who some day may break 100. He hooks and slices, forgets to keep his eye on the ball; that elbow insists on crooking. If there's a golf mistake to be made, he's apt to make it twice." Nixon was an inconsistent golfer but had some surprising moments. In 1952, he shot a 126 at Columbia Country Club; two years later, he shot an 86. Even so, many Washington-area country clubs, including Congressional Country Club in April 1953, extended honorary memberships to the vice president. In 1957, Secretary of the Treasury George M. Humphrey took up the game after being left out of foursomes for nearly five years. He took lessons and in April of that year traveled to Augusta National to spend time with Ike, armed with a new set of golf clubs. With no shortage of golfing buddies, Ike sought more capable opponents.

Ike's golf game brought him many honors. In July 1960, the city of Newport, Rhode Island, changed the name of Washington Square to Eisenhower Park. In 1960, the magazine *Monocle* suggested that, instead of a statue, the nation should build a golf course in Abilene, Kansas, for Ike and that it should be funded with "the sale of lost golf balls, retrieved by caddies all over the Nation." Each hole, then, could be named for one of Eisenhower's policies, suggesting "liberation," "cost of living," and "peace and prosperity."

The golfing world lined up to honor the nation's most famous duffer. On December 7, 1952, the Southern Seniors Golf Association offered Ike an honorary membership. In February 1955, the Golf Writers Association of America (GWAA) awarded Ike the William D. Richardson trophy for his outstanding contribution to golf. Other recipients included Bob Hope, Bing Crosby, Chick Evans, Richard Tufts, Scotty Fessenden, Robert Hudson, and Babe Didrikson Zaharias. Nearly every club and golf association wanted to lay claim to—or at least honor—the nation's first golfer. On January 26, 1956, Ike became the third recipient of the Ben Hogan Trophy (given to a person who overcomes a physical ailment or handicap to continue to play golf) at the annual Metropolitan Golf Writers' dinner in New York. The award, established by Portland businessman Robert A. Hudson, was given by the GWAA. Recovering from his heart attack, Ike could not attend the event, so he asked Jack Westland to accept it on his behalf. The award was established in 1953 by Lincoln A. Werden of the *New York Times*, then president of the GWAA, to honor Ben Hogan, who came back to win the 1950 U.S. Open after a nearly fatal car accident in 1949.

At the ceremony, Westland read a letter that Ike had sent him about the honor: "Dear Jack, I understand that the Golf Writers Association of America has named me the winner, for 1955, of the Ben Hogan Trophy. While I suspect that the award is a little premature, since I have yet to prove to myself that I can again play a respectable game (if indeed I ever did) I am nonetheless apprecia-

187

tive of their action. And I am more than grateful to you for your willingness to accept the trophy on my behalf. With many thanks and warm personal regards, Sincerely, Dwight D. Eisenhower." The award had been previously given to Ed Furgol (1954) and Babe Didrikson Zaharias (1953).

On June 14, 1956, Oak Hill Country Club, site of the fifty-sixth U.S. Open, honored four famous golfers with a tree dedication ceremony. Ben Hogan, Walter Hagen, Bobby Jones, and President Eisenhower had trees named after them in a park near the course's 602-yard par-5 thirteenth green. According to the *New York Times*, "Club officials said trees to be planted on the slight incline near the green would be dedicated to outstanding golfers. The park will be called the Hill of Fame."

In 1958, the World Amateur Golf Council was founded to encourage an international team competition, and it shone the spotlight on two of the nation's most famous amateur golfers, Ike and Bobby Jones. It also further reflects the association of Ike with the game of golf. Joseph C. Dey, executive director of the USGA, suggested an official amateur world championship, similar to the Davis Cup in tennis. Dey presented a plan to his fellow committeemen at the USGA's annual meeting in January and then to the Royal and Ancient Golf Club of St. Andrews in March. In May, the two governing bodies of golf held a planning meeting in Washington, D.C., inviting representatives from thirty-two nations. The U.S. Department of State blessed the idea, and the World Amateur Team Championship was born. The format for the event, to be held every two years, was medal play over seventy-two holes with a single round each day. The winner would receive the Eisenhower Trophy.

The first event, at St. Andrews from October 8 to 11, involved 115 players from twenty-nine countries. The trophy was inscribed, "To foster friendship and sportsmanship among Peoples of the World." By 1958, Jones had not played a full round of golf in a decade. This did not, however, prevent him from being named the nonplaying captain of the American team of the first World Amateur Team Championship. Because of Jones's limited mobility, the organizers of the event obtained a motorized golf cart that would allow him to follow the American team around the course. He was delighted to return to St. Andrews to help his country-men compete for the Eisenhower Trophy because he "felt that this might be my last opportunity to revisit the city and golf course that I love so well." Ike embraced the idea of the tournament but suggested that the duf-fers, of which he counted himself, be invited to play as goodwill ambassadors. On October 13, the Americans lost by two strokes to the Australian team, 222 to 224, in an eighteen-hole play-off.

The second tournament was held at Merion Golf Club in 1960, and the Americans, led by Jack Nicklaus, finished forty-two strokes better than the Australian team to win the trophy. Ike wrote a letter for the pro-gram in which he celebrated the event: "International competitions of this type, encouraging friendly rivalry among athletes of many countries, not only promote interest in the field of sports but also strengthen the tra-dition of fair play. This tradition is the only sound basis for building a world of mutual respect and understand-ing among men and nations." Two years later, the event went to Fuji Golf Course in Kawana, Japan, and the Americans won the Eisenhower Trophy for the second time in a row.

189

In part because it had been such an integral part of Ike's first term, golf became an important issue in his 1956 reelection campaign. Ike's decision to run for a second term was not an easy one. Mamie opposed it, as did Ike at first, largely because of his recent heart attack. His son, John, wrote a long letter to his father on January 19, 1956, detailing all the reasons he should retire. Ike spent the first Christmas after the heart attack in Key West trying to get back in shape by driving golf balls and taking walks, all while mulling over his decision to run again.

On February 11, 1956, four physicians, including Dr. Paul Dudley White of Boston and Colonel Thomas W. Mattingly at Walter Reed Hospital, compared x-rays of his heart before and after the September attack and found little damage. On February 14, they announced that "the President's health continues to be satisfactory." The next day, Ike left for Thomasville, Georgia, to stay at Milestone, the twelve-thousand-acre plantation owned by George M. Humphrey. His agenda included golf, bridge, and hunting. Facing his first drive in five months at the number one tee at Glen Arven Country Club, he quipped, "They ought to handicap fellows according to whether or not they've had a coronary." The press followed his every step and constantly commented on his "zip and zest." The weekend's strenuous activity convinced Ike and the public that he was fit enough to serve. Even Wall Street was relieved; on February 25, 1956, the stock market rose appreciably. The press attributed the rise to three factors, including "investor confidence" that came when "President Eisenhower played golf and laughed and joked at his mistakes as ordered by his physician." The 1956 election was symbolically decided in this small Georgia town. The nation saw that Ike was ready to run.

It came as little surprise, then, that on February 29, 1956, Eisenhower held a press conference outside the Indian Treaty Room to announce his candidacy. But he was not shy about explaining the terms under which he would serve: "The opinions and conclusions of the doctors that I continue to carry the burdens of the Presidency contemplate for me a regime of ordered work activity, interspersed with regular amounts of exercise, recreation and rest . . . readiness to obey the doctors, out of respect for my present duties and responsibilities, is mandatory in my case." Ike would again face a serious health issue on June 9, 1956, when he had to undergo emergency abdominal surgery for ileitis. The crisis gave additional fuel to the Democrats, who were advocating a slogan "A Vote for Eisenhower is a Vote for Nixon." Two months later, Ike seemed to have fully recovered and was at Burning Tree playing four holes of golf with his son, John. He then traveled to California for the Republican National Convention, where most of the news reported on his postconvention rounds at the exclusive Cypress Point Golf Club, a club with only 135 members, most of them millionaires.

In the 1956 election, Adlai Stevenson mocked Ike's love of golf and made it an issue on the campaign trail, but the strategy failed. As historian Richard J. Moss argued in his book *Golf and the American Country Club*, "Stevenson suggested that Eisenhower had become a part-time president and a full-time golfer who escaped behind fences of exclusive country clubs. The *Democratic Digest*, an official organ of the party's 1956 national campaign, issued a thirty-five-page indictment of Eisenhower. . . . Although much of this criticism was typical election year venom, it had a larger significance. By retreating to Augusta National, where he would eventually have his own tree and his

191

own cabin, and to Burning Tree, Ike confirmed many Americans' belief that golf, country clubs, and conservative Republican politics go together naturally." The Democrats hoped that Ike's health and his propensity for golf would sway voters; it had, instead, the opposite effect, as the *Sunday Times* in London reported: "But the health issue, according to the experience of some pollsters, has only further endeared Mr. Eisenhower to the people. The fact that he can afford the time to play so much golf—something many Americans would like to be able to emulate—is to them a sign of his ability to organize his busy life." Joseph and Stewart Alsop, writing for the *Washington Post*, concluded that Stevenson would "have to run against a man whom it is politically dangerous to criticize, on an issue it is even more dangerous to talk about."

Richard Tufts, president of the USGA and Pinehurst Country Club, suggested an unconventional campaign tactic for Eisenhower and Stevenson: "It would save a lot of money if they'd settle it on a golf course. Adlai is a golfer as well as Ike. Both know how to drive. Both have a good approach. The next couple of months will determine which is better at getting out of trouble." While the two men did not heed Tufts's advice, Ike's golf game became a critical asset during his reelection campaign in 1956. It helped prove to voters that he was healthy, though several editorials pointed out the strangeness of such logic. One writer from Silver Spring, Maryland, argued, "It seems to me that the naïve and pathetic interpretation of the outdoor activities—18 holes of golf, mind you! and a three hour shoot to boot!—of the President in his recent ten-day vacation as a significant test of strength and fortitude for another four years in the

White House is shameful." He went on to ask, "Who in his right mind would or could equate the intellectual, emotional and physical demands made on a man by the Presidency of the United States with those made on the same individual in playing a round of golf?" But for the most part, the country liked Ike, especially those with a penchant for the links. The *Washington Post* published a photograph of Frank Strafaci of Garden City, New York, holding a golf bag that he used in the North-South Tournament that said "Putt for Ike in '56."

Ike prevailed, beating Stevenson by an even wider margin than he had in 1952; he carried forty-one of the forty-eight states and won 56 percent of the popular vote, compared to 55 percent in the previous election. With this win, Ike became the first man to run for president after having suffered a heart attack, the fourth Republican elected to a second term, and, at sixty-six, the second oldest man to seek the office. The oldest, William Henry Harrison, was sixty-eight when he died only a month after his inauguration. Eisenhower made some important strides, becoming the first Republican since 1928 to carry the city of Chicago. But he remained unpopular in the Deep South, with the exception of Louisiana. Alabama, Arkansas, Georgia, Mississippi, Missouri, and North and South Carolina supported Stevenson. Ike's inability to win the region over would become a significant issue in the midst of his second term as he faced one of the most important issues of his administration—school desegregation. His first golf trip after the election was, once again, to Augusta National. This time, Bobby Jones was on hand to welcome his old friend.

EIGHT

THE PART-TIME PRESIDENT

It always gets into the papers when I play golf.
Why isn't it mentioned when I stay in the office
and work?

—Dwight D. Eisenhower

Ike used private golf courses to remove himself from the turmoil of the outside world and was frequently criticized for spending too much time on them. He deliberated some of the greatest challenges of his administration—notably, the desegregation of Central High School in Little Rock, Arkansas (1957), and the U-2 spy plane incident (1960)—with a golf club in his hand. Both crises challenged Ike's view of the country, and the public and the media used Ike's love of golf to help frame their understanding of the complex issues at hand. The two events also reveal the uneasy tension between golf (and all it came to represent in the late 1950s) and the nation's future.

As it had a generation earlier, when Bobby Jones graced the front page of newspapers, golf remained a sport dominated by white wealthy men, men like Ike and his favorite golfing partners. Yet, Ike—never far from his hardworking roots in Abilene, Kansas—worried that it was unpatriotic and undemocratic to keep a sport he loved from the people who had elected him to office. He supported efforts that encouraged juniors, women, and seniors to take up the game and was pleased to see that so many new public courses were being built during his presidency. In short, he wanted everyone to play. But his definition of *everyone* was shaped by his generation's filtered view of America, a perception blurred by race, gender, region, and class.

Ike's political philosophy, personal history, and character appealed to middle-class America, average hardworking people who dreamed of trading in their Chevrolet for a Cadillac and upgrading their Rancher home in Levittown for a Country Clubber. Ike eschewed class distinctions; he and his brothers were born into the River Brethren, a Mennonite sect in Kansas that stressed self-reliance, thrift, and simplicity. For all its rules, golf is a relatively simple game that depends solely on individual effort and a strict adherence to fair play. For anyone who has ever played it, golf is a humbling game, and that appealed to Ike as much as anything else about the sport.

Paradoxically, even while he personally embraced democratizing the game, he benefited from its elitism. Ike wanted everyone to play golf, but he didn't want to play golf with just anybody. He played at exclusive private golf clubs that were a far cry from public courses or run-of-the-mill country clubs. He carefully selected his playing partners from among his wealthy and influential peers and tried to keep his game out of public view. But the press would not oblige; they reported on many of his rounds and tried, though often unsuccessfully, to record every shot. More and more, Ike used golf as a refuge, a place to escape the roiling issues that complicated his second term as president. One of these issues—the emerging civil rights movement—was about to change the rules of the game that Ike so loved. There was no golf course on Earth that could shelter him from the coming storm.

When Ike was sworn in for his first term as president, there were more than 156 million Americans, and 10 percent were black. Long before that cold day in January 1953, African American men and women had played golf in America in spite of segregation. Barred from competitions sponsored by the USGA and PGA, black players such as Ted Rhodes and Charlie Sifford competed in all-black tournaments organized by the United Golf Association (UGA), a tour for black golfers founded in 1928. Though African Americans had played in USGA events as early as 1896, by the 1920s, both explicit and informal racial barriers had been erected, precluding them from the same clubs or associations as white players. The Caucasian race clause made things crystal clear for PGA members of color like Dewey Brown. A light-skinned African American golfer from North Carolina, Brown joined the PGA of America in 1928 and remained an active member until his affiliation was unceremoniously terminated in 1934, when the clause went into effect. With new rules freshly printed in black and white, so to speak, Brown—like other non-Caucasian members—was a persona non grata. The game of golf—at least the game Ike played—would remain white-only until Ike left office.

197

The civil rights movement did not begin with Rosa Parks's defiant gesture on a Montgomery bus in 1955. As early as the 1930s, a small group of African Americans became vocal critics of segregation in the armed forces, in restaurants, in public parks, and in sports. By 1955, average men and women were no longer content to remain silent on the issue. Even with the passage of *Brown v. Board of Education* on May 17, 1954, Ike managed to generally steer clear of this issue through his first term, but after his reelection, he could no longer avoid direct confrontations with demands for equality. One of the greatest challenges of Eisenhower's presidency came in September 1957 over the desegregation of Central High School in Little Rock, Arkansas. For two of the main players in this drama—Eisenhower and Arkansas Governor Orval Eugene Faubus—Central High had very little to do with social justice and a great deal to do with the politics of the day.

Little Rock became a battle of historic proportions with two unlikely combatants. At an earlier time, Eisenhower and Faubus could have been friends, even golfing partners. They were both born into poor families. Eisenhower's father had lost his money in a failed business venture in Denison, Texas. The family moved to Abilene in 1891 to allow Ike's father to take a position in a creamery. Ike and his five brothers contributed to the family household, selling vegetables and working odd jobs. Faubus's childhood home was constructed from unfinished sawmill lumber; his mother had to carry water to the kitchen from a nearby spring; and Orval attended a grammar school in one of Arkansas's many one-room schoolhouses. He would be the first Arkansas governor to come from the state's northwest hill country.

198

Ike's support of the nine black students seeking admission to Central High did not reflect his personal politics. He was no more in favor of wholesale desegregation than Lincoln was of quickly emancipating the slaves during the Civil War. Ike took a progressive stand on race for two reasons. First and foremost, it was his responsibility as president to uphold federal law established by the 1954 *Brown* decision. To do less would undermine the very office of the presidency. Second, he was keenly aware that his actions in Little Rock would have far-reaching foreign policy consequences around the world. Prior to Little Rock, the United States had been roundly criticized for its support of white supremacy, and it was often compared to the apartheid regime in South Africa (a regime Ike had openly supported). Indeed, America's rampant racism did threaten to tarnish the nation's reputation as a global power at the dawning of the Cold War. In 1946, a few New York hotels refused to accommodate United Nations delegates from Liberia, Ethiopia, and Haiti because they were black. In 1955, the French press widely condemned the acquittal by an all-white jury of white vigilantes accused of lynching fourteen-year-old Emmett Till in Money, Mississippi, for talking to a white female shopkeeper. That same year, Autherine Lucy, a young black woman who was turned down by the University of Alabama, was offered admission to and financial aid from the University of Copenhagen after her plight was reported internationally. Around the world—from Bombay to Stockholm—the media criticized America's handling of race issues.

Ike and his administration were afraid that continued international scrutiny of the nation's racial policies would impede America's attempts to extend influence

199

over African and Asian nations. Ike worried that these nations were vulnerable to overtures from the USSR and other Communist states as they were transitioning from colonial rule. Historian Cary Fraser argued, "Little Rock had become the Suez of the Eisenhower administration—a moment of crisis that forced a fundamental and radical reassessment of existing approaches to dealing with the world of color." To put it simply, Ike believed that Communists would use evidence of racial strife in the United States as propaganda to persuade countries that had not yet declared their political allegiance to reject the democratic ideals advanced by the United States.

Faubus's decision to prevent black students from attending Central High was not about desegregation but about political survival. Arkansas governors stood for election every two years, and unlike most of his peers in other states, Faubus had neither education nor wealth. If he lost the next election, he would not make a seamless transition into a prestigious corporation, law firm, or university; he would be forced to return to rural Arkansas with his tail between his legs. That fear of failure and the resulting isolation, more than any other factor, drove his actions at Central High. Until Little Rock, Faubus had been a moderate on the question of race, certainly in comparison to other southern governors, such as Marvin Griffin of Georgia and George Wallace of Alabama. His record as governor shows that he appointed more African Americans to state positions than any of his predecessors. Even so, Faubus ultimately allied with Roy Harris, the head of the racist Citizens' Councils, not because of any shared ideology but because, in 1957, it was unclear which way the political tide would turn. Faubus simply had to make his best guess.

Eisenhower and Faubus were headed on a collision course, and there would be little time for concern over the fate of nine children caught between them. Elizabeth Eckford, Ernest Green, Jefferson Thomas, Terrance Roberts, Carlotta Walls, Minnijean Brown, Gloria Ray, Thelma Mothershed, and Melba Patillo were about to be thrown into Central High School as a sacrifice for justice. The widespread media coverage of their arrival on the steps of the formerly all-white Central High turned these students overnight into symbols of the nation's second Reconstruction, like Emmett Till and Rosa Parks before them. The African American community did not randomly select the nine students; they were, in typical fashion, given little choice in the matter. White school superintendent Virgil Blossom, who began with a list of eighty potential candidates and eventually whittled the number down to thirty-two, controlled the whole process. The students had to be both smart and brave. Eventually, the list was reduced to seventeen names and then finally to nine. The chosen ones were coached in the practice of nonviolence. They were not to respond in any way to the taunts and threats that awaited them. They understood that their success, three years after the first *Brown* decision, would shape the nation's approach to desegregation. Though a few other cities had made peaceful transitions, most districts in the South took "all deliberate speed," the timetable set forth in *Brown*, to mean that they could choose when to comply. And nobody seemed to be in a hurry.

Arkansas was the last place in the South that anyone expected the civil rights movement to make the evening news around the nation. That was supposed to happen in Georgia, Mississippi, or Alabama. When the second *Brown* decision was handed down in 1955, Governor

201

Faubus said, "Our reliance must be upon the good will that exists between the races—the goodwill that has long made Arkansas a model for other Southern states in all matters affecting the relationship between the races." Compared to its more overtly racist neighbors, Arkansas in 1957 was a relatively moderate state, one that had already peacefully integrated the state university, several smaller colleges, medical and law schools, some public schools, and the bus system. Few anticipated a conflict in Little Rock, mainly because Faubus had supported the gradual desegregation plan for Central High. He had been in conversation with the school superintendent and understood the plan. Faubus was a moderate, and Arkansas was going to be a model southern state in which to implement *Brown*. What no one saw coming, including Ike or Faubus himself, was the governor's last-minute change in position, brought on by pressure from other southern politicians. On August 22, two weeks before the planned desegregation effort, segregationist Governor Marvin Griffin of Georgia and Roy Harris visited Faubus with the sole purpose of making sure that he toed the line. Recognizing that his political future was in jeopardy, he reluctantly obeyed.

On September 2, 1957—Labor Day and the day before the public schools in Little Rock were scheduled to open—Faubus announced on television that the Arkansas National Guard had been called out to prevent nine black students from attending Central High the next day, ostensibly to avoid violence. When a reporter later asked one of the guardsmen why they were there, he replied candidly, "To keep the niggers out."

The success of Faubus's gamble depended upon Ike's next move. Faubus knew—as did much of the nation—that Ike did not support a radical revision of the racial

order. The governor knew that Ike was a social conservative with divided loyalties, mainly a result of his
upbringing. As a boy in Abilene, he and his brother
Edgar, like many children, played a game called crack
the whip, where one child was designated as black and
then chased and tormented by the other players. As
cadet at the then all-white West Point, Ike befriended
many racist southern officers and was mostly insulated
from the concerns of black America. While serving in
North Africa, he wrote home to his son, John, in 1943:
"I . . . find myself living in a comfortable house, nicely
heated, staffed by Mickey [McKeogh] and a group of
darkies that take gorgeous care of me." Though Ike
worked hard to ensure that black and white troops were
treated fairly under his command, his views on race
were fairly typical. His prejudices were, as historian
Peter Lyon argued, "rooted more in intellectual lazi-
ness than in positive conviction." Ike shared the belief
of many white Americans that blacks were making
adequate progress toward attaining civil rights and that
there was little need to press the issue.

Though he rarely discussed his position in public, Ike
confided his views on race to one of his speechwriters,
Arthur Larson, who reported that Ike had said of *Brown*,
"I personally think the decision was wrong." Ike echoed
the point in a July 22, 1957, letter to his longtime friend
Swede Hazlett: "I think that no other single event has
so disturbed the domestic scene in many years as did
the Supreme Court's decision of 1954." Even though
in his later writings and speeches Ike defended integration, he always thought that the Supreme Court had
overstepped its authority with *Brown*. Ike believed that
fair access and economic opportunity did not necessar-

203

ily mean social equality, indicating that his views on race, like the majority of white Americans, were still rooted in the nineteenth century. He was not one to change his mind easily, and he ultimately blamed himself for *Brown*. After all, he had appointed Earl Warren, governor of California, to be the chief justice of the Supreme Court. Indeed, he privately called it the "biggest damnfool mistake I ever made."

Like no other issue, civil rights stymied Ike. Never one to question authority, he understood his obligation to uphold the 1954 Supreme Court decision. The day after the ruling, Ike gathered the D.C. commissioners and asked them to integrate Washington as an example. After the meeting, he simply said, "The Supreme Court has spoken and I am sworn to uphold the constitutional process in this country; and I will obey." Eisenhower seemed to be trying to convince himself. He even enlisted evangelist Billy Graham to preach "moderation and decency" in all areas involving race relations. He once told Nixon, "No man is discharging his duty if he does nothing in the presence of injustice." He would even go as far as to sign a civil rights bill (albeit a weak one, but the first since Reconstruction) on September 9, 1957, in the midst of the Little Rock crisis. But his heart was not in it.

Eisenhower knew that some blacks suffered under segregation, but he did not believe that the nation should be force-fed such a major change in the status quo. He even hated to use the word *discrimination* in public speeches, believing that it was an overstatement of the situation. He rarely sought the advice of E. Frederic Morrow, special assistant to the president and the first African American man to hold an executive position in the White House, and instead repeatedly resisted meeting with leaders like Martin Luther King Jr. and Adam Clayton Powell. Morrow lamented the unfolding events: "I have been powerless to do anything. The President's advisors have not asked me my thinking on these matters, and I am too well-schooled in protocol to advance any uninvited ideas." Ike once told Earl Warren that segregationists "are not bad people." He continued, "All they are concerned about is to see that their sweet little girls are not required to sit in school alongside some big overgrown Negroes." He was of another generation, and this antebellum cliché was still very much alive for Ike.

In an effort to find common ground with segregationists, who had supported his rise to the White House, Ike frequently reminded southern politicians that he was one of them. He told the same story, over and over again, hoping that it would gain currency. He was born in Texas and had lived in the South, and some of his favorite golf courses were below the Mason-Dixon Line. Yet, as a Mennonite, he abhorred inequality, and his actions reveal his divided allegiances. Though the desegregation of the armed forces began under Truman, Ike oversaw its implementation. He also ended segregation in the Veterans Administration hospitals, schools on military posts, naval bases among civilian employees, and the District of Columbia government—areas directly under his jurisdiction as president. He accomplished all of this without external pressure, public debate, or fanfare. This is how he liked to work—sure, steady, and out of public view. Man to man. That would have been his approach at Little Rock had the media and Faubus not turned Central High into an international showdown over racial equality. When this happened, Ike became unsure and afraid.

205

When Orval Faubus sent in 270 National Guardsmen to keep nine teenagers out of Central High on September 3, Ike was caught off guard, and he hated to be unprepared to face any enemy. This was the man who in June 1941 had drawn up the entire Allied plan for the Pacific in three hours after a brief meeting with General George C. Marshall. He knew war and how to win it. Yet, in the first days of the Little Rock crisis, his skills as a strategist failed him, and he had trouble seeing a clear path ahead. On September 4, Eisenhower left Washington for a Newport vacation, where he believed he could sort this out. A decisive plan was the key to success; a few days of golf and fishing might help. Ike could see the long, beautiful fairways of Newport Country Club beckoning him. The next morning, he walked to the base headquarters to give himself time to think.

Though not one to delegate responsibility to subordinates, Ike decided that the best strategy was to allow someone else to decide how the situation would be handled. His hope was that Ronald N. Davies, the federal district judge assigned to the Little Rock case, would overrule Arkansas's attempt to delay integration. Then Faubus might pull back. Failing that, Attorney General Herbert Brownell Jr. could call in the federal troops and force Faubus to withdraw. Either option would absolve Eisenhower from having to make the decision directly. Ike believed that no law or court case was going to change people's hearts, and more than anything else, he did not want to personally force the issue. Above all, he wished to avoid, as Senator Hubert Humphrey suggested, leading the nine children to the school himself. That would make him a symbol of a cause he did not support. Ike hoped that he could delay any decisions and simply play golf.

Inaction was not Ike's style. Just as the Little Rock situation was becoming a crisis, he made quick a decision to send arms to Jordan, Lebanon, Turkey, and Iraq to help remove the Soviet-dominated Syrian regime. While he could solve one crisis six thousand miles away in two days, he mulled over what to do at home. He could not seem to act. Instead, he read the newspapers and throughout his vacation kept asking his close confidants for advice, something he had always done in his military days. But still he waited and brooded. Little Rock was just one battle; there was a much bigger war raging, and he needed to assemble the troops to thwart the enemy. But they seemed to be coming at him from all sides. Ike was getting insistent telegrams from the NAACP and the National Urban League, urging immediate action. The international press in London, Tokyo, and Paris called Ike's inaction a disgrace. Amis Guthridge, attorney for the Capital Citizens' Council, a local branch of the larger anti-integrationist group, obsessed over the need to "maintain the high principles upon which our Southern society was founded." Those principles were put into action in Birmingham, Alabama, on September 7, when two Ku Klux Klansmen confessed to castrating and torturing an African American boy in anticipation of "race mixing." School integration was not going much better elsewhere. On September 5, an attempt in Charlotte, North Carolina, resulted in a near riot. The next day, nine black students were turned away from schools in Arlington, Virginia. On September 9, a new elementary school in Nashville, Tennessee, was dynamited the day before one black child was scheduled to attend.

In Little Rock, Governor Faubus was reading the same newspapers as Ike, but he was developing a different plan. He worked hard to ensure that he was portrayed as a sympathetic figure, especially in the southern press. Faubus did not care about the *New York Times* or the *Washington Post*. Those readers were not going to end up in a voting booth in Arkansas. Though Ike sympathized with black children who wanted access to a good education, he, too, needed the support of southern politicians and business leaders. They were Ike's golfing partners and campaign donors, and, like Ike, they did not wish to upset the status quo. Ike was convinced he could settle the Little Rock crisis with a little help from Davies and Brownell. This may have been the case had Faubus not forced his hand.

On September 14, more than a week after Faubus challenged federal authority by calling out the National Guard, Ike agreed to meet with him in Newport. Ike was certain, perhaps overconfident, that he could be persuasive and charming enough to solve this problem and get back to his Newport vacation. Faubus would, of course, be reasonable. Would the governor travel that far to defy his commander in chief to his face? Brownell was against it; he knew that Faubus was mainly interested in his reelection campaign and was using Ike. The president asked to meet with Faubus privately to get a measure of the man. Then Brownell and Sherman Adams joined them. For more than an hour, Faubus was contrite and friendly. He said he would comply with the court order but pleaded that he simply needed more time and asked for "understanding and patience." Ike was prepared to consent, even capitulate, until Brownell stopped him. While listening to Brownell's explanation of the timetable set by the courts, Ike finally realized that Faubus was stalling. At that moment, the meeting became much less friendly, as Ike pushed the governor to comply with the planned integration. Faubus finally consented and said as much at a short press conference after the meeting. All seemed well as the Arkansas governor chatted and posed for photographs with Brownell and Eisenhower before Ike headed out for an afternoon of golf.

Ike left the morning meeting believing that he had convinced the governor to reconsider his position. He was relieved because the alternatives were not appealing. According to the Justice Department, Ike had three choices if Faubus refused to comply. He could prosecute the Arkansas governor for a federal crime under Section 252 of Title 18 in the United States Code. He could withhold federal funds from the Arkansas National Guard. Or he could invoke a Civil War statute—50 U.S.C. Section 202—authorizing the use of federal troops or National Guard units of any state to quell a "rebellion against authority of the Government." But Ike firmly believed that none of these options would be necessary. He had won, and with just a firm handshake and some well-intentioned cajoling.

Satisfied, he finished up his morning appointments, had a quiet lunch, played golf, and settled in to watch *The Proud Ones* that evening with William Robinson. Faubus, however, had returned to Little Rock as defiant as ever, determined to keep the troops in place and the students out of Central High. When Ike finally realized that Faubus had lied to him, he acted quickly and decisively. Ike's fear that Little Rock could become a political liability turned to outrage. Faubus's blatant betrayal, as far as Ike was concerned, deserved punishment. Eisenhower, who had been waffling about what to do for several weeks, finally made a decision and began to look more like a five-star general than a politician.

209

No subordinate was going to humiliate him. On September 24, Ike federalized the Arkansas National Guard and sent the 101st Airborne to Little Rock to escort the nine black students to Central High on September 25. When the soldiers finally arrived at Minnijean Brown's house to escort her to school, she said, "For the first time in my life I felt like an American citizen."

As the Little Rock situation made headlines around the world, Ike was accused of running the presidency from a golf course. A brief look at his September calendar that year shows that this was in fact the case. From September 5 to 24, the day he made a national television appearance to address the issue of school integration, Ike played fourteen rounds of golf, many of them at Newport Country Club. Sherman Adams recounted how Ike responded to Faubus's telegram on September 12: "Jim Hagerty brought the wire to him as he was holing out on the first green. They sat down together in a golf cart that the President had used most of the time since his heart attack. Eisenhower studied the telegram and together they worded a reply that Hagerty took back to the naval base. Then the President walked on to the second tee and drove off." Two days later, on September 14, the day he met with Governor Faubus, Ike played an afternoon round at Newport with Robinson, H. G. Cushing, and Norman Palmer. Ike finally returned to Washington ten days later to make a television address to the nation about the crisis, conceding that "it did not sound well to have it said that his speech to the nation came from the vacation White House." Privately, he confessed to Nixon that the "stupidity and duplicity of one called Faubus" was going to end his golfing vacation.

While Ike was golfing, sailing, and fishing in Newport during most of the month of September, nine brave black children in Little Rock were negotiating the dangerous and volatile environment at Central High. They were harassed in the halls, assaulted in the bathrooms, and showered with racial epithets. Even the 101st Airborne could not protect the children from the taunts of their peers, largely because other students either actively participated in the harassment or did nothing to prevent it. Few offered to help the Little Rock Nine, as they came to be known.

Ike paid a high price for his decision to oppose Governor Faubus and the segregationists. For many southerners, he had committed an unpardonable sin. By using federal troops to solve a local social problem, he had undermined states' rights. Most whites below the Mason-Dixon Line believed that Eisenhower had turned on the South. They held Ike personally responsible for images of middle- and working-class white citizens being held at gunpoint by uniformed troops. For some, Little Rock was a second Reconstruction. This was not lost on Ike, who had won the presidency twice with the support of southern Democrats who crossed party lines to elect him. Richard Russell, the stately and racist senator from Georgia and a longtime friend of Ike's, publicly and privately excoriated Eisenhower. He couldn't win. Blacks were no happier than whites. Even Louis Armstrong criticized him, refusing (in protest of Ike's tepid handling of the crisis) to participate in a goodwill tour to the Soviet Union sponsored by the State Department. A Gallup poll taken nine months before Little Rock gave Ike a 79 percent approval rating; in early October, it dropped to 64 percent. Only 36 percent of the South approved of Ike's actions.

The southern press, from Chattanooga, Tennessee, to Jackson, Mississippi, barbecued Ike. One editorial

211

declared, "The Republican party is dead in the South."
Nowhere was it more obvious than in Augusta, Georgia. Ike had joined Augusta National Golf Club, one
of the most exclusive golf clubs in the nation, in 1948,
and his defense of *Brown v. Board of Education* in Little
Rock jeopardized the long friendships he had with men
who mattered to him. Though not all southerners, most
ANGC members, like most Americans, shared Governor Faubus's outlook on civil rights. Privately, so did Ike,
but it was his public actions in Little Rock on which
Augusta—like the nation at large—would judge him.

More than anything, Ike hoped the nation would
understand that his decision in Little Rock was made
in the interest of protecting federal authority (and, by
extension, the office of the president) and in an effort
to combat the spread of Communism. More than anything, Ike hoped the South would forgive him. In the
midst of the crisis, while playing golf at Newport, Ike
said to his longtime friend Slats Slater, "You know, Slats,
people can't dislike or disapprove of me too much when
day after day they come out here just to get a glimpse
of me." He would find out otherwise during his annual
visit to Augusta National in November 1957.

Some historians and journalists have claimed that
when Ike arrived for his sixteenth visit to Augusta as
president, he was booed down Washington Street.
There is little evidence to support this contention, but
he certainly received a cool reception. Two days before
he arrived, the *Augusta Chronicle* printed an editorial
entitled "Advice on the Home Front," where the author
warned that "it is time for the federal government to
stop making war on the south." Worried that the city
might spurn their favorite son, community leaders, on
November 16, 1957, made "special efforts to assure

the President that he was as welcome as ever." Mayor Hugh L. Hamilton explained, "I think there is a great deal of ill-feeling toward the President in Augusta as a result of Little Rock. . . . I may not agree with the President on some occasions, but he is the President of the United States and I certainly respect the office he holds." Slater recalled the reception Ike received after Little Rock two years later in his diary entry for October 22nd to 25th, 1959: "When we drove to the [Augusta] airport Sunday afternoon, there was a large crowd waiting to send him off. As we got into the air you could see hundreds of cars parked in the whole area at the field and along the road. That must have made him feel quite happy, perhaps in contrast to this feeling when we went to Augusta right after the Little Rock/Faubus affair when all of the South was so deeply aroused—to the point where the crowds at Augusta were almost nil."

The South's response to Little Rock should not have come as a surprise. A year before the incident, on November 6, 1956, Richmond County voters, which included the city of Augusta, supported Ike, but the neighboring counties did not. Ike's stand on race in the South may have been understood or even respected, but it was not forgiven. Supporters of integration tried to make Augusta National and the president's membership there a symbol. Three years after the Little Rock crisis, on May 2, 1960, eleven of Augusta's Paine College students were arrested in a series of bus demonstrations and fined $45 for violating a segregation ordinance. Five of the eleven students filed a lawsuit in August against the city, Augusta Coach Company, the mayor, and the police chief. Throughout the year, Paine students protested nonviolently, participating in "kneel-ins" to get equal access to white churches and

213

boycotting downtown restaurants. On December 10, 1960, sixty students and other demonstrators protested the visit of President Eisenhower. They gathered outside Augusta National Golf Club, where they held signs that said, "Wrong will fail, right will prevail."

In 1960, Dwight D. Eisenhower and his administration faced another serious crisis, which stretched Ike's brinkmanship to the limit and would oddly enough also be linked with golf. On the Soviet holiday May Day (May 1) 1960, two weeks before Ike was scheduled to attend a summit intended to improve U.S.–Soviet relations, an American U-2 spy plane was shot down and crashed near Sverdlovsk, an industrial town twelve hundred miles into the heart of the Soviet Union. The U-2 planes, designed by Clarence "Kelly" Johnson to reach an altitude of 100,000 feet and built by Lockheed Aircraft Corporation, had been flying missions since 1955, and the Russians knew it. The planes were equipped with cameras precise enough to take images of serial numbers on the sides of military equipment on the ground. This was not the first crash related to a secret mission for which the United States would have to answer; in 1956, sixteen Americans were killed when a reconnaissance plane plunged into the China Sea. The incident in the Soviet Union, though, was a different story. Ironically, the U-2 flights had been suspended in 1959, but Ike resumed them on April 9, 1960, just a month before the Paris Summit Conference.

The Soviets' sophisticated radar had detected the planes, and Soviet government officials had been protesting the flights, without the knowledge of the American people, through diplomatic channels. When

Gary Francis Powers's plane was lost, the Eisenhower administration at first denied authorizing such a flight. On May 5, the State Department released a misleading statement claiming that the U-2 was an unarmed weather observation plane that accidentally violated Soviet airspace because the pilot, deprived of oxygen, lost consciousness. The administration's hope was that the pilot would have followed protocol, committing suicide by using the poisoned needle hidden inside a silver dollar and beginning the sequence that would help the plane self-destruct. Eventually, Ike was forced to admit that he had supported the clandestine operation after the Soviets announced on May 7 that the pilot, Powers, a CIA operative, had parachuted to the ground and had been captured alive. A statement issued by State Department Press Officer Lincoln White that same day concluded, "It is in relation to the danger of surprise attack that planes of the type of unarmed civil U-2 aircraft have made flights along the Frontier of the Free World for the past four years."

In his book *Eisenhower: Portrait of the Hero,* Peter Lyon argued, "The affair . . . plunged the Eisenhower administration into what was by any test its most embarrassing predicament, a carnival of foolishness, a parade of lies and blunders and self-deceptions that led the government of the United States, for the first time in its history, to the humiliating admission that it had knowingly lied and that it was guilty of espionage and of having deliberately violated the territory of another sovereign power." Ike's dishonesty was such a serious blunder that he told his personal secretary, Ann Whitman, that he wanted to resign. Ironically, just prior to the incident, Ike had advised his cabinet, "when you get caught in

215

this town, don't get cute and try to cover it up. You'll just get more entangled in your own lies." He told his friend Virgil Pinkley, "The greatest asset any occupant of the White House has is the trust of the American people and total credibility. If the president loses this, he has lost his greatest strength. Therefore, I admitted to ordering the flight."

The administration's mishandling put the détente that Eisenhower and Nikita Khrushchev had worked so hard to achieve over the past three years in jeopardy. Following a series of public statements and two weeks after the incident, Ike boarded a plane to Paris for the summit with the Soviet premier and other heads of state. On May 16, Khrushchev denounced Eisenhower for allowing espionage flights, exclaiming, "This man Eisenhower comes here posing as my friend. All the time I was at Camp David, he pretended to be my friend. At the same time, he was directing overflights of our territory by American U-2 airplanes to gather Intelligence information. He calls me a friend. Actually, he stands there with blood dripping from his hands down to his elbows and falling in pools to the floor." With that, the Soviet premier walked out of the Paris summit. Privately, Khrushchev was disappointed. As Piers Brendon reported, "He was definitely looking forward to entertaining Ike in Russia, had built a bijou palace for him overlooking Lake Baikal, had learned golf so that he could play the president, and had even planned to construct his own version of Disneyland outside Moscow."

As the crisis was unfolding and before the summit, the New York Times reported, "Premier Khrushchev's sensational speech shattered the calm of this hesitant spring day in the capital. President Eisenhower was at his Gettysburg farm and he managed to play eighteen holes of golf, but high officials were on the phone to him at various times." Such coverage gave Khrushchev the opportunity to declare, "There is a strained situation after all, and yet the President has chosen to go off to his golf course." To the nation, facing one of the most serious crises of the Cold War, President Eisenhower, at that moment, seemed to be a man who put golf before world peace.

The Soviet people may have been more forgiving. Five months before the incident, on January 4, 1960, the *New York Times* included a brief story about the growth of golf in the Soviet Union, focusing on the establishment of several courses in the Crimea. A course near Moscow was reportedly scheduled to open in the spring of 1960, just as the U-2 incident was unfolding. The story speculated, "If East-West exchanges are accomplishing nothing else, they seem to be popularizing that old Scottish, and now bourgeois game of golf in the Soviet Union. In fact, Moscow is publicly hinting that President Eisenhower and Premier Khrushchev may be able to hold a summit meeting next spring on the first tee of a Moscow golf course." The events in May made such a pairing impossible. Khrushchev expressed his dismay, claiming in August 1960 that he did not know what to do with the golf clubs that an American company sent to him in Moscow to give to Eisenhower. He also quipped, "Your country is sometimes funny, as for example the way you choose your Presidents. Roosevelt proved that a President could serve for life. Truman proved that anyone could be elected. Eisenhower proved that your country can be run without a President." A look at Ike's daily calendar from May 1 to May 14 gives Khrushchev plenty of ammunition; Ike

217

played or practiced golf nine times. On that last day, as he was preparing to leave for Paris, he even attended a golf tournament at Burning Tree Club.

Ike, as always, weathered the storm. Powers, however, was sentenced to two years in jail and finally exchanged for Rudolf Abel, a Soviet prisoner, in February 1962. In hindsight, Richard Nixon may have ultimately paid the price; he later wrote that the U-2 incident was a likely factor in the close election he lost to John F. Kennedy. A few years later, it was a topic of humor at the National Golf Awards dinner in 1963. Senator Hugh Scott joked that Khrushchev cancelled the summer meeting in 1960 with Eisenhower because the U-2 flights exposed "brown spots on the greens of the only golf course in the Soviet Union."

As the events involving Little Rock and the U-2 spy plane reveal, Eisenhower faced some of his greatest challenges on the golf course and was roundly criticized for it. In some ways, he was an easy target, as Louis Galambos argued in the introduction to *Reexamining the Eisenhower Presidency*: "There were the fumbled press conferences—not all of which were products of calculated obfuscation. There were the wealthy friends—a few of whom did indeed take advantage of their privileged positions. There was his slowness to move against the demagogue Joseph McCarthy. His slowness to speak out for civil rights. His lowbrow reading habits. His bridge game and, above all, his golf. What more could a clever journalist posing as a historian need to caricature the man?" Apparently, they simply needed a pen, paper, and a decent rendering of a golf ball.

When he decided, after his heart attack, to run for reelection in 1956, Ike was honest with the American

218

people, confessing that he could only be a part-time president, who needed recreation to help build his strength. He kept his word. Nearly a year after his second inauguration, the *New York Times* reported that "out of 1,777 days as President, Eisenhower had spent 583 days resting, vacationing, or recovering from his illnesses, for a total of a year and a half." Despite full disclosure, Ike's critics routinely called him the "first non-working president in history," "an absentee president," and a "golf player who never lets the presidency interfere with his game." Adlai Stevenson, then governor of Illinois, accused Ike of "gazing down the fairway of indifference." Democratic activist Rexford G. Tugwell once said that while John Foster Dulles, Ike's secretary of state, was "playing God," Ike was "playing golf." In 1960, New York University government professor Louis William Koenig published *The Invisible Presidency*. A question often heard of the era was, "If Sherman Adams dies, who will become president?"

There are countless examples of Ike choosing golf over his official and ceremonial duties. On February 23, 1953, Ike sent Commander Edward L. Beach, a naval aide, to lay a wreath at the tomb of George Washington for Presidents' Day. In the Senate that day, John Sherman Cooper, a Republican from Kentucky, read Washington's Farewell Address. Richard H. Poff, a Republican from Virginia, delivered it to the House of Representatives. Ike was reported to have "followed the example of many fellow Washingtonians on this sunny holiday by avoiding business in favor of a round of golf. He played a round at Burning Tree Club in nearby Maryland." In his second term, Ike was also criticized for not watching Nikita Khrushchev's presentation on disarmament before the United Nations, opting instead

219

for a round of golf. In 1960, the *Chicago Tribune* ran a headline that read, "Ike Golfs with an Ear Cocked Toward Congo."

On April 14, 1953, the *New York Times* reported that the Washington Senators and New York Yankees game, which launched the American League's pennant race, was rained out and rescheduled for Thursday evening. This gave Ike a chance to redeem himself in the eyes of baseball fans. He had earlier declined to pitch the first ball because he was scheduled for a golf trip in Augusta. When asked about the snub, one fan asked, "Who needs him?" Shirley Povich, writing for the *Washington Post*, commented, "For baseball, the last measure of hurt comes not from Mr. Eisenhower's decision to bypass the opener, but from his preference for golf on that day. Golf isn't even a game of the people. It's for zealots only." Fans would have had to accept Richard Nixon as the substitute. But with the rescheduled game, Ike had a chance to mend "his baseball fences." His participation was an important part of the Senators' tradition; a sitting president had thrown out the first ball, with only a few exceptions, since William H. Taft's time. Ike would never make the mistake of allowing his golf schedule to interfere with this important ceremony associated with the nation's pastime again; each spring, Ike made sure he had a baseball in his hand. He would, however, periodically skip other events for golf, such as the 1954 Army-Navy game. On January 29, 1955, Eisenhower declined to attend a dinner hosted by the National Business Publications and present the Silver Quill award to former President Herbert Hoover because he was flying to Augusta that morning.

Much of the criticism may be chalked up to partisan politics. About six months after Ike took office, John

Fitzpatrick, writing for *Golf Digest*, remarked, "Needless to say there has been some criticism of Eisenhower's golfing proclivities. Political opponents have inferred that he seems more interested in breaking 90 on the golf course than in breaking the deadlock in Korea." Throughout his presidency, Ike's golf game was on the front page of nearly every daily newspaper. He was photographed with a golf club in his hands even when the headlines had nothing to do with golf, giving the false impression that he was not engaged with the affairs of state or he was out of touch with ordinary people. Joseph and Stewart Alsop, in a nationally syndicated newspaper column, called Ike "a nice old gentleman in a golf cart." During a press conference on March 27, 1957, regarding the federal budget crisis, one reporter asked Ike if he could do "without that pair of helicopters that have been proposed for getting you out to the golf course a little faster than you can make it by car." Ike responded, "Well, I don't think much of the question because no helicopters have been procured for me to go to a golf course." In 1960, late in his tenure, however, helicopters were being used regularly for precisely that purpose.

Some of the criticism was more personal. Senator Joseph McCarthy said on March 27, 1955, that President Eisenhower should spend "less time with golf" and should give more attention to Communist China. McCarthy then went on to declare that he was "shocked beyond words at the attitude of persons in the White House" on "the sell-out at Yalta." In November 1959, Viscount Alanbrooke, the wartime chief of the Imperial General Staff, published his diaries, *Triumph in the West*, accusing Ike of "taking practically no part in running the war." Alanbrooke claimed that just before the Battle of the Bulge, Ike was "on the golf links at Reims." When called on the criticism, Alanbrooke conceded that Ike was stationed at a course and used the clubhouse as his office outside Reims but had not been able to play the course because of its condition and his intensely busy schedule. Ironically, Alanbrooke did not criticize Viscount Montgomery, who was, according to Montgomery's memoirs, in the middle of a round of golf on December 16, 1944, when the Germans broke the front line of the American First Army.

Senator Matthew M. Neely delivered a stinging critique of Ike, saying he was the "worst President we've ever had." Criticizing Ike's policies on China, domestic farming, and balancing the budget, Neely said the president was "like Alice in Wonderland." He went on to say, "This is not a time for a fishing and golfing President. I want somebody that can keep his mind not on the golf ball, but can keep the American people from being behind the eight ball."

But Ike didn't shy away from criticism. At an April 10, 1957, press conference, he declared, "I don't believe that criticism that is honest and fair hurts anybody. . . . Criticism of public figures is a good thing." He brushed off advice from the likes of Henry Cabot Lodge that he should not be photographed on golf courses and instead believed that relaxation and golf were part of his image. Eisenhower thought that a golfing president who seemed in control of the country was preferable to a harried chief executive who was chained to his desk. And the public initially agreed; a June 26, 1953, Gallup poll revealed that Americans were not concerned about how much time Ike spent on the golf course. In answer to the question, In your opinion do you think President Eisenhower is taking too much time off to play golf?, only 17 percent answered yes, while 73 percent answered no, and 10 percent had no opinion.

As Paul Johnson noted in *Forbes,* a close look at Ike's record shows that he was not a "near-zombie who was always out playing golf while the real decisions were made by Secretary of State John Foster Dulles and aides such as Sherman Adams." Johnson argued that "Ike deliberately cultivated the relaxed, golf-playing image, seeking to lower the political temperature during some of the hottest days of the Cold War." Nixon is quoted in Johnson's article describing Ike as "the most devious man I ever came across in politics." Johnson goes on to argue that Ike's presidential papers and telephone records "prove he was often hard at work early in the morning, when even his press secretary believed he was still asleep." Ike also took his criticism in stride: "I have never answered criticism in my life. In war, I was called reckless one day and a coward the next. And you get used to it."

In *Mandate for Change,* Ike described one of his so-called golf vacations: "But a President is President no matter what his location. For example, during eight weeks in Denver in 1954 my staff and I worked every day other than Sunday, including six that I spent in the mountains at Fraser, Colorado, with Aksel Nielsen. During those weeks I saw 225 visitors, not including my own immediate staff, made four official trips out of Denver, delivered six speeches, made three television appearances, attended five official luncheons or dinners, considered 513 bills from Congress, signing 488 into law and vetoing 25. Finally, I signed 420 other official papers or documents—all of this business of direct concern to the running of the Executive branch."

In keeping such a schedule, it was not surprising that Eisenhower's golf was constantly interrupted. Sherman

223

Adams recounted the disruption of one of his many practice sessions: "I remember that once when I needed a decision on an appointment I went out on the back lawn, where Eisenhower was practicing his golf shots. Dulles was already there ahead of me on a related errand. The President saw me coming and with a simulated sigh said, 'Look, Foster, here comes my conscience!'" On December 30, 1954, Ike's friend and partner Slats Slater reported that Ike began play at Augusta National Golf Club after lunch but was anxiously awaiting the results of the French vote on the rearmament of Germany. A negative vote would mean that Ike would be forced to cut his vacation short and return to the White House. Slater reported, "Well, things turned out well because as we were playing the seventh hole, the security came out and reported the Assembly had voted 287 to 260 to permit Germany to rearm on a twelve division basis—so there was much relief all over the place."

While overt criticism of Ike's game was part of the 1950s political banter, there was an endless supply of jokes. The *New York Times* reported in 1953, "No man can hope to make peace with the Soviet Union, unify the Republican party, and master the game of golf in a single lifetime." Another refrain held, "I suppose that we'll have a national holiday if the President ever makes a hole-in-one." A third began, "An assistant ran into the office of Secretary of State Dulles with the alarming news that Malenkov shot an eighty on the eighteen-hole course at the Kremlin. 'An eighty, you say?' Dulles said grimly. 'This means war. The President had a ninety-six yesterday.'"

Bob Hope was frequently the source of such barbs. He once said, "Ike loved to paint. I always kidded him

224

that he preferred painting to golf because it required fewer strokes." On May 8, 1953, Hope spoke at a White House correspondents dinner and told a joke about the president: "Ike was playing down at Augusta National the other day and he hit a bad shot. His caddie remarked, 'You certainly goofed that one, mister.' The other caddie in the group scolded him. He said, 'You don't talk that way, LeRoy. That's the President of the United States!' On the next hole Ike hit out of bounds. The chastised caddie said, 'You certainly freed that one, Mr. Lincoln.' " When visiting Ike for the last time in Walter Reed Hospital in Washington, Hope wanted to tell a joke to cheer up the general. It was the last one he would share with his old friend. Hope remembered telling it: "Did you hear the one about the guy, I said, despondent over his round, who walked into the locker room and loudly declared, 'I've got to be the worst golfer in the world.' There was another guy sitting there and he said, 'No, I am.' The first guy said, 'What did you have on the first hole?' 'An X.' 'You're one-up.' "

Ike's golf game was almost too easy a target, as the Gridiron Club demonstrated during his second campaign. At their annual dinner at the Hotel Statler in Washington, the members lampooned Ike as running the first "country club front porch campaign in history." The evening's festivities, with short skits and songs, made constant reference to Ike's love for golf. The lyrics of one song, set to the tune of "Summertime" from *Porgy and Bess*, began, "Summer time, time for taking it easy / Fish are biting, and the golfing is fine." A few days later, the Women's National Press Club took a similar approach by performing their skits dressed in golf clothes. In 1957, at the Democratic Party Night dinner in Washington, Jim Glading, an Ike look-alike, sang

225

the following song: "Out we go, into our whirl-y bird-y / Thank the Lord it is for thee / Here we come eager to meet our cad-dy. / On the tee—at Burning Tree."

Not everyone took the jokes or criticism about Ike's golf too seriously. Reverend Dr. John Sutherland Bonnell, the minister at the Fifth Avenue Presbyterian Church in New York, defended Ike's golf game in a sermon entitled "The Lost Art of Meditation." Bonnell explained, "Instead of criticizing him, many Americans would do well to learn from the President's balanced mode of living." Even President Harry Truman defended Ike and encouraged his own party to back off in a November 11, 1958, article in *Look* magazine. Roger Kahn reported on Truman in *Golf* magazine in 1959, "But to criticize the President because he uses a helicopter to fly to his home or to yap at him when he plays a game of golf is unfair and downright picayunish."

Ike's staff, aides, friends, and family strongly encouraged him to continue playing. Dr. Howard Snyder, his physician, claimed, "If that fellow couldn't play golf, I'd have a nut case on my hands." Hillary Rodham Clinton expressed the same sentiment regarding Bill Clinton forty years later. According to the *New York Times*, "In Washington, his staff has seen him weary at noon when he headed for the golf course, and a completely recharged man when he came back around 5 o'clock. So they continually urge him to knock off work around noon at least once a week." The game refreshed Ike; he was fond of saying, "You have to let a little air into the war room now and then."

Ike generally took the criticism in stride, but he did blame the presidency for adding eight strokes to his handicap, mainly because he could never truly escape the job. Though Ike preferred not to discuss the affairs of state on the golf course, they were rarely far away. He was constantly forced to interrupt his play to attend to his endless number of duties. James C. Hagerty, his press secretary, explained, "He'll be going along playing really well—par, par, bogey, par, bogey. All of the sudden his mind comes off golf. You can see it. Suddenly he's thinking about Quemoy, or Lebanon, or Berlin. Then it's triple bogey, and we all might as well go home. It isn't going to be any more fun that day."

NINE

CITIZEN IKE

He's taught this whole country how to relax through golf. Everybody is going at a mad pace—never taking any time out—and it remains for the President to show the rest of the country how to really live and do important work. I think that's a great contribution.
—BABE DIDRIKSON ZAHARIAS

When Ike retired from public life in January 1961 after John F. Kennedy defeated Richard Nixon in the 1960 presidential election, the nation lost its most visible amateur golfer and advocate for the sport. Though a regular player, JFK sought to distance himself as much as possible from Ike and the criticism the sport brought him. Even so, in April 1961, the press reported that Kennedy played golf seven times during the first three months of his administration, compared to Eisenhower's six rounds during the same period in 1953. At the age of forty-three, Kennedy was the youngest president. He was put there by the public who voted for youth, progress, and getting a man into space. Ike was elected in the 1950s to stabilize the nation; Kennedy was elected to change it. Ike looked back, while Kennedy looked forward.

But Ike never fully retired from public life nor the game he so loved. Golf's popularity continued to grow in the 1960s, largely because of the charismatic play of Arnold Palmer. In the wake of Ike's retirement, however, the game would undergo a dramatic change, prompted by the struggle for civil rights that would come to define the decade. Ike delivered his Farewell Address on January 17, 1961, warning his successors against the dangers of the military-industrial complex. He left the nation with a prayer for peace and quietly entered civilian life. That week, dozens of trucks loaded with the Eisenhowers' personal belongings drove to their home in Gettysburg. Papers, documents, and many of the eighteen thousand gifts he had received during his eight years as president—including a golf bag shaped like the Washington Monument—were sent to the Eisenhower Museum in Abilene, Kansas.

On his final day in the White House, Ike arose at 6:15 in the morning for appointments with James C. Hagerty, General Andrew Goodpaster, and a few others. He sent several telegrams, including one to Mary Jones, Bobby Jones's wife, that read, "On this, my last day at the White House, I want to thank you and Bob for all the many kindnesses you have extended to Mamie and me over the past years." He also hosted the Kennedys and the Johnsons for coffee. Ike and JFK rode together to the Capitol for the early afternoon swearing-in ceremony by Chief Justice Earl Warren. Afterward, Ike joined friends at the F Street Club for lunch. Then he and Mamie climbed into their 1956 Chrysler and drove to Gettysburg to occupy the only house they ever owned. On January 21, the Eisenhowers were officially welcomed home to Gettysburg at a dinner at the Gettysburg Hotel. At that event, Ike said that he had visited Gettysburg in 1914 while a cadet at West Point and noted, "I believe that was the last time until today that I was called Mr."

Gettysburg had become accustomed to having the first family as citizens of the town and tended not to make much of their presence. One resident remarked, "But don't forget that Gettysburg was on the map long before any of this here happened. We had a battle here. Remember? And, much as we like him, Ike is not the first president to honor us with his presence." Between their extensive travels, Ike and Mamie settled into life on the farm and had time to devote to their grandchildren. Ike regularly tooled around Gettysburg Country Club in a brightly painted golf cart, and they both worshipped at the same Presbyterian church that Abraham Lincoln visited on November 19, 1863, when he dedicated the national cemetery and delivered the Gettysburg Address. Ike and Mamie decorated their home for comfort rather than style, though they did commission F. Shumacher and Company to design a drapery pattern featuring scenes from Eisenhower's life, including golf clubs and balls. It was called "Eisenhower Epic."

After leaving the White House, Ike was asked how his life had changed since being president, to which he replied, "I don't get as many short putts." His workload declined significantly, but he still had an average of 7,500 pieces of mail to process each month. He also became a regular citizen, albeit a famous one. In his last month in the White House, Ike wrote to his friend Slats Slater demanding that he no longer be called General Eisenhower or Mr. President. "Whether or not the deep friendships I enjoy have had their beginnings in the ante or post-war period, I now demand, *as my right*, that you, starting January 21, 1961, address me by my nickname," he implored. "No longer do I propose to be excluded from the privileges that other friends enjoy."

Longtime White House reporter Merriman Smith described the world Ike faced in retirement: "Amazing as it may seem, he did not upon leaving the White House know how to use a dial telephone. He had no driver's license. The world of laundromats, drive-in theaters, bowling alleys, and supermarkets was an utter mystery to him. He began exploring the stores of Gettysburg with avid interest. And it was hard even for those closely associated with him to realize that during his long Army and White House years, most of the everyday chores of living had been done for him, including the placing of telephone calls and driving the car." Ike once confessed that he shopped at the supermarket for fun and to "bring back things that Mrs. Eisenhower doesn't know what to do about."

The world into which Ike retired shared little in common with his Abilene boyhood. Largely sequestered from the American people from the time he entered West Point to the end of his second term as president, Ike discovered that everything had changed. Historian Piers Brendon described the culture shock: "When Ike was president males had worn charcoal-gray suits and females mid-calf-length dresses; now caftans and miniskirts were in fashion. Elvis Presley had attained a degree of respectability by joining the army; the Beatles lauded the culture of drugs—'Lucy in the Sky, with Diamonds.' Wherever Ike looked he was appalled by new manifestations of decadence, by hippies and Hell's Angels, by pop art and nude theater, by Women's Lib and black power, by pornography and violence." Ike was stunned by the Watts riots in 1965, not realizing that such a public expression of discontent could be a logical outcome of decades of rampant discrimination. He perceived the counterculture movements wholly in moralistic terms; as an aging soldier, he saw campus protests as a breakdown of law and order. They were a long way from vaudeville and *Amos 'n' Andy*, the popular comedy radio series that Ike had enjoyed as a young army officer in the 1920s.

Upon Ike's retirement, Congress reinstated his five-star rank, which he had resigned when he assumed the presidency. He received numerous awards and honorary degrees from universities, and Presidents Kennedy and Johnson periodically asked him for advice in foreign affairs. Barely a month after retiring to Gettysburg, he worked with CBS President William Paley and Fred Friendly, an executive producer, on a documentary series that aired in June 1961 entitled "Eisenhower on the Presidency." Actor Robert Montgomery (media consultant for Ike during his presidency and a longtime friend) assisted with the project. NBC featured Ike on a television special commemorating the centennial of the Civil War, and CBS featured him in its "Biography" series in 1962. In July 1963, CBS hosted a "Town Meeting of the World," in which, through interactive technology and the Telstar II satellite, Ike engaged in a discussion with Sir Anthony Eden in London, Jean Monnet in Brussels, and Heinrich von Brentano in Bonn. In August of that same year, Ike returned to Europe for the filming of a CBS program called "D-Day Plus Twenty Years." Hosted by Walter Cronkite, the program featured Ike driving an Army jeep across

Normandy and to a cemetery that showed the graves of Americans who died on D-day. The program aired on June 5, 1964.

In the midst of his ambitious television schedule in 1963, Ike completed the first volume of his memoirs, *Mandate for Change*. Four years later, he wrote *At Ease: Stories I Tell to Friends*, which became a bestseller. For the most part, however, Ike enjoyed the leisure that came with his retirement. John Eisenhower, Ike's son, remembers, "Very shortly after our return to Gettysburg on January 20, 1961, Dad and Mother left for Augusta. When they returned about two weeks later I was shocked and worried at the Old Man's demeanor. His movements were slower, his tone less sharp. And he had time even during the workday to stop and indulge in what would formerly be considered casual conversation. I feared for his health. Fortunately, I could not have been more in error; the Boss had simply relaxed." In November 1965, Ike suffered another heart attack, after playing eighteen holes at Augusta National. While in the hospital, he warned, "If they order me not to play golf, then there is going to be a real argument." During recovery, Ike's doctors let him play on the par-3 course, but he was not placated and complained that next his doctors would make him play from the ladies' tees.

Despite their declining health, Susan Eisenhower recalled, Ike and Mamie did not become sedentary: "When my grandparents weren't in Gettysburg or traveling to see friends or giving speeches, they spent their time at Augusta National Golf Club in Augusta, Georgia, or at the Eldorado Golf Club in Palm Desert, California. They would usually leave for the West Coast after celebrating Christmas with us at the farm. But

234

twice my family joined them in Palm Desert for the holiday. We swam in the club's pools and took golf lessons, and Granddad took us to Disneyland."

Dorothy Yates, the wife of Charlie Yates, told a story about Ike and Mamie after they left the White House. Mamie hated to fly but agreed to do so while Ike was president. After his retirement, she insisted on taking the train to Augusta, and Dorothy and Charlie, who lived in Atlanta, often accompanied them. Dorothy recalled, "Miss Mamie loved dominos, so Charlie would often play with her. Well, one day they were playing and couldn't remember some of the rules. They called in Arthur, one of the porters, who was a good player. He made a suggestion, and they kept playing. When Ike came back into the car, he was baffled by the game they were playing and asked what they were doing, to which Mamie replied, 'We're playing by Arthur's rules.' "

Home was an elusive term for the Eisenhowers—it could mean the farmhouse in Pennsylvania, a four-bedroom rented home in California, or a cottage in Georgia. As Ike aged, they spent more and more time in California, and it is there that he realized every golfer's dream. On February 6, 1968, at the age of seventy-seven and a year before he died, Ike played at Seven Lakes Country Club in Palm Springs with Freeman Gosden, who had played Amos in the *Amos 'n' Andy* radio show, Leigh Battson, and George Allen. Ike made a hole in one on the 104-yard thirteenth hole—his first and only ace. He hit a 9-iron and it landed in the cup. He called it "the thrill of a lifetime." In a February 15, 1968, letter to his friend Charlie Yates, Ike wrote, "I would certainly like to duplicate it some day when we are partners against a couple of our rich friends from New York." Three days later, President Lyndon B. Johnson's diary

235

detailed a round with Ike in exquisite detail and mentioned the fabled ace:

1:00 p. (Pacific time) President had lunch w/ General
Eisenhower, Mrs. Eisenhower, Joe Carlson. They had
steak, salad, ice tea, and rum chocolate.

1:30 p. Mrs. Eisenhower directed the President to a
room to change for golf session.

1:35 p. President Gen. Eisenhower proceeded to
Seven Lakes County Club where they played 18 holes
of golf . . .

1:45 p. Teed off!

On Hole 9—They had fresh orange juice. Hole 11—
They met up with Mr. Don Kimball, former Sec. of
Navy.

Hole 13—The Gen. told the President that the last time
he played the hole he shot a hole in one.

Hole 18—The President shot a 122 yd. drive down the
green and parred the shot. Gen. Eisenhower also parred
the hole.

Surprised by all of the attention, Ike on February
20 wrote his friend Brigadier General Robert Cutler,
"I did not know that *Time* magazine had noted my
hole-in-one; it seems that I have gotten more publicity
than a movie star gets on his sixth divorce. One thing
is sure—if I ever make another one, it is going to be
the deepest darkest secret of my life." But this would
be his last season of golf. Ike suffered additional heart
attacks on April 29, 1968, and July 15, 1968. He had surgery on February 23, 1969, to remove scar tissue, but in

March he developed congestive heart failure. He died on March 28, 1969, at the age of seventy-eight. He had been an avid golfer for forty-two years, and the game was in no small measure responsible for the quality of life he enjoyed after his first heart attack, in 1955.

In a recent issue of *Golf Digest*, Tom Callahan claimed that Arnold Palmer was the second-most influential person in the history of American golf. He had to take a backseat to Ike. Eisenhower helped shape the destinies of millions of men and women, namely Tiger Woods and Phil Mickelson. Because of Ike, "military golf spread like napalm across the map, from the Tan Son Nhut Air Base course in Ho Chi Minh City to the one-shot DMZ course at Panmunjom." Earl Woods, Tiger's father, had been a tennis player, but he also played golf in Vietnam because there was a Navy course available free of charge for servicemen near where he was stationed. Phil Mickelson's father, a Navy aviator, played at Miramar. Callahan concluded that Ike helped influence the top players in the game today to embrace golf instead of tennis, thus saving America's top golfers from a "life in short pants." In July 1963, in recognition of his service to both the military and the sport he so loved, Ike was invited to dedicate a golf course named in his honor at the U.S. Air Force Academy.

From his retirement to his death, Ike struggled with various physical ailments, notably bursitis and arthritis, which reduced his time on the golf course. In the late 1960s, he limited his playing schedule and played the nine-hole course at Augusta National, rather than the eighteen-hole championship layout. Similar to Bobby Jones after his retirement, Ike became an unofficial ambassador for golf. He made public appearances and

237

participated in one notable charity match. Throughout most of his career, Ike shied away from playing for a public audience, but in 1964 he was persuaded to participate in a tournament at Merion Golf Club in Ardmore, Pennsylvania.

Designed by Hugh Wilson in 1912, Merion's East Course has served as host site for a record seventeen USGA Championships and will be the site of the 2013 U.S. Open. It played a significant role in the career of Eisenhower's longtime friend Bobby Jones. In 1916, at age fourteen, Jones won the Georgia State Amateur Championship and thus qualified for his first national championship—the U.S. Amateur at Merion. Dubbed "the new kid from Dixie" and dressed in long pants and a red and white striped bow tie, Jones led all qualifiers on the West Course with a 74 in the morning round. On the East Course in the afternoon, he shot an 89 and made the cut. In the third round of the competition, Jones lost to reigning amateur champion, Robert A. Gardner, 5 and 3. Eight years later, in 1924, Jones returned to Merion to win his first U.S. Amateur. When he returned for a third time to compete in the 1930 U.S. Amateur and the last leg of what would become the Grand Slam, there was intense international interest about whether Jones could complete an unprecedented sweep of the Open and Amateur Championships of the United States and Great Britain. He did. On the eleventh hole in the final match, Eugene Homans missed a twenty-five-foot putt, giving Jones an 8 and 7 victory and final leg of the Grand Slam. Merion was just the right place for Ike to play an exhibition match.

On May 26, 1964, he and Arnold Palmer, who had just won a fourth Masters Green Jacket, teamed up to play in a charity exhibition match against Jimmy

238

Demaret and singer Ray Bolger. On the first tee, the seventy-three-year-old former president was introduced as a dirt farmer from Gettysburg, Pennsylvania. The match benefited the Heart Association of Southeastern Pennsylvania, an organization for which Palmer was serving as the honorary chairman. Playing alternate shot format, Ike drove 220 yards on the first hole, prompting Bolger to cry "Hustler!" Palmer put Ike's ball on the green, and the former president made a seven-foot putt for birdie. After one shot, a female spectator cried out, "Mr. Eisenhower, you are wonderful. That was a beautiful shot." Ike replied with a broad grin, "I'm full of aspirin today."

On the eighth hole, playing from the back tees, Palmer blasted 320 yards into a downhill lie in the rough in front of a bunker. Worried about the difficult shot he faced, Ike turned to Palmer and said, "Arnie, forgive me for this." Ike placed the ball several feet from the hole, prompting Palmer to exclaim, "That man came to play." On the sixteenth hole, Ike and Palmer won the match 3 and 2, yet they decided to play to the end. Though running late for a dinner engagement at Valley Forge Military Academy, Ike refused to leave and finished the round. *Golf* magazine reported that on the seventeenth hole, Ike sank a 45-foot putt for another birdie and "beamed like a boy with a new bicycle" as the gallery roared with approval. After the match, Palmer said, "The General carried me." Fred Austin, Merion's golf professional, said after watching Ike, "There was nothing in Mr. Eisenhower's swing that I would want to change. It's smooth and easy. He had a good stance and he looks comfortable. You can't beat a natural swing for success." The event raised more than $20,000 for the charity.

239

Ike was a frequent spectator at the Bob Hope Chrysler Desert Classic, a tournament that raised money for the Eisenhower Medical Center in Rancho Mirage and offered a trophy named in his honor. Bob Hope remembered, "When I got involved with the Desert Classic in 1965 Ike became an important part of the tournament. He really enjoyed watching the competition, and he always participated in the presentation ceremonies." In 1968, which would prove to be Ike's last appearance at the Classic, Hope arranged a surprise for the general. "He was sitting in the bleachers with Mamie behind the 18th green at Bermuda Dunes," Hope explained. "Over on the 1st fairway, unknown to Ike, General Bill Yancey, who was the tournament's executive secretary, was assembling a combination of army, navy, and air force bands. The moment that play was completed, the bands moved into position on the 18th fairway and marched in unison toward Ike, playing all of his favorite songs. Ike was deeply moved. Mamie told me, 'That's the first time in years I've seen tears come into his eyes.'"

Ike's health declined in the mid-1960s, and he began to see his friends pass away. In the spring of 1962, a group of his Augusta friends, including Pete Jones, were traveling on a hunting trip when the American Airlines plane they were on crashed. In June 1962, Ralph "Rip" Arnold, the golf professional at Cherry Hills Country Club in Denver, died. In October 1963, Ed Dudley died at the age of sixty-three. Dudley was the golf pro at Augusta during most of Ike's time there; he left in 1957 to become the winter professional at Dorado Beach Club in Puerto Rico until his retirement in 1960.

In February 1969, Ike had intestinal surgery and sub-
sequently contracted pneumonia, dying on March 28.
After three days of funeral ceremonies in Washington,
D.C., Ike's body was taken by train to Abilene. The
Belle Springs Creamery, where he worked as a teenager,
draped their doors in black crepe. Ike was buried on
April 2, 1969, in the Place of Meditation Chapel at the
Eisenhower Center in Abilene, Kansas, at a ceremony
that attracted 100,000 mourners. He was laid to rest in
his World War II uniform with the Army Distinguished
Service Medal, the Navy Distinguished Service Medal,
and the Legion of Merit pinned to his chest. The grave
was next to that of his first-born son, Ikky, whose casket
was moved from Denver to Abilene in June 1966.

Even though Ike never lived again in Kansas after
leaving for West Point, it was always his home. In 1965,
he visited and dined at Lena's Farmhouse Restaurant,
where he watched the first game of the World Series
and received a good-natured paddling from Lena in
advance of his seventy-fifth birthday. Ike signed the
paddle, which hangs today in Mr. K's Farmhouse Restaurant at 407 South Van Buren Street. One of the last
gestures he made as president was to send a gift of one
of his own paintings to the high school he had attended.
In a speech delivered at his alma mater, Ike declared, "I
have wandered far, but never have I forgotten Abilene.
Every boy dreams of the day when he comes back home
after making good. I, too, so dreamed, but my dreams
have been exceeded beyond the wildest stretch of the
imagination. The proudest thing I can say is that I am
from Abilene." Ike came home in a flag-draped coffin,
accompanied by honorary pallbearers—his longtime
valet, Sergeant John Moaney, several officers, and mem-

241

bers of his family. When Mamie died on November 1, 1979, she was buried next to him.

At the 1969 Masters Tournament, a week after Ike's death, Clifford Roberts delivered a eulogy for his old friend, proclaiming, "Very few contributed as much as General Eisenhower toward the enhancement of the popularity of the game of golf." With that, Roberts announced that the club would preserve the cabin where Ike and Mamie had so often stayed. In 1975, Mamie wrote in a letter to Mary Jones, Bobby Jones's wife, of her time there without Ike: "I am grateful that I had the opportunity to stay at 'Mamie's Cabin' six years after Ike died, but with so many new members, new butlers, new maids, etc., somehow it was not the same as when you and Bob and Ike and all the group would be down there for fun." The former first lady did, however, remain active, as she indicated in a May 16, 1972, letter that she mailed from Gettysburg to Charlie Yates: "I am back in the harness of things here and I am on the eve of a ten-day trip that will take me to the big dedication of Eisenhower Hall in West Point on the twentieth, a luncheon in New York for the USO on the twenty-fourth and ending up for the first graduation ceremonies at Eisenhower College on the twenty-eighth."

Countless tributes to Ike have dotted the American landscape since his presidency: the Eisenhower Medical Center in California (dedicated in 1971); Eisenhower College in Seneca Falls, New York (opened for classes in 1968 and closed in the 1980s); a postage stamp in 1969; the Eisenhower Library (opened in 1962); elementary, middle, and high schools; bridges, tunnels, avenues, office buildings, public libraries, and golf courses; Eisenhower Park in Abilene; and even a mountain in New Hampshire. In March 1971, the *Profes-*

sional Golfer, the PGA of America's monthly magazine, advertised a fund-raising effort to help memorialize the president. The money raised was intended to support the Eisenhower Medical Center and Eisenhower College. The PGA and the USGA were cosponsors of the plan and asked for "modest-sized" contributions. For their donations, patrons received a golf bag tag and portrait of General Eisenhower. Mamie remained involved in fund-raising for the college. In the fall of 1969, she made a donation in the amount of $2,500, which she raised from selling her Chrysler and the proceeds for an article written with Ben Hibbs for *Reader's Digest.*

While honors, awards, and tributes have been plentiful, assessments of Ike's presidency have changed with the times. Since the mid-1980s, he has been consistently ranked as one of the top ten leaders in American history—by polls ranging from C-SPAN to the American Psychological Association. Before this, a 1962 poll done by Arthur M. Schlesinger Jr. ranked Eisenhower twenty-second, between Chester A. Arthur and Andrew Johnson. He has been on his way up the list ever since. Murray Kempton's landmark essay, "The Underestimation of Dwight D. Eisenhower," in the September 1967 issue of *Esquire* magazine, began the upward trend. Garry Wills, Richard Rhodes, Stephen Ambrose, Herbert Parmet, and others followed Kempton's lead as they reevaluated Ike. Ike's reputation continued to grow, partly fueled by the Eisenhower Library's release of thousands of manuscripts documenting the daily life of Ike's presidency. Kenneth S. Davis argued, "He gave us the strength of a great reputation, a great character, and an abiding sense of America's mission; gave us, when all is said and done, the chance to live up to the

243

best there is in us. Not very many Presidents have ever given us more." Historian Thomas A. Bailey expressed the same sentiment: "Unlike many other aging military men in civilian office, he proved to be humble, modest, teachable, susceptible to growth, and endowed with common sense. He was not power-hungry. Even more popular at the end than the beginning, he left the country prosperous and peaceful: his proud boast was that no American soldiers had lost their lives fighting on foreign soil during his eight years."

Even though Eisenhower made several grievous mistakes as president—waffling on civil rights, refusing to confront Senator Joseph McCarthy, and initially deceiving the nation about the U-2 spy plane—the public saw Eisenhower for what he was: a decent man who gave his life in the service of his country. In this way, he seemed somehow above party politics. In spite of his mistakes, Ike was able to divorce himself from the office he held, as only few other presidents could do. Ike's popularity barely suffered even in the midst of numerous crises. He remained wholly unpretentious despite his stellar reputation as a leader, and that was his main appeal. Craig Allen explained part of Ike's attraction: "Eisenhower's communication efforts were clear, honest, and consistent. . . . Eisenhower established a remarkable record for telling the people what he was going to do, doing it, and then telling them it was done. For eight years Eisenhower stood for peace, prosperity, and progress—and he delivered." At end of 1959, Ike's approval rating was 76 percent. At the end of his second term, it had dropped to 59 percent. Yet, only FDR and Reagan have enjoyed higher numbers as they left office. In December 1968, a Gallup poll showed that Ike was one of the ten most admired Americans.

Almost immediately after Ike left office, the nation became nostalgic for the "golfer in chief." In 1963, a Pennsylvania company began circulating a button at local country clubs that read, "Ike for President in 1964 ... of the United States Golf Association." Bob Hope compared Ike to the new administration: "President Kennedy is flying to California. His wife is flying to Italy and India. Remember the good old days when you knew where the President was? On the golf course." Thinking that he would find a willing opponent, Fidel Castro challenged Kennedy to a golf game in March 1961. The Cuban leader, who had been nationalizing the small nation's golf courses, wanted to see if JFK would take the bait. Castro's caddie, Delio Rodriguez, reported that Castro's boast was full of hot air, as he was incapable of breaking 150.

Assessing Ike's legacy on the golf course requires a comprehensive view of the sport in the twentieth century and the four men who shaped it. Eisenhower—like Bobby Jones before him and Arnold Palmer and Tiger Woods after him—helped usher in the modern era of golf. Jones influenced Ike, while Palmer benefited from the almost constant media visibility around the game during and after Eisenhower's presidency. Woods directly benefited from Palmer's popularity on television. Each of the four popularized the game for the masses, left an important imprint on the way golf is played and regarded, and influenced future generations of golfers. Jones, with his sportsmanship and intellect, stood shoulders above his fellow athletes of the 1920s. He was far removed from the sporting scandals of the era; it would be impossible to imagine him involved in anything closely resembling the Black Sox scandal of

245

1919. Although Red Grange, Ty Cobb, and Babe Ruth were extraordinary athletes, they were not extraordinary men. Jones was. Even in the Jazz Age's cult of celebrity, he seemed more human and respectable than his famous counterparts Henry Ford, Charles Lindbergh, and Rudolph Valentino. The public respected Jones's commitment to amateurism and celebrated his displays of sportsmanship in the 1920s, after he learned to control his youthful temper. He was the right athlete at the right time.

The nation was reeling from World War I and looking to what sportswriter Grantland Rice considered the innocence of play. The South needed Jones, and he was the most visible and respected personage to come out of the region since the Civil War. Jones filled a void, as Herbert Warren Wind explained: "Everybody adored him—not just dyed-in-the-wool golfers, but people who had never struck a golf ball or had the least desire to. They admired the ingrained modesty, the humor, the generosity of spirit that were evident in Jones' remarks and deportment. They liked the way he looked, this handsome, clean-cut young man, whose eyes gleamed with both a frank boyishness and a perceptiveness far beyond his years." Jones's ability to appeal to the masses made him the first real golf hero in America. Other men, such as Francis Ouimet and Walter Hagen, were popular, but they never held the stature that Jones did. No one would equal his impact on the game until Eisenhower entered the White House.

A March 1971 issue of the *Professional Golfer* illustrated this point: "In the history of golf few men have been credited with giving the game the impact given to it by Dwight D. Eisenhower while he was President. Of course the game had its heroes both before and after General Eisenhower's White House years, from Francis Ouimet in the pre–World War I years, down to Arnold Palmer and Jack Nicklaus today. But they're different. They don't play the same game as the rest of us. The General did, and he played it with gusto and pure enjoyment."

Herbert Warren Wind recounted a telling story from a golfing enthusiast in New York: "Before Ike came in, every time I carried my golf bag down to Grand Central and boarded a train for a golfing weekend, I could count on running into disapproving faces and at least one slur carefully delivered so I could hear it—you know something like, 'Don't strain yourself, Reginald.' Now it's all changed. Strangers look at me as if I were a member of the 4-H Club. And when they speak to me, they give me the warm smile and a cheery word like, 'Looks like a grand weekend to get out of doors.' All of the sudden, I'm on the same level with the Fourth of July and Mom's apple pie, and I like it."

Ike's influence cannot be separated from that of Arnold Palmer and the rise of television. The young man from Pennsylvania who picked up his first golf club at the age of three and was able to break 100 at the age of seven mesmerized the nation. Golfers identified with Ike; they idolized Palmer. Palmer was cut out of the same cloth as Walter Hagen, Sam Snead, and Gene Sarazen—all from working-class backgrounds. Palmer's father, Deacon, was a steelworker turned golf professional. Palmer played golf at Wake Forest University and after winning the 1954 U.S. Amateur accepted a position as a golf course superintendent. Four years later, in Ike's fifth year in office, he won the first of his four Masters Tournaments. Palmer's thirty-five-foot putt at

247

the seventeenth and 6-iron shot to within five feet of the flag on the final hole helped him win over Ken Venturi and gave birth to the "Palmer Charge."

Palmer's record is extraordinary and needs no retelling here—he won sixty-two U.S. events and twenty-nine additional titles throughout the world—but what is significant is how he interacted with the media and the public. Like Ike, Palmer had a common man's touch. But Palmer's appeal was largely a product of the growth of television. While Ike had the White House press corps to chronicle his antics on the course, Palmer had television. In the late 1950s and early 1960s, with the advent of color television, five million Americans were regularly tuning in to golf tournaments. As Herbert Warren Wind explained, "With that sort of interest, one can understand why early in the 1960s the large companies made it a point to get into the golf picture. Beginning in 1961, the Shell Oil Company began to underwrite an annual series of television matches in which the outstanding American and foreign stars met on the great courses of the world, from Gleneagles to Gavea, from Banff to Royal Melbourne. This program was so well received that it lasted for nine years."

Another reason for Palmer's popularity was that, with the possible exception of Ben Hogan and Sam Snead, charismatic golfers did not dominate the sport during the 1950s. Though they were respectable players, Doug Ford, Cary Middlecoff, and Julius Boros did not excite the masses. George Peper claimed, "In a sense, Arnold Palmer sold golf to the American public, and his number one customer was another national hero, Dwight Eisenhower, who picked up the game and brought it to the White House lawn. No one loved golf more than Ike, no one played it better than Arnie, and together they spread the gospel to millions of leisure-minded Americans. Between 1960 and 1970, golf in the United States boomed as never before. As the number of players doubled, from five to ten million, the number of courses exploded from sixty-three hundred to ten thousand: in effect, a new golf course for every day of the year for ten straight years."

While someone like Ben Hogan had many admirable qualities—indomitable courage, perseverance, and focus—and engendered near universal respect, he was a difficult man to adore. His concentration on a golf course was so focused that he generally disregarded how other players were performing in a round. It also meant that he did not interact actively with golf fans. In contrast, a player who was to create new definitions for *sports idol* and *fan favorite* was about to make his entrance. In August 1954, a twenty-four-year-old Pennsylvanian named Arnold Palmer won the U.S. Amateur at the Country Club of Detroit, defeating forty-three-year-old Robert Sweeny on the last hole of the thirty-six-hole match-play event. In November of that year, Palmer turned professional. The following August, he won his first event as a professional, the Canadian Open, then one of the most important events on the professional Tour.

Like Ike, Palmer seemed to have been created by central casting for television. Lithe and athletic, he resembled a football halfback of the era more than the typical golf professional, many of whom were pudgy. Unlike the deliberate and serious Hogan, Palmer's demeanor constantly betrayed his highs and lows during a round. It was easy for a golf fan to relate to Palmer's reaction to a shot because Palmer responded so readily, contorting his face into a grimace after a bad hook would land him in the trees off the fairway or beaming in a large smile when he sank a long putt.

In 1958, the year Palmer won his first Masters by one shot over Doug Ford, the previous year's champion, Eisenhower began what was to be a continuing correspondence with him:

Dear Mr. Palmer,

Because of the general confusion the other day, I failed to realize when Ben Fairless introduced us that you were Arnold Palmer of 1958 Masters fame. I hope you will forgive my lack of reaction and accept, even this belatedly, my warm congratulations on your splendid victory.

Ben suggests that sometime we might have an opportunity to play at Augusta. This I should like very much though, judging from the brand of golf I have recently been displaying, I would be more than embarrassed.

Sincerely,

Dwight D. Eisenhower

The two men had much in common. They came from modest circumstances and were both men of high achievement who were gregarious and unpretentious. Eisenhower's love of golf may have introduced the game to many Americans unfamiliar with the sport, yet in 1952, it was still not a game generally taken up by working-class men and women. Palmer, like Eisenhower, was largely responsible for changing how ordinary Americans viewed the game. His ability to connect with an audience and his emotional displays made the sport appealing and accessible to ordinary people, whether they were golf fans or not. Television brought golf into the homes of people who had never set foot on a golf course. It was thrilling to witness one of the best and certainly one of the most appealing golfers triumph in spectacular fashion. Determined yet approachable and comfortable in a crowd, Palmer radiated the confidence of being an American in the post–World War II era.

Just twenty years before Palmer won at Augusta in 1958, the United States was still in the grips of the Depression, which only started to lift when manufacturing needs of the war began to put people back to work. Palmer embodied the opportunities and achievements available to a large segment of Americans in the postwar era. Although his skill level was actually dramatically superior to any average weekend golfer, his manner seemed to suggest that any ordinary duffer might join Palmer on the first tee of the U.S. Open with a few more hours on the practice range. Like Ike, Palmer inspired millions of people to try the game, and many of them stayed with it. With Eisenhower, Americans saw that golf could become a nearly obsessive activity; with Palmer, Americans saw themselves and went out to the golf course to prove how similar they were to the new champion.

Palmer recalled that he and Ike first got to know each other after the 1960s Masters: "It was our first round together, and I remember mostly that, despite the pressures of the Presidency, he was one of the most congenial and pleasant persons I had ever had the opportunity to play golf with." Though Eisenhower and Palmer did not become close friends during the years of the Eisenhower presidency, once Eisenhower left the White House, the two men played golf together regularly. As their relationship developed through their mutual enjoyment of golf and each other's company, Eisenhower displayed a fondness for Palmer little different from that of millions of fans who eagerly followed Palmer's exploits in tournament play.

If the nation admired Jones, liked Ike, and loved Palmer, it stood in awe of Tiger Woods. His surprise win of the 1997 Masters (making him the first African American champion) became a visible, indisputable signal that the game had changed. Historians can and do argue that golf has been changing all along, becoming more democratic with each new decade as the ranks opened to professionals, women, international players, and minorities. But the general nonplaying public still had a view of golf as a snobbish, white-only sport restricted to country club members. In a 1989 article, Dan Jenkins told a revealing story. An African American man, who had never played golf or attended a championship, was at the Masters Tournament with a friend, who was trying to point out some of the better-known players. When the friend identified Jack Nicklaus and Johnny Miller walking with their caddies, the man responded, "Golf? I get it. A couple of blonde Nazis walking through the woods with two spades carrying their shit." Tiger Woods changed that perception.

On August 27, 1996, Eldrick "Tiger" Woods announced that he was leaving Stanford University and turning professional. In that first year, he won nearly $3 million and was in the top ninety on the career money list. Golf writer Ron Sirak estimated that Tiger's popularity brought $650 million into the golf world in the form of increased ticket sales, television ratings, sponsorships, and equipment purchases in his first year on the Tour.

In 1996, 19.4 million households had tuned in to the four major championships (the Masters, U.S. Open, British Open, and PGA Championship). In 1997, the figure jumped to 29.3 million. Nike's golf division, which sponsors Tiger, grew from a $100 million business to a $250 million business.

Tiger—like Jones and Palmer before him—became a man who transcended his sport, introducing golf to new audiences. In 2000, PGA Tour Commissioner Tim Finchem claimed, "Golf continues to grow globally and is enjoying a period of booming popularity. At the forefront of this charge to unparalleled growth is Tiger Woods. . . . Just as when I was a teenager and was influenced by the popularity of Arnold Palmer, other youngsters are now following golf because of Tiger." Golf also became cool again. In the 1970s and 1980s, many still had the perception that golf was a game played by overweight white men in plaid pants. Tiger's muscular frame and fist-pumping style appealed to youths. Joe Barrow, the national director of the First Tee program that was founded in 1997, explained the long-term impact of someone like Tiger: "The more we have role models who achieve a level of success at the top of the game, the more it reinforces that there are opportunities out there."

Golf in the twentieth century belonged to four men, each unique in his manner, style, and legacy. Bobby Jones put golf on the front page of the newspaper, Dwight D. Eisenhower put it on the White House lawn, Arnold Palmer put it in American living rooms, and Tiger Woods put it within reach of every child in America. It is in this context that we should evaluate the game and those who love to play it.

253

There is no doubt that Ike influenced golf, but it is equally important to see how golf shaped Ike and the nation. Golf kept him fit and happy. After his 1955 heart attack, his ability to get around a course gave voters the confidence they needed to reelect him. It may have, in the end, saved his life. It certainly preserved his sanity. Much of the business of the presidency unfolded on a golf course or with fellow golfers. Ike often viewed the 1950s through the traditional values of golf and selected close friends and advisors who shared that perspective. Those who did not play were not excluded from his inner circle, but they had limited influence. Analyzing Ike's obsession with golf is not the only way to view this complex decade, but it surely is one approach that bears much fruit.

NOTES

PREFACE

viii, **John F. Kennedy, his successor:** Tom Callahan, "The Country's First Golfer," *Golf Digest*, August 2005, 76.

viii, **Labor leader Jacob Potofsky:** Shepherd Campbell and Peter Landau, *Presidential Lies: The Illustrated History of White House Golf* (New York: Macmillan, 1996), 107.

viii, **Fidel Castro predictably:** Richard J. Moss, *Golf and the American Country Club* (Urbana: University of Illinois Press, 2001), 158.

ix, **To a nearly empty:** "President vs. Squirrels and Senator," *New York Times*, March 23, 1955, 1.

ix, **He asked that a fence:** Edward T. Folliard, "White House Halts Eviction of Squirrels," *Washington Post and Times Herald*, March 26, 1955, 1; and "Mr. Hagerty's News Conference, March 25, 1955, at 10:30 A.M. EST," James C. Hagerty, Press Secretary, Papers, 1953–1961, Box 42, Folder 1: James C. Hagerty's Press Conferences, January–March 1955, Eisenhower Library.

CHAPTER 1

1, **One may not agree:** Bus Ham, "Hagen a Country Gentleman," *Washington Post and Times Herald*, August 8, 1954, C1.

2, **By 1939, the numbers:** James M. Mayo, *The American Country Club: Its Origins and Development* (New Brunswick, NJ: Rutgers University Press, 1998), 158.

3, **In addition, new methods:** George Peper, *The Story of Golf* (New York: TV Books, 1999), 153.

4, **By Ike's twentieth birthday:** Richard J. Moss, *Golf and the American Country Club* (Urbana: University of Illinois Press, 2001), 13.

4, The organization recruited members: Benjamin Rader, *American Sports: From the Age of Folk Games to the Age of Televised Sports* (Upper Saddle River, NJ: Prentice Hall, 1999), 101.

4, The Association for the Advancement: Alison Wrynn, "The History of American Health, Hygiene and Fitness." http://personal.ecu.edu/estesst/2323/readings/americanpe.html. Accessed March 18, 2006.

4, In 1877, Dr. E. H. Bradford: Wrynn, 6.

5, A mere ten years later: Moss, 35–44.

5, Robert Hunter wrote: Robert Hunter, *The Links* (New York: Charles Scribner's Sons, 1926), vi–vii.

5, And like Ike: Andrew Carnegie, "Dr. Golf," *Independent* 70 (June 1, 1911): 1181–1192.

5, The focus on the lessons: Charles B. Macdonald, "Golf: The Ethical and Physical Aspects of the Game," *Golf*, January 1898, 20.

6, Writing for *Scribner's Magazine*: Henry Howland, "Golf," *Scribner's Magazine*, May 1895, 546.

6, Historians have dated: Robert B. Browning, *A History of Golf: The Royal and Ancient Game* (London: J. M. Dent and Sons, Ltd., 1955), 116–117.

6, The first national tennis championship: Rader, 65.

6, Historian Benjamin Rader explained: Rader, 65–66.

7, Lockhart has been called: George Peper et al., *Golf in America: The First 100 Years* (New York: Harry N. Abrams, 1994), 10.

7, In 1887, he visited: Peper et al., *Golf in America*, 9.

7, On November 14, 1888: Peper et al., *Golf in America*, 11–12.

8, The USGA had four goals: Peper et al., *Golf in America*, 25.

8–9, An article in the *New York Times*: Peper et al., *Golf in America*, 20.

10, Benjamin Rader argued that golf expanded: Rader, 196.

10, But he offered yet another explanation: Rader, 196.

11, The *Atlanta Journal* once compared: John Strenge, *When War Played Through: Golf During World War II* (New York: Gotham Books, 2005), 140.

12, Golf equipment companies began contributing: Peper et al., *Golf in America*, 192.

12, Setting moral issues aside: Moss, 143.

13, Abercrombie & Fitch: Strenge, 26.

13, On April 9, 1942: Al Barkow et al., *20th Century Golf Chronicle* (Lincolnwood, IL: Publications Unlimited, 1998), 201–202.

13, One story holds: "Military Links," GovExec.com. May 1, 1997. http://www.govexec.com/features/0597s6.htm. Accessed August 19, 2005.

13, Golf writer Herbert Graffis: Strenge, x.

14, The Royal and Ancient Golf Club of St. Andrews had already: Strenge, 30–31.

14, When Judge Kenesaw Mountain Landis: Strenge, 33.

14, In 1943, the PGA of America: Strenge, 169.

14, USGA committeeman Edward Cheney: Strenge, 34; and Barkow et al., 205.

15, Bobby Jones, who reportedly: "Jones Shows Way on Links with 205," *New York Times*, June 8, 1942, 21.

15, By comparison, the U.S. Open: Barkow et al., 198; and Strenge, 63.

15, Coverage of the Miami Open: Strenge, 12–13.

16, And the British government: Dale Concannon, *Bullets, Bombs, and Birdies* (Ann Arbor, MI: Clock Tower Press, 2003), 89.

16, The players at Richmond Park: Concannon, 91.

16, Golfers who played in Kent: Concannon, 96.

16, As supreme Allied commander: Army Lieutenant James "Jimmy" Preston, *General Dwight D. Eisenhower's Golf Caddie* (n.p.: Foolscap Press, 2001).

18, While Ike led the troops: The Churchill Centre, http://www.winston churchill.org/i4a/pages/index.cfm?pageid=971. Accessed July 5, 2006.

18, The USGA donated a new: Strenge, 34.

18, The Women's Golf Association: Strenge, 37.

19, In a speech to the USGA: Strenge, 19.

19, In a letter to O.B. Keeler: Letter from Robert Tyre Jones Jr. to O. B. Keeler, January 12, 1942. Bobby Jones Subject File, Kenan Research Center, Atlanta History Center.

20, Many of the regular Tour players: Herb Graffis, *The PGA: The Official History of the Professional Golfers' Association of America* (New York: Thomas Y. Crowell Co., 1975), 232.

20, They both engaged the crowds: Bob Hope, *Confessions of a Hooker: My Lifelong Love Affair with Golf* (New York: Doubleday, 1985), 40.

21, With perfect timing: Strenge, 112.

21, In recognition of Hope's efforts: Bob Addie, "Column," *Washington Post and Times Herald*, August 15, 1957, C1.

21, Herb Graffis, author of: Graffis, 234.

21, It was one of the best: Strenge, 7.

22, The trophy was made from: Barkow et al., 208.

22, By the end of 1945: Barkow et al., 215.

22, Eleven PGA sections: Graffis, 239.

23, A November 20, 1944: Strenge, 241.

23, The club may have been heartened: Barkow et al., 206.

23, ANGC declared: David Owen, *The Making of the Masters: Clifford Roberts, Augusta National, and Golf's Most Prestigious Tournament* (New York: Simon and Schuster, 1999), 145.

23, As the *New York Times* reported: Quoted in Moss, 143.

24, **The Greenbrier:** Strenge, 83.

24, **Prior to D-day:** "Military Memo: Army Names Now Figures at Resort," *Washington Post*, October 8, 1944, S1.

24, *Golfing Magazine* **made light:** Strenge, 122.

24, **In 1944, twenty-two:** Barkow et al., 204.

25, **He reported:** Bus Ham, "GIs Certain Athletics Can Keep Peace," *Washington Post*, September 27, 1945, 12.

26, **For comparison:** Peper et al., *Golf in America*, 38.

26, **The article quoted:** "President Drives Golf to Fore and Putts Tennis on Wane Here," *New York Times*, August 6, 1953, 25.

26, **Mercer Beasley:** "President Drives Golf to Fore and Putts Tennis on Wane Here," 25.

CHAPTER 2

27, **Fred Corcoran:** Don Van Natta, *First Off the Tee: Presidential Hackers, Duffers, and Cheaters from Taft to Bush* (New York: Public Affairs, 2003), 57.

27, **Sport was one of the few:** Dwight D. Eisenhower, *At Ease: Stories I Tell to My Friends* (New York: Doubleday, 1967), 7.

28, **At Augusta he is remembered:** Peter Andrews, "Ike and the Gang," *Golf Digest*, April 1993, 164.

29, **There he met Ida Elizabeth Stover:** Allan Taylor, ed., *What Eisenhower Thinks* (New York: Thomas Y. Crowell Co., 1952), 1–4; Quentin Reynolds, "The Eisenhowers of Kansas," *Collier's*, December 18, 1948, 95; and John Hertzler, "The 1879 Brethren in Christ Migration from Southeastern Pennsylvania to Dickinson County, Kansas," *Pennsylvania Mennonite Heritage* (1980): 11–18.

29, **Historian Stephen Ambrose described:** Stephen E. Ambrose, *Eisenhower: Soldier, General of the Army, President-Elect* (New York: Simon and Schuster, 1983), 16–18.

30, **Years later, he recalled:** Quoted in Ambrose, 27.

30, **Ike's mother, Ida:** Virgil Pinkley, *Eisenhower Declassified* (Old Tappan, NJ: Fleming H. Revell Co., 1963), 38–39.

30, **Abilene forever shaped:** Piers Brendon, *Ike: His Life and Times* (New York: Harper and Row, 1986), 29.

30, **With some irony:** Quoted in Brendon, 29. Carl Becker, *Everyman His Own Historian: Essays on History and Politics* (New York: Appleton-Century-Crofts, 1935).

31, **Years later, he remembered:** Ambrose, 35.

31, **His 1909 senior yearbook:** Steve Neal, *The Eisenhowers: Reluctant Dynasty* (New York: Doubleday, 1978), 16.

31, **His performance was reviewed:** Eisenhower, *At Ease*, 101.

31, **In 1910, his last year:** Eisenhower, *At Ease*, 104.

32, **He also briefly played:** Carlo D'Este, *Eisenhower: A Soldier's Life* (New York: Henry Holt, 2002), 53; and Thomas B. Koetting, "One Strike on Ike: Secret of Center Field Could Have Changed History," May 1992, Vertical File, Sports and Hobbies, Eisenhower Library.

32, **At five feet eleven inches:** Ambrose, 48–49; and "Eisenhower Chats on Days in Sports," *New York Times*, October 29, 1952, 21.

32, **The *New York Times*:** Natta, 61; and Lester David and Irene David, *Ike and Mamie: The Story of the General and His Lady* (New York: G. P. Putnam's Sons, 1981), 55.

32, **His 1912 record:** Pinkley, 60.

32, **Ike was not too concerned:** David and David, 55.

32, **Ike's graduating class:** Kevin McCann, *Man from Abilene* (New York: Doubleday, 1952), 63; and Kenneth S. Davis, *Eisenhower: American Hero* (New York: American Heritage Publishing Co., 1969), 22.

33, **He described the incident:** "Eisenhower Chats on Days in Sports," *New York Times*, October 29, 1952, 21; Eisenhower, *At Ease*, 14–15; and Ambrose, 48.

33, **In that capacity:** Pinkley, 62.

34, **While serving in World War II:** D'Este, 73; and Dwight D. Eisenhower, *In Review: Pictures I've Kept* (Garden City, NY: Doubleday, 1969), 17.

34, **Those words were etched:** Major General A. S. Sherman, "Many Athletes Become Fine Soldiers," *Army* (March 1978): 57–58.

34, **On July 1, 1916:** Ambrose, 56–58.

35, **On the day of his wedding:** Davis, 25.

35, **He was quickly promoted:** "Gen. Eisenhower Is Expert on Tanks and Maneuvers," *Washington Post*, November 8, 1942, 1.

35, **He finally gave up:** "Eisenhower Chats on Days in Sports," *New York Times*, October 29, 1952, 21.

35, **He was an avid cook:** Joseph A. Loftus, "Eisenhower's Formula for Relaxation," *New York Times*, September 5, 1954, SM10; and Robert J. Donovan, *Eisenhower: The Inside Story* (New York: Harper and Brothers, 1956), 195, 207.

36, **Writing for the *New York Times*:** Minnesota Citizens for Eisenhower, Recipe Card, "President Eisenhower's Old Fashioned Beef Stew," 1956. Folder: DDE Inauguration, 1957. Charlie Yates Private Collection and Loftus, SM25.

36, **He had learned the game:** Raymond Daniell, "He Is Our Eisen and This Is Our Hour," *New York Times*, January 1, 1942, SM7.

36, **He was apt to call:** Dwight D. Eisenhower, *Mandate for Change*, 1953–1956 (New York: Doubleday, 1963), 270.

37, **Ike began copying:** Dwight D. Eisenhower, *In Review: Pictures I've Kept*, 99; Pinkley, 230; and Ira Henry Freeman, "Eisenhower of Columbia," *New York Times*, November 7, 1948, SM37.

37, In a December 14, 1954: Peter Boyle, ed., *The Churchill-Eisenhower Correspondence, 1953–1955* (Chapel Hill: University of North Carolina Press, 1990), 182–183.

37, Churchill replied: Boyle, ed., 184.

37, The pastime helped him: Robert Griffith, ed., *Ike's Letters to a Friend, 1941–1958* (Lawrence: University Press of Kansas, 1984), 89.

37, Because Mamie used her bedroom: Edward Russoli, *Dwight D. Eisenhower: General, President, Cook* (Allentown, PA: Benedettini Books, 1990), 75.

38, Eisenhower thrived: McCann, 81; and Mark C. Bender, *Watershed at Leavenworth* (Fort Leavenworth, KS: U.S. Army Command and General Staff College, 1990), 3.

38, Though in interviews: "Medical History of Dwight D. Eisenhower, 1911–1987," Thomas W. Mattingly Papers, Box 1, Folder: General Health—Addenda," Eisenhower Library.

38, He remembered that: Quoted in Bender, 49–50; and Dorothy Brandon, *Mamie Doud Eisenhower: A Portrait of a First Lady* (New York: Charles Scribner's Sons, 1954), 156.

38, In June 1926: D'Este, 180; and "Eisenhower and Sports," *Overview: Eisenhower Foundation Newsletter* 10:1 (Spring 1984): 1–2.

38, Their son John, who: D'Este, 212; and John S. D. Eisenhower, *Strictly Personal* (Garden City, NY: Doubleday, 1974), 8.

38–39, Butcher laughingly recalled: D'Este, 213; and Neal, 74–75.

39, Ike was delighted: Susan Eisenhower, *Mrs. Ike: Memories and Reflections on the Life of Mamie Eisenhower* (New York: Farrar, Straus and Giroux, 1996), 144, 152.

39, Ike and Mamie returned: Ambrose, 120.

39, When Ike was named: Mack Johnson, "New War Aide Served with MacArthur," *Washington Post*, February 23, 1942.

40, Historian Stephen Ambrose made an: Ambrose, 171–172.

40, In 1942, General George Marshall: Pinkley, 144.

40, Marshall then sent: Pinkley, 144.

40, In 1943, Ike wrote: McCann, 115.

41, He eventually moved: Ambrose, 173.

41, His wartime chauffeur: Drew Pearson, "Golf, Jealousy in World War II," *Washington Post and Times Herald*, November 15, 1959, E3.

41, The conditions on Coombe Hill: John Strenge, *When War Played Through: Golf During World War II* (New York: Gotham Books, 2005), 210.

42, With a smile on his face: Douglas Green, "Ike: The Human Side," *American Legion*, May 1983, 22.

42, General George C. Marshall: Strenge, 276.

42, **Upon leaving the presidency:** Edward T. Folliard, " 'Remarkable Man' Leaving White House," *Washington Post and Times Herald*, January 15, 1961, E1.

43, **During the postwar occupation:** Strenge, 288.

43, **When his hometown:** Walter Winchell, "In New York: Portrait of Ike," *Washington Post*, January 5, 1951, B11.

43, **In July 1945, President Harry Truman:** Ambrose, 409.

44, **Great Britain gave him:** Letter, Kenneth T. Gordon to Charlie Yates, January 10, 1977. Folder: DDE Information, Charlie Yates Private Collection; " 'Ike' Faces Busy Visit in Scotland," *Washington Post*, September 27, 1946; and Strenge, 301.

44, **The honorary life membership:** Letter, Chairman of the Emergency Committee to Dwight D. Eisenhower, November 17, 1945, Dwight D. Eisenhower Pre-Presidential Papers, 1916–1952, Organization Series, Box 188, Folder: Clubs and Associations, St. Andrews Golf Club, Eisenhower Library.

44, **In his reply:** Letter, Dwight D. Eisenhower to M. E. Lindsay, December 21, 1945, Eisenhower Pre-Presidential Papers, 1916–1952, Organization Series, Box 188, Folder: Clubs and Associations, St. Andrews Golf Club, Eisenhower Library.

44, **The first part of the round:** "Eisenhower Sinks Long Putt," *New York Times*, October 10, 1946, 3.

44, **In 1946, while stationed:** Griffith, ed., 39.

44, **He told his friend:** Dwight D. Eisenhower, *Letters to Mamie* (Garden City, New York: Doubleday, 1978), 259.

45, **Under doctor's orders:** "Eisenhowers Off Today for Rest in Florida," *Washington Post*, December 7, 1946, 4.

45, **Upon announcing his newly:** "Celebrities' Golf Draws Big Names," *New York Times*, May 18, 1947, 51; and Morris Siegel, " 'Old Masters' Show Crowd Golf They Came to See," *Washington Post*, May 18, 1947, M8.

45, **In subsequent years:** Siegel, M8; "General Who Said 'Nuts' to Germans Plays in Tourney," *Washington Post*, May 16, 1947, 16; Shirley Povich, "Great Golf Show Starts at 1 O'Clock," *Washington Post*, May 17, 1947, 6; and "Former Champions Play for Eisenhower Cup," *Washington Post and Times Herald*, August 1, 1954, C1.

46, **Ike had been offered:** Griffith, ed., 39.

46, **Afterward, Sandburg announced:** Sam Stavisky, "People in the News," *Washington Post*, October 13, 1948, 2.

46, **They had never lived:** "Eisenhower Flies West," *New York Times*, April 25, 1948, 4; and Travis Beal Jacobs, *Eisenhower at Columbia* (New Brunswick, NJ: Transaction Publishers, 2001), 90.

46, **Characteristically, Ike replied:** Ira Henry Freeman, "Eisenhower of Columbia," *New York Times*, November 7, 1948, SM12.

46, In July, he said: "Leonard Lyons," *Washington Post,* July 15, 1948, B14.

46, In a letter to his friend: Griffith, ed., 50.

47, He played regular rounds: Clarence G. Lasby, *Eisenhower's Heart Attack* (Lawrence: University Press of Kansas, 1997), 53.

47, Ike's philosophy about his: Freeman, "Eisenhower of Columbia," SM12.

47, At the end of his talk: Freeman, SM12.

47, Ike liked Columbia: Freeman, SM12.

48, When the Nashville *Tennessean*: "Ike Issues Statement Reiterating Earlier Stand," *Washington Post,* July 6, 1948, 1.

48, To which Ike replied: Pinkley, 228. See also C. L. Sulzberger, A *Long Row of Candles: Memoirs and Diaries, 1934–1954* (New York: Macmillan Company, 1969), 649.

48, Ike also introduced Russian: Pinkley, 228.

48, In December 1948, Truman: Ambrose, 486.

49, He would hold this position: Davis, 91.

49, Eisenhower also held: C. L. Sulzberger, "Intimate Portrait of a Symbol," *New York Times,* March 25, 1951, 143.

49, The *New York Times* reported: Sulzberger, "Intimate Portrait of a Symbol," 143.

50, As a surprise for Ike: "Penny Ridgeway Sets Her Own Style," *Washington Post,* July 18, 1952, 35; David and David, 176; and John Gunther, *Eisenhower: The Man and the Symbol* (New York: Harper and Row, 1951), 33–34.

50, Golf, however, was difficult: Dorothy McCardle, "Gen. Ike Shifts to Oils from Golf for Relaxation," *Washington Post,* August 8, 1951, B3.

50, By June 1, 1952: Pinkley, 237.

51, Clifford Roberts: Davis, 96.

51, Ike, however, was lukewarm: Robert H. Ferrell, ed., *The Eisenhower Diaries* (New York: Norton, 1981), 168.

51, On February 8, 1951: Pinkley, 238; Susan Eisenhower, 265; and Herbert Brownell with John P. Burke, *Advising Ike: The Memoirs of Attorney General Herbert Brownell* (Lawrence: University Press of Kansas, 1993), 101.

51, Three days later: William B. Pickett, *Eisenhower Decides to Run* (Chicago: Ivan R. Dee, 2000), 170; and Oral History Interview with Jacqueline Cochran, March 28, 1968, by Dr. John E. Wickman, Eisenhower Library.

51, The opening paragraph described: W. G. Clugston, *Eisenhower for President? or, Who Will Get Us Out of the Messes We Are In?* (New York: Exposition Press, 1951), 11.

52, In confidence to Robinson: Ambrose, 517, 518, 521.

52, He resigned and lost: Edward F. Ryan, "Military Welcome Slated at Airport; Truman to Greet Him at White House," *Washington Post,* June 1, 1952, M1.

52, On June 1, 1952: Ambrose, 530.

52, **Bob Hope often told this revealing:** Bob Hope, *Confessions of a Hooker: My Lifelong Love Affair with Golf* (New York: Doubleday, 1985), 75–80.

53, **A week later, he was:** Robert C. Albright, "Ike Leader Charges Mail Defames General," *Washington Post*, June 30, 1952, 2; "Eisenhower to Campaign in Rocking Chair Today," *New York Times*, June 28, 1952, 9; and "Ike Sheds Convention Strain, Sees Dentist and Plays Golf," *Washington Post*, July 17, 1952, 5.

53, **They were so similar that James Reston:** James Reston, "Memo on the Two Presidential Candidates," *New York Times*, August 24, 1952, SM7.

53, **Even so, Reston went on:** Reston, "Memo on the Two Presidential Candidates," SM7.

54, **Dr. Emmet F. Pearson:** David and David, 188.

54, **In a letter to Clifford Roberts:** Louis Galambos, *The Papers of Dwight David Eisenhower: NATO and the Campaign of 1952* (Baltimore: Johns Hopkins University Press, 1989), 575.

54, **Jack Westland:** "Golf Champion Gives Putter to Eisenhower," *New York Times*, October 7, 1952, 39.

54, **A month before the election:** "Sports Stars Organized to Support Ike," *Washington Post*, October 9, 1952, 24.

54, **Fellow Augusta National member:** "Bob Jones Is Stricken," *New York Times*, October 11, 1952, 25.

55, **Regardless of the facts:** Pinkley, 256.

55, **An elderly woman:** Samuel Lubell, "Ye Compleat Political Angler," in *Eisenhower as President*, ed. Dean Albertson (New York: Hill and Wang, 1963), 28.

56, **The Carlisle Country Club:** "For Presidential Divots," *New York Times*, December 11, 1952, 48.

56, **The day after Truman:** "Tunney Says He Predicted in 1948 Ike Presidency," *Washington Post*, July 11, 1952, 40.

56, **Before the inauguration:** Natta, 63.

Chapter 3

57, **The presidential candidate:** Frank Ahrens, "Our Nation's Fore! Fathers," *Washington Post*, June 14, 1997, D1.

57, **On the day in question:** Burt Herman, "South Korean Prime Minister Resigns Over Golf Scandal," Associated Press, March 14, 2006. http://www.signonsandiego.com/news/world/20060314-1642-skorea-primeminister.html. Accessed August 13, 2006.

58, **To complicate matters:** Herman, http://www.signonsandiego.com/news/world/20060314-1642-skorea-primeminister.html.

58, **Bob Hope once said:** Don Van Natta, *First Off the Tee: Presidential Hackers, Duffers, and Cheaters from Taft to Bush* (New York: Public Affairs, 2003), 309.

58, Longtime sports broadcaster: Shepherd Campbell and Peter Landau, *Presidential Lies: The Illustrated History of White House Golf* (New York: Macmillan, 1996), 3.

58, In the 1950s: Al Barkow et al., *20th Century Golf Chronicle* (Lincolnwood, IL: Publications International, Ltd., 1993), 252.

59, The article recounted an episode: James Carney, "The Most Dogged Duffer Since Ike, Clinton Does Some of His Best Work with a Club in His Hands," *Time*, August 28, 1995. http://www.time.com/time/magazine/article/0,9171,983344,00.html. Accessed July 16, 2006.

59, As his predecessor had done: United States Golf Association, Exhibition script, "Presidential Golf: Memorabilia of White House Golfers," 1997, USGA Library and Archives.

60, Ike's predecessor, Truman: Piers Brendon, *Ike: His Life and Times* (New York: Harper and Row, 1986), 228.

60, Harding once responded: Quoted in Paul F. Boller Jr., *Presidential Anecdotes* (New York: Oxford University Press, 1996), 230.

60, No wonder Ike turned: Harold Hinton, "How Presidents Get Away from it All," *New York Times*, April 19, 1953, SM26.

60, Hinton went on to argue: Hinton, SM26.

60, One of Ike's aides explained: Campbell and Landau, 9.

60–61, George Washington had: George Gipe, *The Great America Sports Book* (New York: Doubleday, 1978), 79.

61, One story goes: Hinton, SM26; "Presidential Playtime," *Washington Post*, March 1, 1953, B4; and Gipe, 80.

61, Calvin Coolidge fished: John Hall, "Political Sportsmen," *Los Angeles Times*, November 5, 1968, C3; and Hinton, SM26.

61, A 1954 *Washington Post* editorial: A. H. Hendly Sr., "President's Relaxation," *Washington Post and Times Herald*, May 21, 1954, 22. As a singer, Margaret Truman made her first appearance on television on "Toast of the Town" in 1950. See also "Ike Finds a Fairway," *Life*, February 23, 1953, 26–27.

62, Writing for *Golf Digest*: Peter Andrews, "Ike and the Gang," *Golf Digest*, April 1993, 161.

62, *U.S. News and World Report*: "Ike: The 'Travelingest' President," *U.S. News and World Report*, March 21, 1960, 100–101.

62, In *Golf and the American Country Club*: Richard J. Moss, *Golf and the American Country Club* (Urbana: University of Illinois Press, 2001), 8.

63, He once said: George Dixon, "Washington Scene: Jefferson vs. Eisenhower," *Washington Post*, October 23, 1954, 9.

63, According to the article: "The Golfer in the White House," *USGA Journal and Turf Management* (February 1953): 4.

63, On May 1: Gipe, 82; and "Public Controversy Over Presidential Golf Isn't New," *Boston Daily Globe*, May 10, 1955, 17.

63, Boston's mayor: Edward T. Folliard, "Golfer Ike Won't Make Wilson Error," *Washington Post and Times Herald*, February 17, 1957, E1.

64, Theodore Roosevelt, the most sporting: Campbell and Landau, 12.

64, Frank Ahrens, writing: Frank Ahrens, "Our Nation's Fore! Fathers," *Washington Post*, June 14, 1997, D1.

64, Andrew Mutch: Ahrens, D1.

64, William Howard Taft: "Ike's Golf Again," *Golf World*, January 2, 1953, 5.

64, Taft often remarked: United States Golf Association, Exhibition script, "Presidential Golf: Memorabilia of White House Golfers."

64, One popular joke: Campbell and Landau, 17.

64, Another one was similarly: Dave Rubel, *Mr. President: The Human Side of America's Chief Executives* (Alexandria, VA: Time-Life Books, 1998), 161.

64, When he broke 100: Archibald Willingham Butt, *Taft and Roosevelt: The Intimate Letters of Archie Butt* (New York: Doubleday, 1930), 186–187.

65, In a reply to Travis: Gipe, 83.

65, A second letter from Roosevelt: Edmund Lindop and Joseph Jares, *White House Sportsmen* (Boston: Houghton Mifflin Co., 1964), 100.

66, It helped him survive: "William Howard Taft," http://www.whitehouse.gov/history/presidents/wt27.html. Accessed March 6, 2006.

66, During the 1908 election: Barkow et al., *20th Century Golf Chronicle*, 50.

66–67, When the press speculated: Campbell and Landau, 31.

67, So honored was he: "William Howard Taft," http://www.whitehouse.gov/history/presidents/wt27.html. Accessed March 6, 2006.

67, Paolo E. Coletta: Paolo E. Coletta, *The Presidency of William Howard Taft* (Lawrence: University of Kansas Press, 1973), 2.

67–68, Taft played what he called: Frederick C. Hicks, *William Howard Taft: Yale Professor of Law and New Haven Citizen* (New Haven: Yale University Press, 1945), 120.

68, When told by his staff: Barkow et al., *20th Century Golf Chronicle*, 50.

68, Taft realized: Al Barkow, "Big Bill Taft Presides Over the Game," *20th Century Golf Chronicle*, 50.

68, He once noted: Marquis Childs, "President's Burdens Ripe for Debate," *Washington Post and Times Herald*, June 13, 1956, 12. The quote was drawn from Clinton Rossiter's *The American Presidency* (Baltimore: Johns Hopkins University Press, 1956).

68, Wilson had played: "Ike's Golf Again," *Golf World*, January 2, 1953, 5.

68, He explained: David Lawrence, *The True Story of Woodrow Wilson* (New York: George H. Doran Company, 1924), 129.

69, After an early breakfast: *Burning Tree Club, A History 1922–1962* (Washington, DC: Burning Tree Club, 1962), 219; and Edwin A. Weinstein, *Woodrow Wilson: A Medical and Psychological Biography* (Princeton: Princeton University Press, 1981), 250.

69, According to Grayson: Lindop and Jares, 87.

69, He once described golf: Lindop and Jares, 86–87.

69, Wilson typically shot: Lindop and Jares, 88.

69, He was on the golf course: Lindop and Jares, 88.

70, **The diary of Colonel:** Folliard, "Golfer Ike Won't Make Wilson Error," E1.

70, **This, however, did not:** *Burning Tree Club, A History 1922–1962,* 220.

70, **He also played in the snow:** Lindop and Jares, 86; and "Determined Golfer," *Washington Post,* March 1, 1953, R3.

71, **For Harding, that meant:** Quoted in Paul F. Boller Jr., *Presidential Anecdotes,* 229.

71, **Harding was a betting man:** "A Long Line of Golfing Presidents," *U.S. News and World Report,* April 24, 1953, 22.

71, **In addition, he bet:** Hinton, SM26.

72, **There were plenty of reports:** Shirley Povich, "This Morning," *Washington Post and Times Herald,* September 4, 1956, 16.

72, **Between rounds:** Ahrens, D6; and Lindop and Jares, 89.

72, **Barnes later said:** Fred Byrod, "Executive Golf," *Golf Journal,* January/February 1976, 42.

72, **Walter Hagen played:** Walter Hagen, *The Walter Hagen Story* (New York: Simon and Schuster, 1956), 166.

73, **Every caddie was eventually:** Byrod, 42.

73, **All of which makes:** Quoted in Campbell and Landau, 55.

73, **When his staff finally found:** Campbell and Landau, 53.

74, **In 1926, he complained:** Lindop and Jares, 92.

74, **According to presidential lore:** United States Golf Association, Exhibition script, "Presidential Golf: Memorabilia of White House Golfers."

74, **In *Triumphant Journey*:** Richard Miller, *Triumphant Journey: The Saga of Bobby Jones and the Grand Slam of Golf* (New York: Holt, Reinhart, and Winston, 1980), 5.

75, **In 1927, the *American Golfer*:** Campbell and Landau, 72.

75, **During the New Deal:** United States Golf Association, Exhibition script, "Presidential Golf: Memorabilia of White House Golfers."

75, **FDR was very fond:** Al Barkow, *The Golden Era of Golf: How America Rose to Dominate the Old Scots Game* (New York: St. Martin's Press, 2000), 22.

76, **He once chided:** Ahrens, D6.

77, **But they certainly were prepared:** Campbell and Landau, 15.

77, **A staff member at a public:** Lindop and Jares, 94.

77, **Writing for *Golf Digest*:** John Fitzpatrick, "Ike Likes Golf . . . and It Booms!" *Golf Digest,* July 1953, 33.

78, **Exasperated by the slow play:** Andrews, 161.

79, **In February 1975:** Byrod, 20.

79, **Ronald Reagan worked as a caddie:** United States Golf Association, Exhibition script, "Presidential Golf: Memorabilia of White House Golfers."

79, **A 1993 commentary:** "Commentary," *Runner's World,* April 1993, 6.

CHAPTER 4

82, **"A fellow playing:** Will Grimsley, "Sarazen Wants Golfer Eisenhower to Do Something About Shortage of Golf Links," *Washington Post*, February 6, 1953, 28.

82, **Several editorials printed:** Richard J. Moss, *Golf and the American Country Club* (Urbana: University of Illinois Press, 2001), 52.

83, **In a May 1953 letter:** Don Van Natta, *First Off the Tee: Presidential Hackers, Duffers, and Cheaters from Taft to Bush* (New York: Public Affairs, 2003), 57.

83, **Ike's colleague Jack Westland:** "Elections Supply New Faces for Celebrities," *Washington Post*, November 6, 1952, 25.

83, **Newsweek reported:** "Ike on the Links: The Best Break Golf Ever Had," *Newsweek*, August 31, 1953, 60.

83, **A salesman for a local:** Larry Laurent, "Golf Salesmen, Pros Agree President Causes New Boom," *Washington Post*, March 4, 1953, 16.

83, **Newt Priestly:** Laurent, 16.

84, **In the words of professionals:** Laurent, 16.

84, **Sports historian:** Benjamin Rader, *American Sports: From the Age of Folk Games to the Age of Televised Sports* (Upper Saddle River, NJ: Prentice Hall, 1999), 287–288.

85, **According to the June 1954:** "The President's Green," *USGA Journal and Turf Management* (June 1954): 2.

85, **On May 14, 1954:** Al Barkow et al., *20th Century Golf Chronicle* (Lincolnwood, IL: Publications Unlimited, 1998), 266.

85, **A month later, USGA:** Letter to Isaac B. Granger from Dwight D. Eisenhower, June 14, 1954. Reprinted in the Minutes of the Meeting of the Executive Committee of the United State Golf Association, June 17, 1954, United States Golf Association Library and Archives.

86, **During the Clinton administration:** E-mail between Stan Zontek and Jenean Todd, January 15, 2002, United States Golf Association Library and Archives.

86, **Never one to shy away:** Edmund Lindop and Joseph Jares, *White House Sportsmen* (Boston: Houghton Mifflin Co., 1964), 98.

86, **That initiated, Hope explained:** Bob Hope, *Confessions of a Hooker: My Lifelong Love Affair with Golf* (New York: Doubleday, 1985), 73.

86, **Hope once quipped:** Shepherd Campbell and Peter Landau, *Presidential Lies: The Illustrated History of White House Golf* (New York: Macmillan, 1996), 97.

87, **He recounted one story:** "The Pro and the President," Program for the Eisenhower International Golf Classic, Hollytree Golf Club, Tyler, Texas, May 11, 1987, 7–8.

87, **An exacting player:** Al Barkow and David Barrett, *Golf Greats* (Lincolnwood, IL; Publications International, Ltd., 1998), 222.

Notes

88, **In his book *Golf Anecdotes*:** Robert Sommers, *Golf Anecdotes* (New York: Oxford, 1995), 193.

89, **Ike shot a 94:** "Ike Golfs with Top Professionals on Augusta Course," *Washington Post*, April 15, 1953, 9; and Ben Hogan and Tim Cohane, "How Ike Can Play in the 80's," *Look*, June 2, 1953, 31.

89, **Hogan complimented:** Campbell and Landau, 97.

89, **That may be why:** "Burning Tree Golf Course Haven from Politics for Eisenhower," *New York Times*, July 3, 1955, S3.

89–90, **In New York in the 1930s:** John Companiotte, *Jimmy Demaret: The Swing's the Thing* (Chelsea, MI: Clock Tower Press, 2004); and Barkow and Barrett, 61.

90, **A regular player with Ike:** Campbell and Landau, 97.

90, **On May 25, 1955:** "President Plays with Middlecoff, Byron Nelson," *Washington Post and Times Herald*, May 15, 1955, 49.

90, **'Dear Ike':** Sommers, 185.

91, **Al Barkow and David Barrett:** Barkow and Barrett, 176.

91, **In addition, the advent:** Rader, 233.

92, **Ike once said:** "Dwight D. Eisenhower—He Loved to Play," *Golf Journal*, May 1969, 21.

92, **When Arnold opened it:** Arnold Palmer, *Arnold Palmer: Memories, Stories, and Memorabilia from a Life On and Off the Course* (New York: Stewart, Tabori, and Chang, 2004), 95.

92, **In his book *Arnold Palmer*:** Palmer, 93.

93, **When she asked about his golf:** "Ike and Babe Zaharias Open Cancer Drive, Chat About Golf," *Washington Post*, April 3, 1954, 14.

94, **Samuel Rauworth:** Jack Mabley, "Strictly for Women," *Washington Post and Times Herald*, February 28, 1956, 21.

94, **In his book *American Sports*:** Rader, 128.

95, **On April 9, 1947:** Rader, 294.

95, **In an article published:** Rader, 295.

95, **Rader explained that these:** Rader, 296.

95, **When other players complained:** George Peper, *The Story of Golf* (New York: TV Books, 1999), 169.

96, **The few African Americans:** Moss, 112.

96, **In 1934, the PGA of America:** Steve Eubanks, *Augusta: Home of the Masters Tournament* (Nashville: Rutledge Hill Press, 1997), 152.

96, **Agitation for change:** Peper, *The Story of Golf*, 169–171.

97, **In his book, *Just Let Me Play*:** Charlie Sifford with Jim Gullo, "Bitter Memories," *Golf Magazine*, June 1992, 106.

97, **In one titled:** "President's Drives Send Golf in Capital Over Par," *New York Times*, November 16, 1953, 7.

97, **Bob Hope once joked:** Hope, 73.

98, **Bill Wilson, the club's manager:** "4 Negroes Test City Parks Ban," *Atlanta Constitution*, July 20, 1951, 4.

98, **By 1890, East Lake:** Gail Anne D'Avino, "Atlanta Municipal Parks, 1882–1917," Ph.D. dissertation, 1988, 74, 95.

99, **The desire for recreational facilities:** D'Avino, 142, 80.

99, **Lincoln Country Club:** Herman Mason, *Going Against the Wind: A Pictorial History of African Americans in Atlanta* (Atlanta: Longstreet Press, 1992), 106.

99, **When it opened in 1927:** Karen Harris, "Arson Does Heavy Damage at Lincoln Country Club," *Atlanta Journal Constitution*, January 2, 1985, A8; and "Lincoln Country Club Gutted by Fire; Officials Rule Arson," *Atlanta Daily World*, January 3–4, 1985, A1.

100, **When the four black men:** "Park Named in Holmes' Memory Sounds Historic Tone for Atlanta," *Atlanta Daily World*, August 23, 1983, 1.

100, **On December 24, 1955:** "Racial Equality Goes to Tee on Atlanta Public Links," *New York Times*, December 25, 1955, 12.

100, **When asked about the historic moment:** "Racial Equality Goes to Tee on Atlanta Public Links," 12.

100, **Georgia Governor Marvin Griffin:** "Mayor Says Majority of People to Accept City Golf Decision," *Atlanta Journal*, December 23, 1955.

101, **The governor was frustrated:** "Atlanta to Open Links," *New York Times*, December 24, 1955, 13.

CHAPTER 5

103, **My first day:** Dwight D. Eisenhower wrote this in his diary on January 21, 1952. Virgil Pinkley with James F. Sheer, *Eisenhower Declassified* (Old Tappan, NJ: Fleming H. Revell, 1979), 273.

104, **He advocated peace:** Piers Brendon, *Ike: His Life and Times* (New York: Harper and Row, 1986), 3.

104, **He was a strong supporter:** Public Papers of the Presidents, Dwight D. Eisenhower, 1960, 1035–1040. http://coursesa.matrix.msu.edu/~hst306/documents/indust.html. Accessed July 16, 2006.

104, **His critics jokingly:** Thomas A. Bailey, *Presidential Greatness: The Image and the Man from George Washington to the Present* (New York: Appleton-Century-Crofts, 1966), 325.

104, **Toward the end of his:** Bailey, 327–328.

105, **In the same book:** Brendon, 5–6.

105, **Samuel Lubell, a 1950s:** Samuel Lubell, *The Revolt of the Moderates* (New York: Harper and Brothers, 1956), 4.

Notes

106, **The gross national:** William H. Young and Nancy K. Young, *The 1950s* (Westport, CT: Greenwood Press, 2004), xv–xxi.

106, **Kentucky Fried Chicken:** Edward Russoli, *Dwight D. Eisenhower: General, President, Cook* (Allentown, PA: Benedettini Books, 1990), 114.

106, **From 1948 to 1958:** Beth Bailey and David Farber et al., *The Fifties Chronicle* (Lincolnwood, IL: Publications International, Ltd., 2006), 15.

106, **In addition, twenty-nine million:** Richard Reeves, "America Looked Good to a High School Senior Then," *American Heritage* 45:8 (December 1994): 30–38.

106, **Consumerism became a ubiquitous:** Reeves, 30–38.

107, **The future seemed so promising:** Shirley Anne Wardshaw, ed., *Reexamining the Eisenhower Presidency* (Westport, CT: Greenwood Press, 1993), xvii.

107, **As Charles Price:** Charles Price, "Why Golf Really Grew," *Golf Digest*, April 1989, 46.

108, **Eisenhower's principal contribution:** Eisenhower Library and Museum website, http://www.eisenhower.archives.gov. Accessed April 15, 2006.

108, **It was the largest public works:** J. Ronald Oakley, "Good Times: The American Economy in the Fifties," in *The Eisenhower Presidency and the 1950s*, ed. Michael S. Mayer (Boston: Houghton Mifflin Co., 1998), 202.

108, **The American Society of:** Eisenhower Library and Museum website, http://www.eisenhower.archives.gov. Accessed August 13, 2006.

108, **To showcase the nation's efforts:** Stephen Ambrose quoted in Richard Weingroff, "The Man Who Changed America, Part II," *Public Roads* 66:6 (May–June 2003): 22–38. In a letter to his friend Charlie Yates, Ike confessed that he was glad that trip was over: "I never thought I would make such an assertion, but it is a relief, after ten days of Mr. Khrushchev, to get back to some of the politicking that goes on in the United States as illustrated by the letter from your Democratic friend." Letter from Dwight D. Eisenhower to Charlie Yates, September 29, 1959. Folder: Yates/Eisenhower Scrapbook, Charlie Yates Private Collection.

109, **Before Levittown, the majority:** David Halberstam, *The Fifties* (New York: Villard Books, 1993), 132.

110, **Though being Jewish himself:** Halberstam, 135, 141.

110, **Writing for *Fortune* magazine:** Lucian K. Truscott IV, "More Than Just a Car," *Fortune*, September 18, 2000, 182.

111, **During the 1950s:** Ken Hess, "The Growth of Automobile Transportation," 1984, updated 1996. http://www.klhess.com/car_essy.html. Accessed July 16, 2006. And Bureau of the Census, "Historical Statistics of the United States: Colonial Times to 1970" (Washington, DC: U.S. Government Printing Office, 1975). http://www2.census.gov/prod2/statcomp/documents/CT1970p1-01.pdf. Accessed July 16, 2006.

111, **Historian David Halberstam:** Halberstam, 143.

112, **Magazines, newspapers, and television:** Bailey and Farber et al., 149.

112, **Mamie Eisenhower was the perfect:** Bailey and Farber et al., 148.

112, **While visiting New York:** Robert J. Donovan, *Confidential Secretary: Ann Whitman's 20 Years with Eisenhower and Rockefeller* (New York: E. P. Dutton, 1988), 129.

113, **For their husbands in private:** Reeves, 30–38.

113, **In 1952, women became:** Reeves, 30–38; and Estelle Jackson, "GOP an Agency for America," *Washington Post*, April 9, 1954, 47.

114, **Ike supported these trends:** Malvina Lindsay, "Need of Presidents to Combat Tension," *Washington Post*, April 15, 1953, 16.

114, **Even Nikita Khruschev:** Drew Pearson, "Ike's Golf Praised by Khrushchev," *Washington Post and Times Herald*, September 29, 1958, B19.

114–15, **As one reporter noted:** Marvin L. Arrowsmith, "Ike Invites Many to 'Fitness' Talk," *Washington Post and Times Herald*, September 18, 1955, B12.

115, **Norman Palmer, the golf professional:** Norman Palmer, *Five Star Golf* (New York: Duell, Sloan and Pearce, 1964), 84.

115, **At first, the magazine focused:** Bailey and Farber et al., 217.

115–16, **Historian Benjamin Rader explained:** Benjamin Rader, *American Sports: From the Age of Folk Games to the Age of Televised Sports* (Upper Saddle River, NJ: Prentice Hall, 1999), 289.

116, **The U.S. Open was the first:** George Peper et al., *Golf in America: The First 100 Years* (New York: Harry N. Abrams, 1994), 280.

116, **Arthur Krock, writing for:** Robert Wright, "Eisenhower's Fifties," *Antioch Review* (Summer 1980): 283.

117, **At his 1953 inauguration:** Bailey and Farber et al., 152.

117, **In 1951, the Federal Civil Defense Administration:** Bailey and Farber et al., 69.

117, **In 1954, Oklahoma A&M College:** Lance Morrow, "Dreaming of the Eisenhower Years," *Time*, July 28, 1980, 33.

117, **In the summer of 1959:** Elaine Tyler May, "Cold War-Warm Heart," in *The Eisenhower Presidency and the 1950s*, ed. Michael S. Mayer, 207.

118, **On December 28:** Robert Pavy, "A Look at the 20th Century," *Augusta Chronicle*, August 1, 1999. http://chronicle.augusta.com/stories/080199/cy2_152-1859.000.shtml. Accessed September 11, 2005.

118, **The birth control pill:** Reeves, 30–38.

118, **Secretary of Commerce Sinclair Weeks:** Edward T. Folliard, "Launching of Satellite Made Lasting Impact," *Washington Post and Times Herald*, September 30, 1958, A1; and NASA, http://history.nasa.gov/sputnik/. Accessed August 13, 2006.

119, **In 1958, he supported the:** Dwight D. Eisenhower, *In Review: Pictures I've Kept* (Garden City, NY: Doubleday, 1969), 190.

119, **Ike's close friend:** Quoted in Brendon, 347–348.

119, **One political cartoon:** Reprinted in the *New York Times*, October 13, 1957, E3.

271

119, *Explorer V*, the American: Folliard, "Launching of Satellite Made Lasting Impact," A1.

119, On July 29, 1958: "National Aeronautics and Space Act of 1958," Public Law #85-568, 72 Stat, 426. Signed by the president on July 29, 1958, Record Group 255, National Archives and Records Administration, Washington, DC, available in the NASA Historical Reference Collection, History Office, NASA Headquarters, Washington, DC.

120, During his entire eight years: Gunter Bischof and Stephen E. Ambrose, *Eisenhower: A Centenary Assessment* (Baton Rouge and London: Louisiana State University Press, 1995), 25.

120, In their book *Reevaluating Eisenhower*: Richard A. Melanson and David Mayers, *Reevaluating Eisenhower: American Foreign Policy in the 1950s* (Urbana: University of Illinois Press, 1987), 4.

120, His accusations resulted: Young and Young, 14.

121, The most regrettable incident: Marquis Childs, *Eisenhower: Captive Hero* (New York: Harcourt, Brace and World, Inc., 1958), 144.

121, Loathing McCarthy as Eisenhower: Stephen E. Ambrose, *Eisenhower: The President* (New York: Simon and Schuster, 1984), 634.

121, He never spoke out: Ambrose, *Eisenhower: The President*, 634.

122, A white woman, who had: Pete Daniel, *Lost Revolutions: The South in the 1950s* (Chapel Hill: University of North Carolina Press, 2000), 193.

122, On September 25, 1953: Robert J. Donovan, *Eisenhower: The Inside Story* (New York: Harper and Brothers, 1956), 207.

122, Even children criticized: "Survey Among Farm Youths Shows Fear for Prosperity," *Washington Post*, October 18, 1953, M1.

122, In 1958, Senator William Proxmire: "Proxmire Lists Issues in Campaign," *Washington Post and Times Herald*, April 20, 1958, A25.

123, He turned it into much: Donovan, *Eisenhower: The Inside Story*, 202; "President to Keep Yacht," *New York Times*, March 12, 1953, 19; and Ellis D. Slater, *The Ike I Knew* (New York: The Ellis D. Slater Trust, 1980), 53.

123, Film noir features: Foster Hirsch, *Film Noir: The Dark Side of the Screen* (New York: DeCapo Press, 1981), 9.

124, The next year, Jack Kerouac: Brendon, 277.

124, James Reston, in a September: Robert Wright, "Eisenhower's Fifties," *Antioch Review* (Summer 1980): 281.

124, Journalist Merriman Smith: Merriman Smith, *Meet Mister Eisenhower* (New York: Harper and Row, 1955), 176.

125, Historian Thomas Bailey: Bailey, 145.

CHAPTER 6

127, If I go anywhere: Ellis D. Slater, *The Ike I Knew* (New York: The Ellis D. Slater Trust, 1980), 32. Mamie made this reply to Ellis "Slats" Slater in

February 1953 when he urged Mamie to travel to Arizona to help her recover from a cold.

127, **Woodrow Wilson lived:** Bill Kirby, "Presidents Visited City Frequently," *Augusta Chronicle*, February 22, 1998; and "Biographies Tie to Augusta," *Augusta Chronicle*, May 29, 1999. http://chronicle.augusta.com/ stories/052699/met_142-2261.000.shtml. Accessed September 11, 2005.

128, **At a public address:** Stan Byrdy, *Augusta and Aiken in Golf's Golden Age* (Charleston: Arcadia Publishing, 2002), 18, 72.

128, **By April 1923:** James Gallagher, "A Tale of Two Hotels," *Augusta Chronicle*, April 20, 2005. http://chronicle.augusta.com/stories/050105/ bus_3876696.shtml. Accessed September 11, 2005; and Byrdy, 110.

128, **Franklin Roosevelt is reported:** Kirby, http://chronicle.augusta.com/ stories/052699/met_142-2261.000.shtml.

129, **As Stan Burdy explained:** Byrdy, 9.

129, **The Bon Air Golf Club:** David Westin, "Book Captures Augusta History," *Augusta Chronicle*, January 7, 2003. http://chronicle.augusta .com/stories/010803/wes_041-6665.000.shtml. Accessed September 11, 2005.

130, **Al Barkow explained:** Al Barkow, *The Golden Era of Golf: How America Rose to Dominate the Old Scots Game* (New York: St. Martin's Press, 2000), 66.

131, **The population in 1950:** Mercer Bailey, "Ike's Visits Cause No Augusta Furor," *Washington Post*, April 10, 1953, 38.

131, **It would be Ike's first:** Virgil Pinkley with James F. Sheer, *Eisenhower Declassified* (Old Tappan, NJ: Fleming H. Revell, 1979), 279; Travis Beal Jacobs, *Eisenhower at Columbia* (New Brunswick, NJ: Transaction Publishers, 2001), 62; and Robert Griffith, ed., *Ike's Letters to a Friend*, 1941–1958 (Lawrence, Kansas: University Press of Kansas, 1984), 49.

131, **Robinson flew Ike:** William B. Pickett, *Eisenhower Decides to Run* (Chicago: Ivan R. Dee, 2000), 42.

132, **Years later, Eisenhower:** Dwight D. Eisenhower, *At Ease: Stories I Tell To My Friends* (New York: Doubleday, 1967), 325.

132, **Ike's book was later:** Peter Andrews, "Ike and the Gang," *Golf Digest*, April 1993, 161.

132, **Dudley often remarked:** "Ed Dudley, First Pro for Eisenhower Dies," *Washington Post and Times Herald*, October 27, 1963, C5; and Will Grimsley, "Round of Golf Makes New Man of Eisenhower," *Washington Post*, March 22, 1953, C3.

132, **At the end of the year:** Curt Sampson, *The Masters: Golf, Money, and Power in Augusta, Georgia* (New York: Villard Books, 1998), 123.

133, **Roberts said that Mamie:** Shepherd Campbell and Peter Landau, *Presidential Lies: The Illustrated History of White House Golf* (New York: Macmillan, 1996), 108.

273

133, **Roberts first played golf:** David Owen, *The Making of the Masters: Clifford Roberts, Augusta National, and Golf's Most Prestigious Tournament* (New York: Simon and Schuster, 1999), 46.

134, **On April 18, 1948:** "Eisenhower's Sanctuary," *Masters Journal*, 1999, 7.

134, **The photograph was inscribed:** Sampson, 122.

134, **Twenty years later:** "Eisenhower's Sanctuary," 8; and Oral History Interview with Clifford Roberts, September 12, 1968, 1 of 15, Columbia University Oral History Project, 6, Eisenhower Library.

135, **A year later, Jones:** Letter from Dwight D. Eisenhower to Robert Tyre Jones Jr., October 10, 1960, Eisenhower folder. Atlanta Athletic Club Collection.

135, **To reflect Ike's esteem:** Bob Considine, "How Ike Lives," *Washington Post and Times Herald*, October 3, 1954, AW7.

135, **In one dated May 19, 1953:** Letter from Mamie Eisenhower to Mary Jones, May 19, 1953, Eisenhower folder. Atlanta Athletic Club Collection.

136, **At the ceremony, Totten Heffelfinger:** Lincoln A. Werden, "Eisenhower Pays Tribute to Jones," *New York Times*, February 1, 1953, S1.

136, **When Ike was finished:** "Scores 'About a 96,'" *New York Times*, March 1, 1953, 74. Stephens painted Ike's portrait at least twice. One hangs in the National Portrait Gallery Hall of Presidents and the other is in Gettysburg.

136, **He later joked:** Edward T. Folliard, "Ike Presents Oil Portrait to Bobby Jones," *Washington Post*, March 1, 1953, M1.

136, **Historian Stephen Ambrose described:** Stephen E. Ambrose, *Eisenhower: Soldier, General of the Army, President Elect, 1890–1952* (New York: Simon and Schuster, 1983), 476.

137, **In it, he detailed how:** Letter from Clifford Roberts to Dwight D. Eisenhower, Dwight D. Eisenhower, Papers as President (Ann Whitman File), 1953–1961, Name Series, Box 27, Folder: Roberts, Clifford, 1952–3 (2), Eisenhower Library.

137, **So frequent did Ike:** Owen, 169.

138, **Robinson and Roberts led:** Andrews, 161.

138, **They were to be men:** Letter, Clifford Roberts to Dwight D. Eisenhower, December 5, 1951, Dwight D. Eisenhower, Pre-Presidential Papers, 1916–1953, Principal File, Box 98, Folder: Roberts, Clifford (3), Nov. 1951–Dec. 1951, Eisenhower Library.

138, **The initial list was made:** Letter, Clifford Roberts to Dwight D. Eisenhower, November 15, 1951, Dwight D. Eisenhower, Pre-Presidential Papers, 1916–1953, Principal File, Box 98, Folder: Roberts, Clifford (3), Nov. 1951–Dec. 1951, Eisenhower Library.

139, **The gang also helped:** Jacobs, 73, 247.

139, **Slats Slater recounts:** Slater, 151.

139, **In 1959, the *Washington Post*:** "Eisenhower Phones N.Y. at 3 A.M. to Get Two Golf Cronies to Scotland," *Washington Post and Times Herald*, September 6, 1959, A1.

139, **Woodruff said in a 1950:** Sampson, 59–60.

139, **Woodruff had long admired:** Sampson, 61.

139, **Historian Piers Brendon:** Piers Brendon, *Ike: His Life and Times* (New York: Harper and Row, 1986), 196.

140, **The gang's main role:** Andrews, 162–164.

140, **Ike described his Augusta friends:** Dwight D. Eisenhower, *Mandate for Change*, quoted in Andrews, 164.

140, **Eisenhower even wrote:** Allan Taylor, ed., *What Eisenhower Thinks* (New York: Thomas Y. Crowell Co., 1952), 36–38.

140, **Ohio Senator Robert Taft:** Andrews, 162.

141, **Not until someone yelled:** Dorothy McCardle, "Question of the Hour: Will Eisenhower Put a Woman in Cabinet?" *Washington Post*, November 9, 1952, S1.

141, **Roberts recalled the scene:** "Eisenhower's Sanctuary," 8.

141, **Ike was well protected:** Edward T. Folliard, "Ike Finds Complete Seclusion Except for Increased Guard," *Washington Post*, November 11, 1952, 1.

141, **After a strenuous campaign:** William R. Conklin, "General Arrives in Georgia to Rest," *New York Times*, November 6, 1952, 1.

141, **Ike took a different:** William R. Conklin, "General Gratified," *New York Times*, November 7, 1952, 1.

142, **He spent much of his time:** Marin Durkin (Secretary of Labor) was the former head of a plumbers union. The others cabinet members were John Foster Dulles (Secretary of State), Charles E. Wilson (Secretary of Defense), Douglas McKay (Secretary of Interior), George M. Humphrey (Secretary of the Treasury), Ezra Taft Benson (Secretary of Agriculture), Herbert Brownell (Attorney General), Arthur Summerfield (Postmaster General), Oveta Culp Hobby (Secretary of Health, Education and Welfare), and Sinclair Week (Secretary of Commerce). Pinkley, 261.

142, **But Ike did describe the telegram:** Conklin, "General Gratified," 4.

142, **They had their breakfast:** Conklin, "General Gratified," 4.

143, **Pope Pius XII cabled:** "White House Note Flown by Courier to General," *Washington Post*, November 8, 1952, 1.

143, **Two Secret Service agents:** "Eisenhower's Sanctuary," 9.

144, **"He sent telegrams to the parents:** Dayton Moore, "Ike Names 3 To Seek Peace in Rail Dispute," *Washington Post*, November 26, 1954, 23.

144, **In spite of these significant decisions:** Andrews, 161.

144, **That year, he bought:** Robert J. Donovan, *Eisenhower: The Inside Story* (New York: Harper and Brothers, 1956), 39, 194.

144, **Clifford Roberts remembered:** "Dwight D. Eisenhower—He Loved to Play," *Golf Journal*, May 1969, 21.

145, **Augusta became, during Ike's:** "Fort Gordon: Dwight D. Eisenhower Memorial Hospital," *Augusta Chronicle*, June 28, 1972, 1.

145, Ann Whitman, Ike's personal: Robert J. Donovan, *Confidential Secretary: Ann Whitman's 20 Years with Eisenhower and Rockefeller* (New York: E. P. Dutton, 1988), 74.

145, On New Year's Day: Donovan, *Confidential Secretary,* 74.

146, Others called him Dead Man: Edward T. Folliard, "Augusta Hails Ike on 3-Day Golfing Visit," *Washington Post,* February 27, 1953, 1. See also Ward Clayton, *Men on the Bag: The Caddies of Augusta National* (Ann Arbor, MI: Sports Media Group, 2004), 46–58; and Eugene Kinkead, "Caddy to the President," *Life,* May 11, 1953, 111–116.

146, Perteet never wavered: Ed Dudley and William A. Emerson Jr., "I Like Ike's Golf," *Collier's,* April 18, 1953, 20–21.

146, During one ten-day visit: Clayton, 52.

147, The *New York Times* reported: W. H. Lawrence, "Eisenhower in South for a Rest and Golf," *New York Times,* February 27, 1953, 1.

147, During the trip, Roberts: Lawrence, "Eisenhower in South for a Rest and Golf," 1.

147, In March, the *New York Times* published: "Break That Ninety!" *New York Times,* March 1, 1953.

148, Taft was no stranger to: W. H. Lawrence, "Taft Plays Golf with Eisenhower," *New York Times,* April 20, 1953, 14.

148, The next day, however: James Reston, "President Putts the Party in an Impossible Dilemma," *New York Times,* April 23, 1953, 21; and Barkow, 260.

149, He added that seven putts: W. H. Lawrence, "Eisenhower Shoots 88 as He Ends Vacation," *New York Times,* April 22, 1953, 1.

149, Eisenhower's five-year-old grandson: W. H. Lawrence, "President Joins Under-90 Golfers: 86 Best Taft in First of Two Rounds," *New York Times,* April 21, 1953, 1.

149, Roberts described Ike's spirited: Joseph E. Loftus, "Eisenhower's Formula for Relaxation," *New York Times,* September 5, 1954, SM10.

150, On April 8, 1953, ANGC: Augusta National Golf Club, News Release, November 25, 1953, Augusta National Golf Club Archives.

150, The second-floor dormers: "Eisenhower's Sanctuary," 8; and "Eisenhower's Cabin to Be Ready in Fall," *New York Times,* April 9, 1953, 29.

151, The company that manufactured: Slater, 33.

151, When asked about the new: John D. Morris, "Eisenhowers Plan a Quiet Holiday," *New York Times,* November 26, 1953, 6.

151, Right after they moved in: Slater, 57.

151, He had not known their: Slater, 244; and Invitation, Special Improvements Group Reunion Dinner, May 6, 1961, Dwight D. Eisenhower, Post-Presidential Papers, 1961–1969, 1961 Principal File, Box 16, Folder: PAR (1), Eisenhower Library.

152, The typical sermon began: W. H. Lawrence, "Young Georgian Meets the President," *New York Times*, March 2, 1953, 1; and Jim Davis, *Reid Memorial Presbyterian Church*, history booklet, 2003.

152, When complimented on his: Marvin L. Arrowsmith, "Ike Lays Cornerstone After Easter Service," *Washington Post*, April 19, 1954, 1–2.

153, When the tree was removed: E-mail from L. Phillip Christman II to Catherine Lewis, July 18, 2006.

153, The *New York Times* reported: Lincoln A. Werden, "Spotlight on Augusta," *New York Times*, March 15, 1953, X19.

153, Ike and Hogan won: Fred Byrod, "Executive Golf," *Golf Journal*, January/February 1976, 42.

153, Palmer quipped during the round: Richard Lyons, "Eisenhower Plays Golf with Arnold Palmer," *Washington Post and Times Herald*, April 12, 1960, A19.

154, Still a part of the course: Kamille Bostick, "Ike's Pond Provides Peaceful Setting," *Augusta Chronicle*, April 7, 2005; and Letter, Clifford Roberts to Jerry A. Franklin, September 30, 1949, Dwight D. Eisenhower, Pre-Presidential Papers, 1916–1953, Principal File, Box 98, Folder: Roberts, Clifford (7), January 1949–January 1950, Eisenhower Library.

154, While in Walter Reed Hospital: Letter from Dwight D. Eisenhower to Charlie Yates, December 9, 1965, Folder: DDE Letters and Information about Mamie D. Eisenhower, 1960s–1970s, Charlie Yates Private Collection.

154, Bob Sommers recounted: Robert Sommers, *Golf Anecdotes* (New York: Oxford, 1995), 193; and "Dwight D. Eisenhower—He Loved to Play," *Golf Journal*, May 1969, 21.

155, When Ike was asked in 1958: Letter from Dwight D. Eisenhower to Charlie Yates, May 8, 1958, Folder: Yates/Eisenhower Scrapbook. Charlie Yates Private Collection.

155, When asked about it, O'Meara: Dave Anderson, "Ike's Tree Re-Enlists as Augusta Hazard," *New York Times*, April 8, 1999, D4. The hole was lengthened again in 2005.

155, At a sendoff party: Slater, 10; and letter from Dwight D. Eisenhower to Charlie Yates, March 30, 1953, Folder: Yates/Eisenhower Scrapbook, Charlie Yates Private Collection.

156, It was presented to Ike: W. H. Lawrence, "Humphrey Presents 'Eisenhower Cracker Barrel,' " *New York Times*, November 18, 1957, 1.

156, Humphrey was a Cleveland: Lawrence, "Humphrey Presents," 1.

156, Humphrey joked with: Lawrence, "Humphrey Presents," 1.

157, The band gave Eisenhower: "Fort Gordon: Dwight D. Eisenhower Memorial Hospital," *Augusta Chronicle*, June 28, 1972, 3.

157, The *Augusta Chronicle* reported: "Fort Gordon: Dwight D. Eisenhower Memorial Hospital," 3.

157, *Atlanta Journal* columnist Paul Hemphill: "Operation Ike," *Atlanta Journal*, November 15, 1965, 2.

157, While Ike was recuperating: Virginia Norton, "Prayers of a President," *Augusta Chronicle*, April 11, 2003. http://chronicle.augusta.com/stories/041203/rel_223-2535.000.shtml. Accessed September 10, 2005.

158, On the day of his: "Augusta Club Likes Ikes," *New York Times*, January 21, 1953, 36.

158, An *Augusta Chronicle* columnist: Randy Russell, "All in the Game," *Augusta Chronicle*, January 22, 1953, B6.

158, "Fans didn't like the Ikes": "Ike's Out: Ball Club Seeks New Name," *Augusta Chronicle*, January 29, 1953, 3B.

158, Objections came from all sides: "Ike's Out: Ball Club Seeks New Name," 3B; and "Game Is Never Over Until the Last Out," *Augusta Chronicle*, February 11, 1953, 8B.

159, During and after the Korean War: Eisenhower Army Medical Center, "History of Eisenhower Army Medical Center." http://www.ddeamc.amedd.army.mil/Visitor/history.htm. Accessed September 13, 2005.

159, At the event, he remarked: "Fort Gordon: Dwight D. Eisenhower Memorial Hospital," *Augusta Chronicle*, June 28, 1972, 1.

159, Afterward, he went to Augusta: "Fort Gordon: Dwight D. Eisenhower Memorial Hospital," 1, 3.

160, The monument, which was moved: Eisenhower Army Medical Center, "History of Eisenhower Army Medical Center." http://www.ddeamc.amedd.army.mil/Visitor/history.htm. Accessed September 13, 2005. And "Drive for Eisenhower Memorial Is Successful," *Augusta Chronicle*, April 9, 1972.

CHAPTER 7

161, Some of us worship: "Humorous Quotes About Golf." http://www.workinghumor.com/quotes/golf.shtml. Accessed August 31, 2005.

161, Cullen then turned to the cosmetician: John Crosby, "TV Quiz Contestants Have More Fun than People," *Washington Post and Times Herald*, September 13, 1954, 11.

161, Upon winning the 1952 election: Virgil Pinkley with James F. Sheer, *Eisenhower Declassified* (Old Tappan, NJ: Fleming H. Revell, 1979), 259.

162, One was written by a young girl: Pinkley, 281.

162, He broke 80 at least: Shepherd Campbell and Peter Landau, *Presidential Lies: The Illustrated History of White House Golf* (New York: Macmillan, 1996), 97.

162, Though he struggled: Norman Palmer and William V. Levy, "Eisenhower on the Tee," *Golf Digest*, December 1964, 71; and Campbell and Landau, 96–97.

162, This remark prompted: Campbell and Landau, 106.

163, **Not to be outdone:** "Don't Ask What I Shot," *Golf Digest*, July 1953, 45–48.

163, **Mamie once said:** Marie Smith, "Sixty Signals Start of Fast Social Pace for the First Lady," *Washington Post and Times Herald*, January 31, 1960, F1.

163, **Democratic congressman Omar Burleson:** Campbell and Landau, 105; and Robert C. Albright, "A Filibuster Foe Finds Use for One," *Washington Post*, March 22, 1953, B1.

163–64, **The January 2, 1953:** "Ike's Golf Again," *Golf World*, January 2, 1953, 5.

164, **Roger Kahn described:** *Burning Tree Club, A History 1922–1962* (Washington, DC: Burning Tree Club, 1962), 225; and Roger Kahn, "Take a Mulligan, Mr. President!" *Golf*, April 1959, 58.

164, **A potential member's name:** "Ike on the Links: The Best Break Golf Ever Had," *Newsweek*, August 31, 1953, 60–61.

164, **One member quipped:** Kahn, 58.

165, **The pale green walls:** Kahn, 58.

165, **Charter members contributed:** Edward T. Folliard, "Ike's Golf Club Is a 'Sanctuary' to Its Members," *Washington Post*, July 26, 1953, B1, 7.

165, **In the words of the New York Times:** "Burning Tree Golf Course Haven from Politics for Eisenhower," *New York Times*, July 3, 1955, 53.

166, **Ike mostly played in a threesome:** "Burning Tree Golf Course Haven from Politics for Eisenhower," 53; "Ike on the Links: The Best Break Golf Ever Had," 62; and *Burning Tree Club, A History 1922–1962*, 225.

166, **Toward the end of Ike's term:** *Burning Tree Club, A History 1922–1962*, 227.

166, **Most of his fellow golfers:** Merriman Smith, *Meet Mister Eisenhower* (New York: Harper and Row, 1955), 176–177.

167, **In a letter dated June 18, 1954:** "That Elusive Ace: The Hole-in-One and Who's Been There, Done That," Pasturegolf.com. http://www.pasture golf.com/archive/ace.htm. Accessed August 31, 2005.

167, **By the sixteenth green:** Campbell and Landau, 110.

168, **The caddie answered:** Robert Sommers, *Golf Anecdotes* (New York: Oxford, 1995), 192.

168, **The caddies, upon learning:** Campbell and Landau, 111.

168, **As Ike was paying:** Don Van Natta, *First Off the Tee: Presidential Hackers, Duffers, and Cheaters from Taft to Bush* (New York: Public Affairs, 2003), 70.

169, **His friend Slats Slater:** "Ike Installs 1-Hole Golf Course at Camp David," *Washington Post*, August 14, 1954, 15; Owen, 171; and Ellis D. Slater, *The Ike I Knew* (New York: The Ellis D. Slater Trust, 1980), 76.

170, **Encoded messages were sent:** Edward T. Folliard, "Work-Play Vacation," *Washington Post and Times Herald*, August 26, 1954, 13.

170, **He would typically work:** "Ike Returning to Capitol Late Today," *Washington Post*, September 19, 1953; and Joseph E. Loftus, "Eisenhower's Formula for Relaxation," *New York Times*, September 5, 1954, SM10.

170, Thornton often said of Ike's: Will Grimsley, "Round of Golf Makes Man of Eisenhower," *Washington Post*, March 22, 1953, C3.

170, Evenings at the hotel: "Golf, Bridge, and Food—But Little 'Shop Talk,'" *U.S. News and World Report*, September 23, 1955, 61.

170–71, During that lengthy vacation: Richard Tanner Johnson, *Managing the White House: An Intimate Study of the Presidents* (New York: Harper and Row, 1974), 117.

171, The event shook the nation: David Rubel, *Mr. President: The Human Side of America's Chief Executives* (Alexandria, VA: Time-Life Books, 1998), 203.

171, A group of newspaper reporters: "Ike Sends Thanks for Floral Golf Club," *Washington Post and Times Herald*, October 23, 1955, A6; and Pinkley, 325.

171, Merriman Smith and Laurence H. Burd: Robert J. Donovan, *Eisenhower: The Inside Story* (New York: Harper and Row, 1955), 376.

171, Most surprisingly, a group: Eleanor Harris, "Ike—As a Woman Sees Him," *Washington Post and Times Herald*, August 19, 1956, AW8.

171, In *Eisenhower: The Inside Story*: Edward T. Folliard, "Ike's Choice," *Washington Post and Times Herald*, July 3, 1956, 11.

172, His personal physician, Dr. Howard Snyder: Dwight D. Eisenhower, *Mandate for Change, 1953–1956* (New York: Doubleday, 1963), 544.

172, Remarking on the round: "How the President Keeps Himself Healthy," *U.S. News and World Report*, August 23, 1957, 60; and Natta, 68.

172, Snyder said, "Golf is: Natta, 68.

173, Historian Clarence Lasby: Clarence G. Lasby, *Eisenhower's Heart Attack: How Ike Beat Heart Disease and Held on to the Presidency* (Lawrence: University Press of Kansas, 1997), 262.

173, The USGA's magazine: Lasby, 262; *U.S. News and World Report*, August 23, 1957, 60; and Byrod, 23.

173, The cofounder of E-Z-Go: Damon Cline, "Making It E-Z," *Augusta Chronicle*, June 23, 2002.

174, Upon first playing: Marvin L. Arrowsmith, "Sand Traps, Wind Spoil Ike's Golfing," *Washington Post and Times Herald*, September 6, 1957, A2.

174, The course, which provided: Edward T. Folliard, "Ike Picks Narragansett Bay Isle, Site of Naval Base, for Vacation," *Washington Post and Times Herald*, July 10, 1957, A2.

174, The year-round residents: Edward T. Folliard, "President Seems Chock Full of Healthy Vigor Two Years After His Heart Attack in Denver," *Washington Post and Times Herald*, September 23, 1957, A2.

174, Norman Palmer commented: Norman Palmer, *Five Star Golf* (New York: Duell, Sloan and Pearce, 1964), 20.

175, But Palmer, as with Ike's: Patrick J. Sloyan, "Ike Golfed in 80s, Instructor Reveals," *Washington Post and Times Herald*, November 30, 1964, A3.

175, Ike began his vacation: Edward T. Folliard, "Crowd Hails Eisenhower at Newport," *Washington Post and Times Herald*, September 5, 1957, A1.

175, Club professional Norman Palmer: Palmer and Levy, 71.

175, The day before Adams's visit: Palmer, *Five Star Golf*, 53.

175, Palmer often said of Ike's: Palmer and Levy, 72.

176, It was a logical place: George Gipe, *The Great America Sports Book* (New York: Doubleday, 1978), 85; Bob Considine, "How Ike Lives," *Washington Post and Times Herald*, October 17, 1954, AW22; and Letter, Dwight D. Eisenhower to Nancy Murdock and Carolyn Musselman, March 25, 1964. Dwight D. Eisenhower, Post-Presidential Papers, 1961–1969, Convenience File, Box 1, Folder: DDE—Personals. Eisenhower Library.

176, Ike was given so much: Jeanne Rogers, "Twining to Report to Ike on Look at Red Air Force," *Washington Post and Times Herald*, July 4, 1956, 2; and Drew Pearson, "Presents to Ike Are Most Lavish," *Washington Post and Times Herald*, June 20, 1958, B15.

176, In 1954, for their thirty-eighth: Merriman Smith, *Meet Mister Eisenhower*, 191.

176, But they were not championship: "Golf Club Sends Ike Honorary Membership," *Washington Post*, December 11, 1952, 22; and Merriman Smith, 193.

177, In 1955, the *Washington Post*: Ed Creagh, "Gettysburg Taking Ike in Stride," *Washington Post and Times Herald*, August 22, 1955, 23.

177, During one round: "Ike's 'Shot' Interferes with His Golf Shot," *Washington Post and Times Herald*, June 15, 1958, A2.

177, To minimize distractions: "Gettysburg Club Puts Ike at Ease," *Washington Post and Times Herald*, May 15, 1955, A13.

177, Ike played at dozens: Merriman Smith, 169–170.

178, *Golf* magazine once declared: Kahn, 7.

178, *Golf World* reported: "Ought to Be a Law," *Golf World*, March 6, 1953, 10.

178, During a round at the Ottawa Hunt Club: Eddie McCabe, "Caddy Turns Out to Be Writer, Reports Details of Ike's 90," *Washington Post and Times Herald*, July 12, 1958, A9.

179, Benveniste asked Yates: Author interview with Charlie Yates, Atlanta History Center, July 26, 2000.

179, Ike's longtime friend Slats Slater: Slater, 39.

180, **When the foursome asked:** Campbell and Landau, 95.

180, **Max Elbin at Burning Tree:** Campbell and Landau, 100.

180, **While playing for the first time:** "Old Zest Shown By Ike at Golf," *Washington Post and Times Herald*, February 24, 1956, 17.

180, **There is no record of Ike:** Robert G. Nixon, "Pup Grabs Ike's Golf Ball, Secret Service Regains It," *Washington Post and Times Herald*, May 27, 1956, A1.

181, **James C. Hagerty, Ike's:** Kahn, 7–8.

181, **He used to say:** Edward T. Folliard, "Golf on Capitol Hill," *America* (February 14, 1959), 565.

181, **He would, as one partner said:** Campbell and Landau, 102.

181, **At the end of the round he roared:** Campbell and Landau, 102; and Bob Hope, *Confessions of a Hooker: My Lifelong Love Affair with Golf* (New York: Doubleday, 1985), 75.

182, **Augusta National golf professional:** Ed Dudley and William A. Emerson Jr., "I Like Ike's Golf," *Collier's*, April 18, 1953, 20–22. The Augusta set is still on display in the library at Augusta National.

182, **According to Roger Kahn:** Kahn, 59.

182, **In 1955, retired Air Force:** "Gift of Souped Up Golf Balls Make Ike 250-Yard Driver," *Washington Post and Times Herald*, February 5, 1955, 15.

182, **As Ed Dudley remembered:** Campbell and Landau, 98–99.

182, **Ike's brother Edgar:** John McCallum, *Six Roads from Abilene: Some Personal Recollections of Edgar Eisenhower* (Seattle: Wood and Reber, 1960), 11.

183, **The inventor, Dr. Luis Alvarez:** Drew Pearson, "Ike's Electronic Golf Gadget," *Washington Post and Times Herald*, October 12, 1954, 39.

183, **As James Reston of the *New York Times*:** James Reston, "President Putts the Party in an Impossible Dilemma," *New York Times*, April 23, 1953, 21.

183, **He favored muted colors:** Walter Hagen, *The Walter Hagen Story* (New York: Simon and Schuster, 1956), 138.

183, **After playing a round:** Ed Dudley and William A. Emerson Jr., "I Like Ike's Golf," *Collier's*, April 18, 1953, 22; Patricia Wiggins, "They Like It Down on the Farm," *Washington Post and Times Herald*, July 14, 1955, 33; and Robert G. Nixon, "Eisenhower's Pink Cap Sets a New Golf Style," *Washington Post and Times Herald*, July 10, 1955, A12.

184, **Ben Hogan once said:** Campbell and Landau, 101.

184, **When David, Ike's grandson:** McCallum, 3; and Robert G. Nixon, "Grandson Chauffeurs Ike at Golf, and Grandpa Pays Him 50 Cents," *Washington Post and Times Herald*, May 19, 1957, A1.

185, **Ike made his decision:** Drew Pearson, "Mystery Huddle Was on Golf," *Washington Post*, January 7, 1954, 8; George Dixon, "Washington Scene: Something to Investigate," *Washington Post*, December 11, 1954, 11; George Dixon, "Washington Scene: Old School Thai," 29; Murial

Bowen, "It's a Foine Cup o'Tea We Brew, Says Costello," *Washington Post and Times Herald*, March 17, 1956, 17; and Edward T. Folliard, "Aide Held Best Fitted for Difficult Moscow Post," *Washington Post*, March 27, 1953, 1.

185, **At an April 30, 1954:** Donovan, *Eisenhower: The Inside Story*, 200.

185, **After the round, Ike gave:** Drew Pearson, "It's Odd What Golf Ball Can Do," *Washington Post and Times Herald*, October 30, 1954, 39.

185, **He justified his request:** Drew Pearson, "Light Urged on President's Pals," *Washington Post*, April 29, 1953, B.

186, **After accepting the nomination:** "Nixon Secret Out; He, Too, Is a Golfer," *New York Times*, April 26, 1953, 47.

186, **The *Washington Post* confirmed:** "Vice President Nixon Likes Golf, Too; Tries to Break 100," *Washington Post*, April 26, 1953, C5.

186, **Nixon was an inconsistent golfer:** Bus Ham, "Nixon Says Golfers Can Be Diplomats," *Washington Post and Times Herald*, June 9, 1955, 49.

186, **He took lessons and in April:** Richard L. Lyons, "Dulles Making 'Major' Speech," *Washington Post and Times Herald*, April 22, 1957, A2.

186, **In July 1960, the city:** "Newport Names Park in Honor of President," *Washington Post and Times Herald*, July 23, 1960, A7.

187, **Each hole, then, could be:** Rasa Gustaitis, "Humor Magazine Suggests Memorial to Ike—Golf Course," *Washington Post and Times Herald*, September 27, 1960, C3.

187, **On December 7, 1952:** "Golfers Vote for Eisenhower," *New York Times*, December 7, 1952, S2.

187, **In February 1955, the Golf Writers:** "Writers Honor Ike for Golf Contribution," *Washington Post and Times Herald*, February 7, 1955, 16.

188, **According to the *New York Times*:** "Four Golfers Honored," *New York Times*, June 14, 1956, 44.

188, **The U.S. Department of State:** Will Grimsley, *Golf: Its History, People and Events* (Englewood Cliffs, NJ: Prentice-Hall, 1966), 241.

189, **Ike wrote a letter:** "Second World Amateur Team Championship for the Eisenhower Trophy," Merion Golf Club, September 28–October 1, 1960, Gordon Keen Private Collection.

189, **Two years later, the event:** Grimsley, 242–243.

190, **His son, John, wrote:** John S. D. Eisenhower, *Strictly Personal* (Garden City, NY: Doubleday, 1974), 384–388.

190, **On February 14, they announced:** Donovan, *Eisenhower: The Inside Story*, 402.

190, **The press followed his every step:** "Ike Talks Often About His Heart Attack as He Plays First Golf in Five Months," *Washington Post and Times Herald*, February 18, 1956, 1; and "Old Zest Shown by Ike at Golf," *Washington Post and Times Herald*, February 24, 1956, 17.

190, **The press attributed the rise:** "Varied Factors Cited," *Washington Post and Times Herald*, February 26, 1956, C11.

191, **It came as little surprise:** Donovan, *Eisenhower: The Inside Story*, 403–404.

191, **But he was not shy:** Stewart Alsop, "Matter of Face . . . the President and the Crisis," *Washington Post and Times Herald*, April 29, 1957, A11.

191, **He then traveled to California:** Robert G. Nixon, "Ike Shows Gain, Plays Four Holes," *Washington Post and Times Herald*, August 5, 1956, A2; and Robert C. Albright, "Politics Put Aside as Ike Golfs Again," *Washington Post and Times Herald*, August 25, 1956, 1.

191, **The *Democratic Digest*:** Richard J. Moss, *Golf and the American Country Club* (Urbana: University of Illinois Press, 2001), 158.

192, **The Democrats hoped that:** Henry Brandon, "Ike's Popularity Stymies Democrats," *Washington Post and Times Herald*, May 11, 1956, 26.

192, **Joseph and Stewart Alsop, writing:** Joseph and Stewart Alsop, "The Democrats' Double Dilemma," *Washington Post and Times Herald*, July 1, 1956, E5.

192, **Richard Tufts, president:** Shirley Povich, "This Morning," *Washington Post and Times Herald*, September 4, 1956, 16.

192, **One writer from Silver Spring, Maryland:** J. W., "Letters to the Editor," *Washington Post and Times Herald*, March 6, 1956, 24.

193, **The *Washington Post* published:** "Photo Standalone—1 No Title," *Washington Post and Times Herald*, April 29, 1956, C6.

193, **Ike prevailed, beating:** Kenneth S. Davis, *Eisenhower: American Hero* (New York: American Heritage Publishing Co., 1969), 108.

193, **The oldest, William Henry Harrison:** Edward T. Folliard, "His Victory Over Adlai May Surpass That in '52," *Washington Post and Times Herald*, November 7, 1956, A1.

193, **Ike's inability to win the region:** Dwight D. Eisenhower, *In Review: Pictures I've Kept* (Garden City, NY: Doubleday, 1969), 161.

Chapter 8

195, **It always gets into the papers:** George Dixon, "Washington Scene: Where Is the News—in Golf or Work?" *Washington Post and Times Herald*, May 20, 1958, A17.

196, **Ike eschewed class distinctions:** C. B. Palmer, "Ike in Abilene and the Abilene in Ike," *New York Times*, June 1, 1952, SM11.

197, **When Ike was sworn in:** Peter Lyon, *Eisenhower: Portrait of the Hero* (Boston: Little Brown, 1974), 589.

198, **Ike and his five brothers:** Palmer, "Ike In Abilene and the Abilene in Ike," SM11.

198, **He would be the first Arkansas governor:** David Halberstam, *The Fifties* (New York: Villard Books, 1993), 672.

200, **Historian Cary Fraser argued:** Cary Fraser, "Crossing the Color Line in Little Rock: The Eisenhower Administration and the Dilemma of Race," *Diplomatic History* (Spring 2000): 245.

201, **And nobody seemed to be:** Halberstam, 688.

201, **When the second *Brown* decision:** Halberstam, 668.

202, **Compared to its more overtly:** Pete Daniel, *Lost Revolutions: The South in the 1950s* (Chapel Hill: University of North Carolina Press, 2000), 252; and Virgil T. Blossom, *It Has Happened Here* (New York: Harper and Brothers, 1959), 1–7, 16–18.

202, **Faubus was a moderate:** Halberstam, 672–673.

202, **When a reporter later asked:** Halberstam, 674.

203, **While serving in North Africa:** Lyon, 591.

203, **His prejudices were:** Lyon, 592.

203, **Though he rarely discussed:** Arthur Larsen, *Eisenhower: The President Nobody Knew* (New York: Scribner, 1968), 124.

203, **Ike echoed the point:** Robert Griffith, ed., *Ike's Letters to a Friend, 1941–1958* (Lawrence, Kansas: University Press of Kansas, 1984), 186.

204, **After the meeting, he simply:** Lyon, 598.

204, **He even enlisted evangelist Billy Graham:** Piers Brendon, *Ike: His Life and Times* (New York: Harper and Row, 1986), 278.

204, **He once told Nixon:** Quoted in Brendon, 278.

204, **He rarely sought the advice:** Brendon, 280. Morrow was for a while denied an office in which to work.

205, **Morrow lamented the unfolding:** E. Frederic Morrow, *Black Man in the White House* (New York: Coward-McCann, 1963), 170.

205, **He continued, "All they are:** Earl Warren, *The Memoirs of Earl Warren* (Garden City, NY: Doubleday, 1977), 291.

207, **While he could solve one:** Lyon, 795.

210, **When the soldiers finally arrived:** Halberstam, 688.

210, **Sherman Adams recounted:** Sherman Adams, *Firsthand Report* (New York: Harper and Row, 1961), 344.

210, **Ike finally returned to Washington:** Quoted in Brendon, 345.

210, **Privately, he confessed to Nixon:** Brendon, 346.

211, **Even Louis Armstrong criticized:** "Armstrong May Tour," *New York Times*, September 20, 1957, 15.

211, **Only 36 percent of the South:** Lyon, 798.

211, **The southern press, from Chattanooga:** "GOP Dead in South, Adams Is Told in Chattanooga; Troop Use Criticized," *Washington Post and Times Herald*, October 3, 1957, A15.

212, **In the midst of the crisis:** Ellis D. Slater, *The Ike I Knew* (New York: The Ellis D. Slater Trust, 1980), 161.

212, **Two days before he arrived:** "Advice on the Home Front," *Augusta Chronicle*, November 15, 1957, 6A.

212, **Worried that the city might spurn:** Pat Kelly, "President Receives 'Usual' Welcome," *Augusta Chronicle*, November 16, 1957, 1.

Notes

213, **Mayor Hugh L. Hamilton:** Kelly, 2.

213, **Slater recalled the reception:** Slater, 207.

214, **They gathered outside Augusta National:** Kamille Bostick, "Paine Students Worked to End Segregation," *Augusta Chronicle*, February 5, 2005. http://chronicle.augusta.com/stories/020605/met_3201913.shtml. Accessed September 11, 2005.

214, **The planes were equipped:** Virgil Pinkley with James F. Sheer, *Eisenhower Declassified* (Old Tappan, NJ: Fleming H. Revell, 1979), 337.

214, **The Soviets' sophisticated radar:** Brendon, 388.

215, **A statement issued by State Department:** "Department of State on U-2 Incident at May 7 Lincoln White Press Conference," http://www.eisen hower.archives.gov/dl/U2Incident/DepartmentStatementonU25760 .pdf.

215, **In his book *Eisenhower*:** Lyon, 860.

215, **Ironically, just prior to the incident:** Brendon, 391; and Stephen E. Ambrose, "Overreacting, Once Again," *U.S. News and World Report*, February 2, 1998, 20–25.

216, **He told his friend Virgil Pinkley:** Pinkley, 341.

216, **On May 16, Khrushchev:** Pinkley, 336.

216, **As Piers Brendon reported:** Brendon, 392; and Oral History Transcripts, Harrison Salisbury, October 6, 1972, 42, Eisenhower Library.

217, **Such coverage gave Khrushchev:** Shepherd Campbell and Peter Landau, *Presidential Lies: The Illustrated History of White House Golf* (New York: Macmillan, 1996), 95.

217, **The events in May:** "Random Notes in Washington; Kremlin Adopts Bourgeois Golf," *New York Times*, January 4, 1960, 15.

217, **He also quipped:** Drew Pearson, "Khrushchev Has a Golfing Problem," *Washington Post and Times Herald*, August 19, 1960, D11.

218, **Senator Hugh Scott joked:** Shirley Povich, "This Morning," *Washington Post and Times Herald*, January 13, 1963, C1.

218, **In some ways, he was an easy target:** Louis Galambos and Shirley Anne Warshaw, eds., *Reexamining the Eisenhower Presidency* (Portsmouth, NH: Greenwood Publishing Group, 1993), xi.

219, **Nearly a year after his second inauguration:** Thomas A. Bailey, *Presidential Greatness: The Image and the Man from George Washington to the Present* (New York: Appleton-Century-Crofts, 1966), 131.

219, **Democratic activist Rexford G. Tugwell:** Bailey, 246.

219, **In 1960, New York University:** Pinkley, 325.

219, **On February 23, 1953:** "Eisenhower Golfs," *New York Times*, February 24, 1953, 16.

219, **Ike was reported to have:** "Eisenhower Golfs," 16.

219, **In his second term:** Bob Considine, "Diplomat Named Ike," *Washington Post and Times Herald*, November 8, 1959, AW6.

220, In 1960, the *Chicago Tribune*: "GOP Leaders Worry Over Loss of 'Peace Issue' in '60 Campaign," *Washington Post and Times Herald*, July 22, 1960, A1.

220, When asked about the snub: Gary Peterson, "Ronald Reagan: Above All, the Gipper Was a Good Sport," *Augusta Chronicle*, June 10, 2004. http://chronicle.augusta.com/stories/061104/oth_1172579.shtml. Accessed September 11, 2005; and Shirley Povich, "This Morning," *Washington Post*, April 7, 1954, 29.

220, Shirley Povich, writing for the: Shirley Povich, "This Morning," *Washington Post*, April 6, 1953, 10.

220, But with the rescheduled game: John Drebinger, "President Will Make First Pitch at Re-Schedule of Capital Opener," *New York Times*, April 14, 1953, 33.

220, His participation was an important: "President to Miss Season Opener; Nixon Will Pitch in Relief Role," *New York Times*, April 3, 1953, 29.

220, He would, however, periodically: " 'Impartial' Ike Liked Army," *Washington Post*, November 28, 1954, C2.

220, On January 29, 1955: Drew Pearson, "Ike Chose Golf Over Hoover's Dinner," *Washington Post and Times Herald*, February 14, 1955, 35.

221, Political opponents have: John Fitzpatrick, "Ike Likes Golf . . . and It Booms," *Golf Digest*, July 1953, 33.

221, Joseph and Stewart Alsop: Brendon, 265.

221, Ike responded, "Well, I don't: Vern Haugland, "President Gets Two Helicopters for Flights to Burning Tree Club," *Washington Post and Times Herald*, March 4, 1957, A1; and "Ike Uses 'Copter to Fly Home from Golf Course," *Washington Post and Times Herald*, June 10, 1960, A19.

221, McCarthy then went on to declare: "McCarthy Criticizes President on Yalta," *New York Times*, March 27, 1955, 60.

222, Ironically, Alanbrooke did not: "But Germany Lost the War," *New York Times*, November 1, 1959, E10; and "Ike Didn't Play Golf in France, Hagerty Says," *Washington Post and Times Herald*, November 6, 1959, A19.

222, He went on to say: Damon Stetson, "U.A.W. Exhorted to Build Defense," *New York Times*, March 29, 1955, 20.

222, At an April 10, 1957: Thomas Bailey, *Presidential Saints and Sinners* (New York: Free Press, 1981), 232.

222, In answer to the question: Fred I. Greenstein, *The Hidden-Hand Presidency: Eisenhower as Leader* (New York: Basic Books, 1982), 256. See footnote #45. *The Gallup Poll: Public Opinion 1935–1971*, 3 vols. (New York: Random House, 1972).

223, As Paul Johnson noted in: Paul Johnson, "Strong, Silent Men Make Good Presidents," *Forbes*, March 1, 2004, 33.

223, Johnson goes on to argue: Johnson, 33.

223, **Ike also took his criticism:** Edward T. Folliard, "Ike's Acting as 'Scared' as FDR Was of Landon," *Washington Post and Times Herald*, September 23, 1956, E1.

223, **In *Mandate for Change*, Ike described:** Dwight D. Eisenhower, *Mandate for Change, 1953–1956* (New York: Doubleday, 1963), 267.

223, **Eisenhower's golf was constantly:** Sherman Adams, "At Work in the White House," in *Eisenhower as President*, ed. Dean Albertson (New York: Hill and Wang, 1963), 6; and Sherman Adams, *Firsthand Report* (New York: Harper and Brothers, 1961), 82.

224, **Slater reported, "Well, things:** Slater, 90.

224, **The *New York Times* reported:** James Reston, "President Putts the Party in an Impossible Dilemma," *New York Times*, April 23, 1953, 21.

224, **Another refrain held:** Don Van Natta, *First Off the Tee: Presidential Hackers, Duffers, and Cheaters from Taft to Bush* (New York: Public Affairs, 2003), 64.

224, **A third began:** Merriman Smith, *Meet Mister Eisenhower* (New York: Harper and Row, 1955), 163.

224, **He once said, "Ike loved:** Bob Hope, *Confessions of a Hooker: My Lifelong Love Affair with Golf* (New York: Doubleday, 1985), 80.

225, **On May 8, 1953:** Hope, 75.

225, **Hope remembered telling it:** Hope, 82.

225, **The lyrics of one song:** "Ike and His Cabinet Get Lively Grilling," *Washington Post and Times Herald*, May 13, 1956, F1.

225, **In 1957, at the Democratic Party Night:** Maxine Cheshire, " 'Ike' Made Democrats See Double," *Washington Post and Times Herald*, May 22, 1957, C1.

226, **Bonnell explained:** "Eisenhower's Golfing Defended in Sermon," *New York Times*, September 19, 1955, 23.

226, **Roger Kahn reported on Truman:** Roger Kahn, "Take a Mulligan, Mr. President!" *Golf*, April 1959, 59.

226, **Dr. Howard Snyder:** Campbell and Landau, 108.

226, **According to the *New York Times*:** Joseph E. Loftus, "Eisenhower's Formula for Relaxation," *New York Times*, September 5, 1954, SM10.

227, **James C. Hagerty, his press secretary:** Natta, 74.

288

CHAPTER 9

229, **He's taught this whole country:** Bob Addie, "Sports Addition," *Washington Post and Times Herald*, October 29, 1954, 64.

229, **Even so, in April 1961:** "GOP Leaders Plan Tee Talk with Ike," *Washington Post and Times Herald*, April 7, 1961, A17.

230, **He sent several telegrams:** Telegram from Dwight D. Eisenhower to Mary Jones, January 20, 1961, Eisenhower folder. Atlanta Athletic Club Collection.

231, At that event, Ike said: Richard Weingroff, "The Man Who Changed America, Part II," *Public Roads* 66:6 (May–June 2003): 22–38; and Elsie Carper, "Ike Welcomed into Private Life," *Washington Post and Times Herald*, January 22, 1961, A1.

231, One resident remarked: Ed Creagh, "Gettysburg Taking Ike in Stride," *Washington Post and Times Herald*, August 22, 1955, 23.

231, Ike regularly tooled around: Creagh, 23.

231, Ike and Mamie decorated: "One Peek at Gettysburg," *Washington Post and Times Herald*, February 21, 1956, 63.

231, After leaving the White House: Don Van Natta, *First Off the Tee: Presidential Hackers, Duffers, and Cheaters from Taft to Bush* (New York: Public Affairs, 2003), 76.

231, His workload declined: Ellis D. Slater, *The Ike I Knew* (New York: The Ellis D. Slater Trust, 1980), 259.

231, In his last month in the White House: Slater, 235.

232, Longtime White House reporter: Kenneth Davis, *Eisenhower: American Hero* (New York: American Heritage Publishing Co., 1969), 137.

232, Ike once confessed: Davis, 130.

232, Historian Piers Brendon described: Piers Brendon, *Ike: His Life and Times* (New York: Harper and Row, 1986), 414.

233, Actor Robert Montgomery: Craig Allen, *Eisenhower and the Mass Media: Peace, Prosperity, and Prime-Time TV* (Chapel Hill: University of North Carolina Press, 1993), 192.

233, In July 1963, CBS: Allen, 192.

233, Hosted by Walter Cronkite: Allen, 193.

234, Four years later, he wrote: Allen, 198.

234, John Eisenhower, Ike's son: John S. D. Eisenhower, *Strictly Personal* (Garden City, NY: Doubleday, 1974), 293.

234, In November 1965: Nicholas C. Chriss, " 'Snoot of Fresh Air' Enjoyed by Eisenhower," *Washington Post and Times Herald*, November 21, 1965, A1.

234, During recovery, Ike's doctors: Peter Andrews, "Ike and the Gang," *Golf Digest*, April 1993, 166.

234, Despite their declining health: Susan Eisenhower, *Mrs. Ike: Memories and Reflections on the Life of Mamie Eisenhower* (New York: Farrar, Straus and Giroux, 1996), 307.

235, Dorothy recalled: Interview with Dorothy Yates, July 19, 2006.

235, He called it "the thrill: Shepherd Campbell and Peter Landau, *Presidential Lies: The Illustrated History of White House Golf* (New York: Macmillan, 1996), 113; and Robert Sommers, *Golf Anecdotes* (New York: Oxford, 1995), 193.

235, In a February 15, 1968, letter: Letter from Dwight D. Eisenhower to Charlie Yates, February 15, 1968, Folder: DDE Letters and Information, 1960s–1970s, Charlie Yates Private Collection.

235, Three days later: "That Elusive Ace: The Hole-in-One and Who's Been There, Done That," Pasturegolf.com. http://www.pasturegolf.com/archive/ace.htm. Accessed August 31, 2005.

236, Surprised by all of the attention: Letter from Dwight D. Eisenhower to Brig. Gen. Robert Cutler, February 20, 1968. Dwight D. Eisenhower, Post-Presidential Papers, 1961–1969, Special Name Series, Box 3, Folder: Cutler, Robert, Eisenhower Library.

237, He had been an avid golfer: Davis, 130.

237, Eisenhower helped shape: Tom Callahan, "The Country's First Golfer," *Golf Digest*, August 2005, 76.

237, Because of Ike: Callahan, 76.

237, Callahan concluded that Ike: Callahan, 76.

237, In July 1963, in recognition: "Ike Dedicates Air Force Golf Links," *Washington Post and Times Herald*, July 9, 1963, A21.

237, In the late 1960s, he limited: Davis, 137.

239, After one shot: Will Grimsley, "Eisenhower's Fine Shots Capture Palmer's Army, Demaret, Bolger," *Washington Post and Times Herald*, May 27, 1964.

239, Worried about the difficult shot: Natta, 77.

239, *Golf* magazine reported that: Natta, 77.

239, The event raised: Desmond Tolhurst and updated by Gary Galyean, *Golf at Merion* (Ardmore, PA: Merion Golf Club, 2005), 81; and "Ike, Palmer Play Exhibition for Heart Fund," *Washington Post and Times Herald*, April 17, 1965, D5.

240, Ike was a frequent spectator: George Peper et al., *Golf in America: The First 100 Years* (New York: Harry N. Abrams, 1994), 247.

240, In 1968, which would prove: Bob Hope, *Confessions of a Hooker: My Lifelong Love Affair with Golf* (New York: Doubleday, 1985), 80.

240, Ike's health declined: David Owen, *The Making of the Masters: Clifford Roberts, Augusta National, and Golf's Most Prestigious Tournament* (New York: Simon and Schuster, 1999), 177.

240, Dudley was the golf pro: "Ralph Arnold Dies, Ike's Golf Partner," *Washington Post and Times Herald*, June 12, 1962, A19; and "Ed Dudley, First Pro for Eisenhower, Dies," *Washington Post and Times Herald*, October 27, 1963, C5.

241, The Belle Springs Creamery: Edward Russoli, *Dwight D. Eisenhower: General, President, Cook* (Allentown, PA: Benedettini Books, 1990), 119.

241, He was laid to rest: Henry B. Jameson, *They Still Call Him Ike* (New York: Vantage Press, 1972), 80.

241, Ike signed the paddle: Complimentary Collector's Menu, Mr. K's Farmhouse, Abilene, Kansas, October 2005.

241, **In a speech delivered:** Jameson, 82.

241, **Ike came home:** Jameson, 86.

242, **At the 1969 Masters Tournament:** Natta, 78.

242, **In 1975, Mamie wrote:** Letter from Mamie Eisenhower to Mary Jones, April 29, 1975, Eisenhower folder. Atlanta Athletic Club Collection.

242, **The former first lady did:** Letter from Mamie Doud Eisenhower to Charlie Yates, May 16, 1972, Folder: DDE Letters and Information about Mamie D. Eisenhower, 1960s–1970s, Charlie Yates Private Collection.

243, **Mamie remained involved:** "Golf's Tribute to Ike," *Professional Golfer*, March 1971, 13; and Letter from Mamie Doud Eisenhower to Charlie Yates, October 23, 1969, Folder: DDE Letters and Information about Mamie D. Eisenhower, 1960s, Charlie Yates Private Collection.

243, **Before this, a 1962 poll:** Arthur M. Schlesinger Jr., "Our Presidents: A Rating of 75 Historians," *New York Times Magazine*, July 29, 1962, 12, 40–41.

243, **He has been on his way up:** A 1970 poll conducted by Gary Maranell and Richard Dodder (see "Political Orientation and Evaluation of Presidential Prestige," *Social Science Quarterly* 57 [September 1970]: 418) showed Ike had moved up to number twenty. A *Chicago Tribune* poll in 1982 (see *U.S. News and World Report*, January 25, 1982, 29) put Ike at number nine.

243, **Murray Kempton's landmark essay:** Murray Kempton, "The Underestimation of Dwight D. Eisenhower," *Esquire*, September 1967, 108–109, 156; and Richard A. Melanson and David Mayers, *Reevaluating Eisenhower: American Foreign Policy in the 1950s* (Urbana: University of Illinois Press, 1987), 3.

243, **Kenneth S. Davis argued:** Davis, 5.

244, **Historian Thomas A. Bailey:** Thomas A. Bailey, *Presidential Greatness: The Image and the Man from George Washington to the Present* (New York: Appleton-Century-Crofts, 1966), 325.

244, **Craig Allen explained part:** Allen, 212.

244, **In December 1968:** Russoli, 119.

245, **In 1963, a Pennsylvania company:** Maury Fitzgerald, "Pitches and Putts," *Washington Post and Times Herald*, June 9, 1963, C4.

245, **Bob Hope compared Ike:** "At 60, Bob Hope Faces Busiest Year," *Washington Post and Times Herald*, May 30, 1963, B14.

245, **The Cuban leader:** R. Hart Phillips, "Castro Tries Sport of 'Idle Rich,' " *New York Times*, March 31, 1961, 1.

245, **Castro's caddie, Delio Rodriguez:** "Kennedy Can Shoot in 70's," *New York Times*, March 31, 1961, 3.

246, **Jones filled a void:** Quoted in Catherine Lewis, *Bobby Jones and the Quest for the Grand Slam* (Chicago: Triumph Books, 2005), 118.

246, **A March 1971 issue:** "Golf's Tribute to Ike," *Professional Golfer*, March 1971, 13.

247, Herbert Warren Wind recounted: Herbert Warren Wind, "What Ike Did for Golf," January 24, 1955, attached to a letter from Ann C. Whitman to Clifford Roberts, August 25, 1955, Dwight D. Eisenhower, Records as President (White House Central Files), 1953–1961, President's Personal Files, Box 949, Folder 453: Roberts, Clifford, Eisenhower Library.

248, Palmer's record is extraordinary: George Peper, *The Story of Golf* (New York: TV Books, 1999), 167.

248, As Herbert Warren Wind explained: Herbert Warren Wind, *The Story of American Golf* (New York: Knopf, 1975), 491.

248, Though they were respectable players: Peper, *The Story of Golf*, 168.

250, In 1958, the year Palmer won: James Dodson, *A Golfer's Life* (New York: Ballantine, 1999), 172.

251, Palmer recalled that he and Ike first: E-mail to author from Doc Giffin, August 30, 2006.

252, When the friend identified Jack Nicklaus: Dan Jenkins, *You Call It Sports, But I Say It's a Jungle out There* (New York: Simon and Schuster, 1989), 129.

252, In that first year, he won: Ron Sirak, "The Tiger Effect: A $636.5 Million Impact on Golf in First Year," Associated Press, August 27, 1997. http://www.texnews.com/tiger/effect082792.html. Accessed May 30, 2006.

252, Golf writer Ron Sirak: Sirak, http://www.texnews.com/tiger/effect082792.html.

253, In 1996, 19.4 million: Sirak, http://www.texnews.com/tiger/effect082792.html.

253, Nike's golf division: S. L. Price, "Tiger Woods Has Pared Down His Life So That He Can Focus on Golf," *Sports Illustrated*, April 3, 2000. http://sportsillustrated.cnn.com/features/2000/sportsman/flashbacks/woods/tunnel_vision. Accessed May 30, 2006.

253, In 2000, PGA Tour Commissioner Tim Finchem: "Finchem: 'Woods Boost for Golf,' " BBC Sport, January 8, 2001, http://news.bbc.co.uk/sport1/hi/golf/1106672.stm. Accessed May 30, 2006.

253, Joe Barrow, the national director: Jerry Potter, "In All Facets of the Game: Tiger Leads the Way," *USA Today*, January 8, 2004. http://www.usatoday.com/sports/golf/2004-0108-impact_x.htm. Accessed May 30, 2006.

253, Bobby Jones put golf: "Dwight D. Eisenhower—He Loved to Play," *Golf Journal*, May 1969, 20.

INDEX

Index

303

Index

AUGUSTA NATIONAL GOLF CLUB

Date OCT 1 1949 194__

Dear Sir:

Your Indebtedness to the Club is as follows:

ACCOUNTS PREVIOUSLY RENDERED:		
DUES $ 200. INT. REV. TAX $ 40.		
HOUSE ACCOUNTS		
TOTAL	$240.00	

To

    General Dwight D. Eisenhower
    535 West 116th St.
    New York, N. Y.

MAKE ALL CHECKS PAYABLE TO THE AUGUSTA NATIONAL GOLF CLUB

12 October 1949

MEMO FOR GENERAL EISENHOWER:

The above amount is available in your running
expenses account. I will forward check immediately unless you desire to pay it some other
way.

        Schulz

OK   ✓

Other _____

Eisenhower joined Augusta National
Golf Club in 1948 and became a dues-
paying member, as this 1949 bill reveals.
COURTESY DWIGHT D. EISENHOWER LIBRARY.

Ike's membership cards from Cherry Hills
Country Club, Gettysburg Country Club,
and Augusta National Golf Club.
COURTESY DWIGHT D. EISENHOWER LIBRARY.

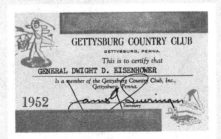

Ike at his desk. Many of his critics felt he should have spent more time attending to the nation's affairs and less time on the fairways. COURTESY LIBRARY OF CONGRESS.

Senator Robert Taft (left) stands by as President Eisenhower tees off on the first green to begin their game at Augusta National Golf Club, April 20, 1953. Courtesy Corbis.

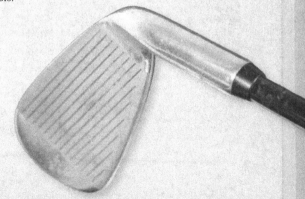

Byron Nelson, Eisenhower, Ben Hogan, and Clifford Roberts at Augusta National Golf Club on April 29, 1953. COURTESY LIBRARY OF CONGRESS.

Governor Dan Thornton, President Eisenhower, L. M. Pexton, and James Murphy at Cherry Hills Country Club in Denver, August 1953. COURTESY IRA GAY SEALY, DENVER POST.

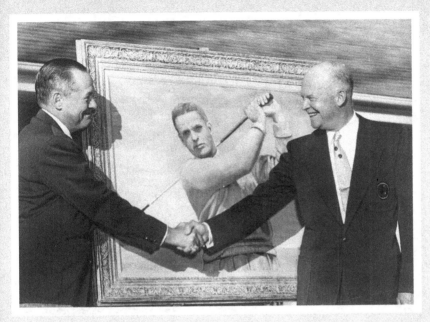

Eisenhower presenting Bobby Jones with a painting that he copied from a portrait done by Thomas E. Stephens, 1953. COURTESY ATLANTA ATHLETIC CLUB.

In 1953, *Golf Digest* printed thousands of these buttons to protect the president from having to reveal his golf score. He is shown at Augusta National Golf Club with the button before teeing off for a round with Senator Robert Taft. COURTESY ASSOCIATED PRESS.

A caricature by Mildred D. and L. E. Tilley from Providence, Rhode Island, of Eisenhower's face, using implements from his favorite hobbies: golf and fishing. COURTESY LIBRARY OF CONGRESS.

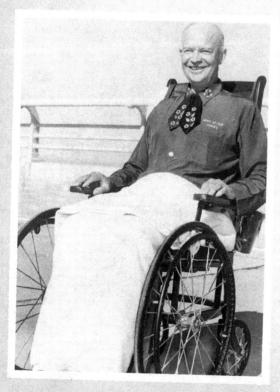

Eisenhower recuperating in Denver after his first heart attack. COURTESY CORBIS.

Bobby Jones, Eisenhower, and Clifford Roberts (seated) with other
Augusta National Golf Club members in the dining room at the club
on February 14, 1957. COURTESY ATLANTA ATHLETIC CLUB.

President Eisenhower playing at Newport Country Club on September 10, 1957, during the Little Rock crisis. COURTESY CORBIS.

Eisenhower and Governor Orval Faubus in Newport
on September 14, 1957, during the Little Rock crisis.
COURTESY CORBIS.

HOLE	MINIMUM YARDS	MAXIMUM YARDS	PAR	HANDICAP RATING	Ike DDE	Charlie Yates	Bill Robinson	Slats	HOLE	MINIMUM YARDS	MAXIMUM YARDS	PAR	HANDICAP RATING	DDE	CY	BR	S
1	375	400	4	9	5	4	5	5	10	445	470	4	6	6	5	5	6
2	475	555	5	1	6	5	5	5	11	365	445	4	12	5	4	4	5
3	330	355	4	11	5	5	5	5	12	130	155	3	16	4	3	3	5
4	170	220	3	15	4	(2)	3	4	13	455	475	5	4	6	5	5	6
5	420	450	4	5	6	4	5	6	14	400	420	4	8	5	4	5	5
6	170	190	3	17	4	(2)	3	3	15	465	520	5	2	6	5	5	6
7	315	365	4	13	6	5	5	5	16	125	190	3	18	4	3	3	4
8	475	530	5	3	6	5	5	6	17	345	400	4	14	5	4	5	5
9	395	420	4	7	5	(3)	4	5	18	395	420	4	10	5	4	5	6
OUT	3125	3485	36		47	35	40	44	IN	3125	3495	36		46	37	40	48

SCORER	Augusta National			TO'L	6250	6980	72	47	35	40	44
ATTEST											
DATE	11/26/58			HANDICAP	93	72	80	92			
				NET SCORES							

NOTE: Minimum distances, as shown, represent yardage from front of tees to nearest pin locations. Maximum distances represent measurements from back of tees to the farthest pin locations.

Scorecard from a November 26, 1958, round at Augusta National Golf Club between Eisenhower, Charlie Yates, William Robinson, and Ellis "Slats" Slater. COURTESY YATES FAMILY.

This rural farm scene painted by Eisenhower was printed on the family's 1958 Christmas card. COURTESY ATLANTA ATHLETIC CLUB.

President Eisenhower with one of his frequent golf companions,
Ed Dudley, pro at Augusta National Golf Club.
COURTESY ATLANTA ATHLETIC CLUB.

Dwight and Mamie Eisenhower with other Augusta National Golf
Club members and their wives. Clifford Roberts is pictured in the
center. COURTESY ATLANTA ATHLETIC CLUB.

A cartoon by Packer and Harry Hershfield signed to Eisenhower. COURTESY ATLANTA ATHLETIC CLUB.

President Eisenhower playing a round of golf at White Sulphur Springs during the North American Summit. Sam Snead is pictured in the background under the umbrella, on the left. COURTESY ASSOCIATED PRESS.

Ike with a football
signed by members of
the NFL champion
Green Bay Packers.
COURTESY ATLANTA
ATHLETIC CLUB.

Arnold Palmer and Eisenhower playing a round at Gettysburg
Country Club, September 9, 1960. COURTESY NEW YORK HERALD
TRIBUNE/ASSOCIATED PRESS.

Ike standing in front of the clubhouse at Burning Tree Club, October 5, 1960. COURTESY UNITED STATES NAVY.

WESTERN UNION
TELEGRAM
W. P. MARSHALL, PRESIDENT

1201

The filing time shown in the date line on domestic telegrams is STANDARD TIME at point of origin. Time of receipt is STANDARD TIME at point of destination.

WUF42 GOVT PD=THE WHITE HOUSE WASHINGTON DC JAN 20 823A EST

MRS ROBERT TYRE JONES=

    3425 TUXEDO RD ATLA=

DEAR MARY:

  ON THIS, MY LAST DAY AT THE WHITE HOUSE, I WANT TO
THANK YOU AND BOB FOR ALL THE MANY KINDNESSES YOU HAVE
EXTENDED TO MAMIE AND ME OVER THE PAST YEARS. I KNOW HOW
SADDENED YOU ARE BY THE DEATH OF BOB'S MOTHER, BUT I
STILL DARE HOPE THAT WE SHALL SEE YOU SOON AND OFTEN, IN
THE FUTURE WITH AFFECTIONATE REGARDS=

    IKE.

941A   THE COMPANY WILL APPRECIATE SUGGESTIONS FROM ITS PATRONS CONCERNING ITS SERVICE

Telegram that Eisenhower sent to Mary and Bobby Jones upon leaving the White House in January 1961. COURTESY ATLANTA ATHLETIC CLUB.

Jane Powell, Gary Player, Eisenhower, and Jack Nicklaus at
the Desert Classic on February 2, 1964. COURTESY DWIGHT D.
EISENHOWER LIBRARY.

Ike sinking a putt on the first green at Merion Golf Club and being congratulated by playing partner Arnold Palmer on May 26, 1964. Courtesy Corbis.

President Eisenhower holding the ball that he hit for a hole in one on the thirteenth hole at Seven Lakes Country Club on February 6, 1968.
Courtesy Corbis.

CPSIA information can be obtained
at www.ICGtesting.com
Printed in the USA
JSHW041656190621
16071JS00001B/30